Newtown Public Library

Presented by

Vram Nedurian Jr.

July 1993

WITH LIBERTY
AND JUSTICE
FOR SOME

WITH LIBERTY AND JUSTICE FOR SOME

A *Critique of*
the Conservative Supreme Court

DAVID KAIRYS

THE NEW PRESS

Published in the United States by The New Press, New York
Distributed by W. W. Norton & Company, Inc.
500 Fifth Avenue, New York, NY 10110

LIBRARY OF CONGRESS CATALOGING-IN-PUBLICATION DATA

Kairys, David.
With liberty and justice for some : a critique of the
conservative Supreme Court / David Kairys.
p.   cm.
Includes index.
ISBN 1-56584-071-2 (cloth) : — ISBN 1-56584-059-3 (pbk.)
1. Civil rights—United States. 2. United States. Supreme Court.
I. Title.
KF4749.K35   1993
342.73'085—dc20
[347.30285]   92-50820

First Edition.

Book design by Laura Lindgren

Established in 1990 as a major alternative to the large, commercial
publishing houses, The New Press is intended to be the first full-scale
nonprofit American book publisher outside of the university presses.
The Press is operated editorially in the public interest, rather than for
private gain; it is committed to publishing in innovative ways works of
educational, cultural, and community value, which, despite their
intellectual merits, might not normally be "commercially viable."

To Antje Mattheus and our children,
Marah and Hannah,
and to the best parents anyone could hope for,
Bernard and Julia Lovett Kairys.

◀ ACKNOWLEDGMENTS ▶

Research assistance was provided by Temple University law students Susan Killam and David Tedhams and, on articles leading up to the book and related projects, Gregory Armstrong, Tia Burke, James Dilsheimer, and Sherri Miller. Helpful comments on drafts of the whole manuscript or specific chapters were provided by Haywood Burns, Spencer Coxe, Robert Gordon, Richard Greenstein, Sylvia Law, Antje Mattheus, Mark Rahdert, Robert Reinstein, David Rudovsky, Adam Thurschwell, and Arthur Waskow. I also appreciate input and encouragement from Edwin Bronstein, Morgan Henderson, and Rodney Napier.

In a larger sense, this book is the result of my experience litigating civil-rights and civil-liberties cases for over twenty years and teaching at Temple Law School for the last three years. For this I am indebted to the people and groups I represented, whose insight, courage, and persistence taught me more about freedom, equality, and life than any school or book; to my colleagues at Kairys & Rudovsky, David Rudovsky, Ilene Kalman, Jules Epstein, and until recently Adam Thurschwell; to Anthony Amsterdam, for a good start; and to the students (particularly those in my political and civil-rights course), faculty and staff at Temple Law School, for collegiality, dialogue, and support, including a research grant from the Temple University Law Foundation.

Finally, I appreciate the contribution of The New Press, which has pioneered nonprofit, public-interest publishing at a time when the commercial media have greatly narrowed the range of ideas and information available to the public (see chapter 3); André Schiffrin, publisher and editor of this volume, a dedicated and talented New Press staff, and design and composition by Laura Lindgren; and the foundations whose generous grants made possible this exciting new development in publishing.

❦ CONTENTS ❦

Introduction 1

1 • WARTIME BOOKENDS AND CONSTITUTIONAL CHOICES 13
WARTIME BOOKENDS
    A Fixed Star • Citizenship Has Its Responsibilities
CONSTITUTIONAL CHOICES

2 • EXPRESSION 39
THE SURPRISING HISTORY OF FREE SPEECH IN THE UNITED STATES
    Public Parks and Private Houses • In Trust for the Use of
    the Public • The Constitution and the Early Popular Under-
    standing • The Liberal Paradigm
FREE SPEECH ISN'T FREE (AND NO ONE IS LISTENING)
THE CONSERVATIVE RETRENCHMENT
    An Eyesore, a Safety Hazard, and Additional Cleanup
    Work • Secondary Effects • The Costs of Security • Teenage
    Girl Students • Not a Case of Suppressing a Dangerous
    Idea • Fighting Words and Racist Speech

3 • PARTICIPATION IN THE POLITICAL PROCESS 83
    The Integrity of the Democratic System • The Voices of
    People and Interest Groups Who Have Money to Spend •
    Nothing to Do with Voting • The Function of Editors

4 • RELIGION 99
FREE EXERCISE
    An Unavoidable Consequence of Democratic Government

ESTABLISHMENT

Jefferson Was of Course in France • *A Secular Purpose* • *A Plausible Secular Purpose*

RELIGIOUS FREEDOM AND THE WALL OF SEPARATION

5 • EQUALITY 129

Undesirable Traffic • *Best Presented to the Legislative Bodies* • *Smoke Out Racism* • *An Additional Risk Unique to Women*

6 • PRIVACY 147

Penumbras and Emanations • *What Are You Doing in My Bedroom?* • *No Legitimate Expectation of Privacy* • *More Than One Should Have to Bear*

7 • DUE PROCESS 167

Watch for These Subjects • *Unfortunate Encounters* • *Harmless Error* • *A Policeman Perched on the Top of a Truck or a Two-level Bus* • *A Basis for Exonerating the Defendant*

CONCLUSION 181

CONSERVATIVE LEGAL THOUGHT AND PRACTICE
LEGAL REASONING, DEMOCRACY, AND THE RULE OF LAW
FREEDOM, EQUALITY, AND DEMOCRACY

Appendix: The Bill of Rights 213
Notes 217
Table of Cases 233
Index 239

⁋ INTRODUCTION ⁋

Conservative ideas about law are no longer only successful material for criticizing liberals and winning elections. We have been in a period of conservative dominance for some time, and there is a substantial record of conservative legal practice. Only one sitting Supreme Court justice was selected by a Democrat—President John Kennedy chose Byron White, whose votes and opinions have been mainly conservative. President Richard Nixon selected William Rehnquist (later made chief justice by President Ronald Reagan) and Harry Blackmun. President Gerald Ford chose John Stevens. President Ronald Reagan selected Sandra O'Connor, Antonin Scalia, and Anthony Kennedy; and President George Bush added David Souter and, with much tumult, Clarence Thomas. The majority of lower federal court judges were also selected by Presidents Reagan and Bush. Regardless of the change in the administration brought about by the 1992 election, the federal judiciary will be dominated by conservatives for at least the next decade, as it has been for almost all of our history.

This book focuses on thirty-one leading Supreme Court cases covering rights of expression, participation in the political process, religion, equality, privacy, and due process. The emphasis is on the stories of the people involved (which are often ignored in court opinions), the reasoning and results of the conservatives and earlier liberal decisions, and some roads not taken. The underlying question throughout is whether, after over a decade of conservative retrenchment of our individual rights far deeper and broader in scope than is generally understood, we as a nation still treasure these rights that are the favorites of Fourth of July speeches, and still have common ground about their content and enforcement. This is about the meaning of American freedom, equality, and democracy.

Much has been promised (or at least implied by the conservative critique) and can fairly be expected from conservative judges and public officials: the demise of judicial intervention without strictly construed authority, a return to democracy and the rule of law, and legal decision making driven by legal rather than political methodology. These facets of the conservative approach have been emphasized by conservative writers, jurists, and politicians and are central to their legal and popular thrust. The basic message is that conservative rules and results are not only preferable but *legally required,* and that other rules and results can only be reached by distorting or perverting the law and the legal process.[1]

This message about law, usually interwoven with a generalized hostility to government, is integral to the conservative approach and vision. President Reagan regularly emphasized the necessity of limiting the power and discretion of judges in order to preserve democracy: "[T]he question involved in judicial restraint was not—and it is not—will we have a liberal or conservative court? . . . The question was, and is, will we have a government by the people?" Edwin Meese III, Reagan's close advisor and attorney general, emphasized in his recent memoir conservative efforts "to depoliticize the courts, to ensure they played a truly judicial role, rather than usurping the authority of the elected branches of our constitutional system."[2]

Reagan's solicitor general, Charles Fried, started his recent memoir with a familiar Reaganesque critique of government and liberal legal thinking. The "Reagan Revolution" sought "a less intrusive government" by two principal means, tax reduction and restraint of courts. Liberal judges were substituting the "judgments and values of the nonproductive sector of society—lawyers, judges, bureaucrats, politicians—for the self-determination of the entrepreneurs and workers who create wealth." "Courts should be the impartial tool for doing justice between man and man . . . [not the] political engines of the left-liberal agenda." Ours is a "government of laws and not men."[3]

If government intrusiveness is the central problem, it is strange that the liberal courts of the 1960s have become the prime villains. Their judicial activism was largely aimed at stopping government intrusion on individuals. The liberal courts provided the individual, usually regardless of wealth or position, with wide-ranging protection from government intrusion. For example, confronted with Connecticut's ban on contraceptives, the Supreme Court of the 1960s established a new constitutional right to privacy in *Griswold v. Connecticut* (chapter 6).

The hated judicial activism is seldom defined specifically. But judicial activism is not the same as government intrusion. The liberal courts intervened to prevent other parts of the federal, state, or local governments from intruding on the people. And they did so in the absence of prior authority and often in spite of established rules and precedents to the contrary. These two factors—intervention and innovation—characterize judicial activism. A court's willingness to engage in either is usually sufficient to earn the label, or accusation, of judicial activism. Liberal judges were judicial activists, but their activism was used to stop government intrusion on individuals in matters of personal freedom.

Conservative judges and lawyers have attempted to reverse this judicial protection of the people from the government. As a result, the government now has enhanced power to intrude in matters usually thought to be within the essential domain of American freedom. These changes have been far deeper than the media and politicians have acknowledged. Conformity can increasingly be compelled in the most personal and private aspects of our lives, and equality and due-process rights have been depleted of meaningful content.

At the same time, conservative justices have shown no reluctance to overrule precedents, to break new judicial ground, or to invalidate legislation. One major conservative goal has been deregulation—for example, to reduce or eliminate environmental restrictions on businesses. Judicial interference with legislation to stop government intrusions into the economy—judicial activism— in service of this goal is very much a part of the conservative agenda.[4] In the civil-rights and civil-liberties cases examined in this book, we will also see conservative judicial activism when, for example, the issue is campaign-financing reforms, bias-motivated crime, or affirmative action.

The conservatives on the Supreme Court did not even address judicial restraint when the Court invalidated acts of Congress and state legislatures that limited campaign contributions and expenditures to reduce the role of money in elections. In addition to undercutting long-established individual rights, the conservative justices are erecting a free-speech barrier to legislative enactments of electoral, economic, and social reforms that increase public participation in our institutions and reduce the influence of wealth on elections and public discourse (chapters 2 and 3). Bias-motivated crime statutes have been invalidated based on another novel interpretation of the First Amendment (chapter 2). Affirmative-action plans adopted by local legislatures have been invalidated based on a novel interpretation of the Fourteenth Amendment that effectively equates good-faith attempts to compensate for current or past discrimination with the legally sanctioned segregation and malicious racism against minorities that characterized our not-so-distant past (chapter 5). Fried was quite explicit, without apparent recognition of the contradiction, about the conservatives' shift to judicial activism: "With the loss of the Senate in the 1986 midterm election, legislative relief became unthinkable, so that the Supreme Court was the only available forum for our views."[5]

Judicial activism is not consistently liberal, and judicial restraint is not consistently conservative. If one looks at the purposes and effects of particular government intrusions and places judicial activism and restraint in specific contexts, the most apparent patterns and the best generalizations are more complicated and have more to do with substantive goals than judicial means.

Conservatives tend to favor less-intrusive government when it comes to regulation or interference in a free-market economy (which I will call "entrepreneurial" freedom) and more-intrusive government when it comes to compelled conformity to religious, moral, cultural, and life-style norms. They champion judicial activism to prohibit government intrusion on the unrestrained operation of the market and to invalidate electoral and other reforms that tend to interfere with property rights or the advantages of wealth. Liberals tend to favor less-intrusive government when it comes to individual autonomy in matters of religion, morality, culture, and life-style (which I will call "personal" freedom) and more-intrusive government when it comes to regulation of the economy and electoral and other democratic reforms. They champion judicial activism to prohibit government intrusion on personal freedom or imposition of compelled conformity. Both conservatives and liberals see themselves as protecting freedom and see each other as favoring impermissible government intrusion. Neither conservatives nor liberals seem seriously bothered by judicial creativity or abandonment of established rules and precedents in furtherance of their higher goals.

These patterns are not new. Probably the most determined and successful advocates of judicial restraint in our history were liberals in the first half of this century. The conservative Supreme Court of that period invalidated economic legislation aimed at protecting working people and providing the economic safety net that we have until recently taken for granted. For example, laws limiting the

5

hours of labor were invalidated by the Supreme Court as unconstitutional infringements on the rights of employers and employees to enter into contracts. The courts were interfering with legislative intrusions into the economy. Liberals opposed this interference by advocating judicial restraint, conceived—like the conservative conception of our time—as a neutral, independent, and overriding principle that transcends substantive goals or politics.[6]

Conservatives and liberals have each tended to advocate judicial restraint when they lose control of the courts, typically justified with the lofty stated goal of stopping the courts from interfering with the will of the people, as manifested directly or through their representatives in legislatures. The most successful recent version of this has been conservatives over the last two decades condemning liberal judges for substituting their values for the will of the people. But conservatives (like liberals before them) apply this restraint only selectively, and the conservative embrace of democracy and empowerment of the people is suspect.

There is a deep distrust of democracy in the conservative tradition and among the framers of the Constitution. The record of the constitutional convention reflects considerable contempt for ordinary people and popularly elected legislatures. The people are "less fit" to choose legislators than the elite of each state, defined as white men with substantial property, according to Charles Pinckney. John Dickinson saw danger in "the multitudes without property and without principle." John Jay, who with James Madison and Alexander Hamilton authored *The Federalist Papers*, thought "the people who own the country ought to govern it." In the famous Federalist Number 10 essay, Madison emphasized how the constitutional scheme protected against "the mischief of factions" that stem from the "unequal distribution of property." The Constitution reflects these views: there was direct election of only members of the House of Representatives; and state qualifications for voting, which usually required ownership of land or substantial property, were incorporated. Racial minorities, all women, and even most white men could not vote.[7]

The predominant theme of the amendments to the Constitution subsequent to the Bill of Rights has been inclusion of all our people in the political process—African-Americans and other minorities, women, white men irrespective of property holdings, and anyone who has reached the age of eighteen (see chapter 3). But these amendments were consistently opposed by the conservatives of each era in which they were adopted. Their adoption was not required by the Constitution or by law; nor was it inevitable. Americans who supported these changes—from all levels of society and with a range of political, moral, and religious beliefs—took often difficult and courageous actions, and succeeded.[8] Ours is a history of progressive inclusion, equality, and protection of individual freedom, for which we can rightly be proud of our people—rather than any legacy from the founders, language in the Constitution, or legal reasoning.

The Reagan and Bush administrations continued the conservative tradition, seeking greatly enhanced powers for the president and the executive agencies, and diminished congressional power. Fried is quite explicit about this, strongly criticizing conservatives whose "celebration of majority rule" abandons the conservative tradition. Chief Justice Rehnquist, in a recent book on impeachment, shared with the framers a concern for "overarching and bullying by the legislative branch." The Reagan and Bush administrations set up executive agencies that reviewed regulations opposed by business and industry, most recently Vice President Dan Quayle's Council on Competitiveness, regardless of the congressional mandates in statutes or the effects on ordinary Americans.[9]

The enhancement of the power of the executive branch and its administrative agencies and the diminution of congressional power have been accommodated and encouraged by conservative justices who have declined to discharge the courts' traditional function of monitoring bureaucracies, a task specifically intended to ensure that congressional statutory mandates are being honored and enforced.[10] This amounts to placing bureaucrats above the laws that created their agencies—and above the legislature that enacted those laws. The conservative justices have also continued the conservative tradition of opposition to popular participation and inclusion of all our people in the political process with recent decisions that limit voter participation and choice and undermine the Voting Rights Act (see chapter 3).

This all may be a combination of the long-standing conservative tradition of distrust of Congress, democracy, and ordinary people and an opportunistic attempt to enhance the power of the branches of government they controlled and to decrease that of the branch they did not. In any event, the conservative emphasis on judicial restraint and deference to legislatures as a necessity of democracy and representative government is certainly open for further investigation.

As in the case of government intrusiveness and judicial restraint, the positions of conservatives and liberals toward democracy or majority rule seem to depend on what government action is being interfered with and whose freedom is being compromised. When a legislature regulates the economy and limits entrepreneurial freedom, conservatives tend to favor business people over the elected representatives of all the people. Liberals tend to favor limits on the majority's power to suppress or discriminate against dissidents or minorities.

Rhetoric aside, neither conservatives nor liberals have concretely favored increased democracy or participation by the people. For example, although the Democrats have favored some liberalization of registration requirements (such as the "motor voter" bill vetoed by President Bush in 1992), both major parties have regularly rejected basic measures that would increase our dismally low levels of participation in elections—such as dispensing with the requirement of registering to vote, which is unique to us among major democratic countries. [11]

There is a blandness, a trivialization of politics in American life. To a large extent, we have replaced politics with law, or more precisely, ordinary politics with legal politics, turning over many of our important disputes and controversies to courts and lawyers. This antidemocratic project has been a major feature of both conservative and liberal politics for most of our history. Conservatives are very much in this tradition, although they often blame liberals for giving lawyers too much power.

Perhaps the most difficult challenge is to break out of the cycle of alternating liberal and conservative accusations of inappropriate legal methodology that has so deformed legal and social discourse. We should be talking about substance, values, and visions, and the extraordinary role of law and the decay of democracy in our society and culture.

This book is primarily about the rules, results, and approaches of the conservative justices on a wide range of civil-rights and civil-liberties issues. The major cases investigated are organized in separate chapters on expression, participation in the political process, religion, equality, privacy, and due process. In each area, the techniques, approaches, and results of the conservatives and earlier liberal decisions are analyzed and criticized. The conservative claim that their rules, results, and methods are legally required is examined. A range of alternatives, including but not limited to liberal ones, are considered, and an alternative approach and vision are developed further in the conclusion.

To establish a framework and provide a brief introduction to some basic concepts and the variety of approaches, rules, and terms that recur throughout the book, the first chapter focuses on two decisions that were the most and least protective of individual rights in the modern era and develops from them the two principal visions or models of freedom, justice, and equality that emerged from World War II. This chapter is more abstract than the rest of the book, although I have tried to make it and the whole book understandable and accessible to nonlegally trained readers. In the succeeding chapters, substantive and process questions common to several areas are taken up either in the discussion of the area and cases in which they first arise or to which they are most central. For example, the "strict scrutiny" standard that characterizes the liberal approach is discussed when it first arises, in chapter 1; "original intent," which arises in many areas and decisions, is discussed in most detail in chapter 4, on religion.

In each chapter, selected themes and cases are stressed without attempting to cover the entire subject or all the major cases. I selected cases and opinions that best demonstrate the rules and results and social and constitutional vision of the conservative justices. There are, of course, important differences among some of the conservative justices, and the rules and results emphasized here could only achieve majority status as various conservative justices took their seats on the Court, replacing liberals or moderates, over the last two decades. I have not focused on the effects of each new justice's votes or the historical progression of the Court's conservative decisions.[12] Rather, the focus is on the approaches, rules, and results adopted, or likely to be adopted in the near future, by the array of convervatives who now dominate the Court.

✳ Most of the opinions emphasized were majority decisions in the 1990s or late 1980s. However, on some issues, a conservative majority was achieved in the 1970s, before conservatives clearly dominated the Court; on others, a dissent presents the clearest picture of where the dominant conservative majority is headed. I regularly contrast earlier liberal approaches, rules, and results and consider other alternatives. Because my emphasis is on the conservatives, often I have not focused on the specific opinions differing with them or the reasoning of liberals who sometimes voted with conservatives. The significance of conservative votes and opinions is not undercut by some liberal justices joining in conservative opinions and providing them majority status before conservatives fully dominated the Court.

Civil rights and civil liberties (what I call "personal" freedom) is a terrain in which conservatives tend to favor judicial restraint and liberals tend to favor judicial activism. These tendencies are not without interesting exceptions, however. For example, as noted above, conservatives become judicial activists when the civil-rights issue is limits on campaign financing, bias-motivated crime, or affirmative action (or gun control). Typically, when one side takes a contradictory position on a particular issue, the other side also does. So we find liberals on these civil-rights issues tending to favor judicial restraint. Another recent example of what might be called a "double flip" was evident in the Clarence Thomas/Anita Hill hearings—the conservative transformation to staunch support for the rights of the accused and the pro-prosecution liberal position when the issue is sex harassment.[13] As we will see, loyalty to supposed legal principles—both substantive principles and principles of decision making—is selective, value laden, and result oriented.

◀ 1 ▶

WARTIME BOOKENDS AND CONSTITUTIONAL CHOICES

WARTIME BOOKENDS

Some events in human history lead nations and cultures to question their foundations and alter their basic precepts. World War II, with its new technologies of destruction and old theories of racial superiority, was such an event. The United States emerged as the world's predominant military and economic power, but it was a different United States. As such events often do, the unfolding changes brought out the best and the worst in our nation and people. Within a period of just over a year—from mid 1943 to late 1944—the Supreme Court issued both its most ringing declaration of freedom and equality and its most chilling acquiescence in authoritarianism and racial oppression of the twentieth century. The competing visions of American society that these cases embody are very much with us as we approach and enter the twenty-first.

A Fixed Star

Marie and Gatha Barnett of Kanawha County, West Virginia, had a difficult problem for elementary-school children.[1] Their country was at war, and they knew which side they were on. But at school the teachers asked something of the Barnett sisters that they could not do. As Jehovah's Witnesses, they could not salute the Stars and Stripes, or any other flag.

Jehovah's Witnesses—described in a typical newspaper account of that time as an "often unpopular, even despised, religious sect"— interpret the Bible literally and strictly. To them the command in Exodus against any "graven image" of God forbids a salute or pledge of allegiance to any flag. Marie and Gatha's father, Walter Barnett, a pipe fitter for DuPont, explained to them that no disrespect to the flag or the nation was intended. The Jehovah's Witnesses proposed a substitute pledge that emphasized allegiance to God but included: "I respect the flag of the United States and acknowledge it as a symbol of freedom and justice to all."

But West Virginia law was quite clear. The law specified a particular way to salute the flag and the exact words of the pledge. The salute had been modified to accommodate some parents and community groups who thought it looked too much like Hitler's salute. The discarded salute, described in great detail in a statewide board-of-education regulation, consisted of raising and extending the right hand up toward the flag, with the palm turned upward, at the point in the pledge when the flag is mentioned. The regulation was changed in 1942 to require a salute consisting of placing "the right hand over the heart with forearm horizontal and elbow extended." But there would be no other accommodations or exceptions. Failure to salute the flag and recite the pledge each day at school was "insubordination" and subjected a child to expulsion and his or her parents to a $50 fine or thirty days in jail. Many Jehovah's Witness children, including the Barnett sisters, refused and were expelled from school, and some of their parents were fined.

We were at war. Americans were rallying and making sacrifices everywhere; many had already died. Anything that appeared to dampen the war effort—any crack in the unanimity of commitment and sacrifice—was extremely upsetting to many people. The refusal of the Jehovah's Witnesses to salute the flag was greeted with hostility, including, according to contemporary press accounts, occasional "mob violence." At least two thousand Jehovah's Witness students were expelled from school, and the Justice Department received reports on more than eight hundred incidents involving violence or harassment. Teachers, students, and police frequently ridiculed and taunted the Jehovah's Witness children, sometimes making a public spectacle of their refusal to salute the flag. In Richwood, West Virginia, seven Jehovah's Witness children were forced to drink castor oil and paraded through the town on a rope.

The issue was clear as the case of *Barnette v. West Virginia Board of Education* came before the Supreme Court in 1943.[2] The West Virginia flag-salute requirement, pursuant to a law duly enacted and broadly supported in that state and probably throughout the country, was challenged as a violation of freedom of religion and speech. Only three years earlier, the Court had upheld a similar flag-salute requirement because national security is an "interest inferior to none . . . [and n]ational unity is the basis of national security."[3] But the outcome this time would be different.

Justice Robert Jackson wrote the majority opinion. Jackson had come to Washington from New York with Franklin D. Roosevelt and had served the New Deal as solicitor general, attorney general and, later, lead prosecutor of Nazi war criminals. He generally subscribed to a nineteenth-century version of individualism that was not easily susceptible to the usual contemporary labels; the *New York Times* article reporting his death included descriptions of him as "middle of the road," an "increasingly conservative bent of mind," and "a man of liberal convictions."[4]

Jackson emphasized that Jehovah's Witness children had only refused to participate in a ceremony. Their inaction may be upsetting, but they had not said or done anything that directly affected others. "The freedom asserted . . . does not bring them into

collision with rights asserted by any other individual. . . . The sole
conflict is between authority and rights of the individual." He
referred to the history of Christians "persecuted for their refusal
to participate in ceremonies" and the fate of William Tell, who
was sentenced to shoot an apple off his son's head because he
refused to salute a bailiff's hat. The individual rights at stake were
not only religious. The state law amounted to "a compulsion of
students to declare a belief." This Jackson found constitutionally
unacceptable based on a principle stated in the opinion's most
quoted passage:

> If there is any fixed star in our constitutional constellation, it
> is that no official, high or petty, can prescribe what shall be
> orthodox in politics, nationalism, religion, or other matters of
> opinion or force citizens to confess by word or act their faith
> therein. If there are any circumstances which permit an
> exception, they do not now occur to us.

The principle, and Jackson's direct and elegant style, may
warm our hearts; but it was relatively new, and its source is not
clear. No such language appears in the Constitution or the Bill of
Rights, and no majority had previously articulated such a broad
restraint of government in the name of personal freedom. Further,
Jackson's "fixed star" has a distinct antimajoritarian aspect: he
invalidated a law duly enacted by the representatives of the people
of West Virginia. This, too, he addressed directly:

> The very purpose of a Bill of Rights was to withdraw certain
> subjects from the vicissitudes of political controversy, to
> place them beyond the reach of majorities and officials and
> to establish them as legal principles to be applied by the
> courts. One's right to life, liberty, and property, to free
> speech, a free press, freedom of worship and assembly, and
> other fundamental rights may not be submitted to vote; they
> depend on the outcome of no elections.

The idea that democracy only works if certain basic matters, like free speech and religion, are beyond majoritarian control was certainly not new.[5] A society in which speech and debate are restricted or citizens fear punishment if they express their views cannot claim to be truly democratic or free. But neither was this concept explicitly incorporated into the constitutional scheme, although it can fairly be viewed as inherent in the nature of the Bill of Rights. The Bill of Rights imposes limits on majoritarian as well as nonmajoritarian aspects of government.

The activist role that Jackson assigns to the courts is uniquely American and has been with us since Chief Justice John Marshall announced judicial review—which is also nowhere mentioned in the Constitution—in 1803.[6] However, it has been used in the particular fashion Jackson advocates—to broadly protect personal freedom—in only two periods of our history, from about 1937 to 1944 and from about 1961 to 1973.

From what source, then, does Jackson draw his principle and reasoning? They are, like those that preceded and followed, judicial creations very much tied to the social and historical context and the particular values and experiences of the individual justices. Jackson's vision of American society is, again, spelled out in the opinion:

> These principles grew in soil which also produced a philosophy that the individual was the center of society, that his liberty was attainable through mere absence of government restraints, and that government should be entrusted with few controls and only the mildest supervision over men's affairs.

This is the heart of the matter, and it is both liberal and conservative. If one applies it to the economy, it's laissez-faire economics, deregulation, Reaganomics—all quite conservative. Applied to government attempts to compel conformity to religious, moral, or cultural norms, it's a scheme for protection of civil rights and civil liberties—liberal.

17

Jackson's vision goes beyond mere tolerance of cultural and intellectual differences among our people: "We apply the limitations of the Constitution with no fear that freedom to be intellectually and spiritually diverse or even contrary will disintegrate the social organization." Freedom and diversity are "not limited to things that do not matter much" or to times and places where they are not controversial. Our "rich cultural diversities" are not a problem to be overcome; our strength and our hope for the future reside there.

Justice Felix Frankfurter dissented, offering perhaps the best articulation of judicial restraint in the Court's history. Frankfurter was an immigrant who became an effective advocate for the labor movement and civil liberties, a brilliant professor at Harvard Law School, and a member of Roosevelt's "brain trust." He did not doubt the importance of freedom of speech or religion or differ with the majority's social vision, but he saw the Court's role very differently:

> Of course patriotism can not be enforced by the flag salute. But neither can the liberal spirit be enforced by judicial invalidation of illiberal legislation. Our constant preoccupation with the constitutionality of legislation rather than with its wisdom tends to preoccupation of the American mind with a false value. . . . [T]his Court's only and very narrow function is to determine whether within the broad grant of authority vested in legislatures they have exercised a judgment for which reasonable justification can be offered.

We will achieve freedom when and as long as the people are convinced it should be so; no court should impose it on us. The individual's rights, according to Frankfurter, lie in the ability to participate in politics and lawmaking—the *processes* of government—and in our individual, internal control over our beliefs and consciences. "The individual conscience may profess what faith it chooses," but the government can compel conduct as long as its compulsions have been democratically arrived at and are generally and equally applicable to all.

This is more or less the way most democratic governments and nations have operated. In some, a tradition of protection of individual freedom and equality develops among legislators and the public. This is usually sporadic, and least reliable when it is most needed—in the midst of controversy and emergency. It is Jackson's conception that is unusual, and peculiarly American. Jackson's vision can claim roots in the Bill of Rights, the Declaration of Independence, and Jefferson's proposed draft of the Virginia Constitution of 1776 (which would have abolished slavery and recognized some basic rights of women). But Jefferson, for example, opposed judicial review, whether on personal freedom or other issues, and favored states' rights [7] Jackson, like Frankfurter and Jefferson, is concerned about government restraint, but he wished to protect individual liberty or personal freedom—get the government off the backs of the people—by means of active intervention by the courts.

Although the current Court has embraced Frankfurter's conception of judicial restraint, it is unlikely that a majority would now vote, as he did, to uphold a compelled flag-salute law. As our notions of freedom have evolved, *Barnette,* on its narrow facts, is an easy case, because it involved a state compulsion to express a required belief and to participate in an officially mandated ritual. However, a recent case has repudiated the principles and vision of *Barnette* (chapter 4).

This debate is, of course, still with us, although the level of constitutional—and electoral—discourse has surely declined. One can only imagine what Jackson or Frankfurter would make of the Souter and Thomas confirmation hearings, the technocratic style of today's judicial opinions, and the thirty-second campaign spot. But this still leaves the question of why a majority of the justices on this occasion overruled a very recent precedent and set forth a new, broadly stated principle and vision.

This is not addressed in the opinions explicitly. However, amidst the rhetorical flourishes, sweeping visions and broad principles, there is a decidedly ominous tone to the *Barnette* opinions. The majority said that their ruling is not only better legally and socially, but also that dire consequences could result from a failure to recognize and enforce fundamental individual rights irrespective of popular majorities. Jackson, focusing on attempts throughout history to "coerce uniformity," said this:

> As first and moderate methods to attain unity have failed, those bent on its accomplishment must resort to an ever-increasing severity . . . . Ultimate futility of such attempts to compel coherence is the lesson of every such effort from the Roman drive to stamp out Christianity as a disturber of its pagan unity, the Inquisition, as a means to religious and dynastic unity, the Siberian exiles as a means to Russian unity, down to the fast failing efforts of our present totalitarian enemies. Those who begin coercive elimination of dissent soon find themselves *exterminating dissenters*. Compulsory unification of opinion achieves only the *unanimity of the graveyard*. (Emphasis added.)

This is, of course, about World War II, but the decision upholding mandatory flag salutes only three years earlier also came during the war. Something else had changed: the news of the Holocaust, long withheld by the government and the press, finally emerged in mid-1942.[8] The majority was reacting to and addressing the shocking news of the extermination of millions whose only offense had been their officially and popularly disfavored religion, ancestry, political views, or life-style. West Virginia authorities had not considered extermination or graveyards, but they had coerced children to salute the flag to achieve the appearance of unity and unanimity. Although unity in wartime is a laudable goal, compelled conformity was an impermissible and extremely dangerous path toward totalitarianism.

Justice Frankfurter's dissenting opinion was also unusual, unique as far as I am aware, in a revealing way. He began his opinion by stating his religion: "One who belongs to the most vilified and persecuted minority in history is not likely to be insensible to the freedoms guaranteed by our Constitution. Were my purely personal attitude relevant I should wholeheartedly associate myself with the general libertarian views in the [majority's] opinion. . . ." He offered an explanation of why, based on judicial restraint, even a Jewish justice might vote to uphold the compelled flag salute. The Holocaust is on their minds, but then how could it not be.

The justices, like other Americans, had just learned what one of the most accomplished Western democracies was capable of, and they were resolved to cut off the totalitarian path at its early stages and to create an institutional mechanism for guaranteeing freedom that does not depend on unreliable popular majorities or yield to exaggerated claims of necessity or emergency.

Citizenship Has Its Responsibilities

As a young man, Fred Korematsu, an American citizen born in Oakland, California, in 1919, attended school and helped his Japanese-immigrant parents run a plant nursery and sell roses. When Japan attacked Pearl Harbor and Congress declared war in December 1941, Korematsu was struck with a combination of surprise, confusion, and embarrassment that many Americans of German, Italian, and Japanese ancestry shared during World War II. He considered himself a loyal American, but, like the Barnett sisters, he would be tested in a way that he could not have imagined. It began right away: no one would buy the family's roses, and Korematsu lost a job as a welder in a shipyard and was excluded from a regular Friday-night poker game with his high-school friends.[9]

In 1942, General J. L. DeWitt was designated military commander of the western states. Martial law was never declared in the West or anywhere else in the country, but there were widespread stories and rumors about subversion. Backed up by an executive order and an act of Congress, DeWitt issued a series of orders placing restrictions on all people of Japanese ancestry on the West Coast, most of whom were American citizens. First there was a curfew, then an order to stay within their residential areas, and finally, an order that they leave their homes and report to designated detention centers or camps for indefinite imprisonment. The government called these detention facilities "concentration camps" until that term came to be associated with the German death camps.

Fred Korematsu refused to go to the camps because he felt that he had done nothing wrong and wanted to maintain his relationship with a girlfriend. He was arrested and served over two years in a camp in the Utah desert, where he joined his family in a one-room tarpaper shack with no furniture, and, he later said, "nothing but wind and dust blowing around." The general, with the support of Congress and President Roosevelt (and the governor of California, Earl Warren, later the most liberal chief justice in the Court's history), had imprisoned all people of Japanese ancestry on the West Coast, without proof that they had violated any law or done anything wrong.

The public reaction to this mass imprisonment was resounding approval. There were few demonstrations, no sit-ins, no marches on Washington. This was before the 1960s; the commitment to civil rights was isolated and sporadic, at best. The range of religious and community groups, churches, unions, and the press stood silently by, or joined in. The only national group of substantial size or stature that publicly condemned and actively opposed this imprisonment of a racial or ethnic group, which we still regularly refer to with the sanitized phrase "Japanese internment," was the Quakers, whose American Friends Service Committee issued an eloquent and courageous denunciation and actively aided the imprisoned.[10]

We now know that the government's claims of necessity and emergency based on the dangers of sabotage and espionage were exaggerated and even fabricated. I will return to this. But to understand and assess the Court's decision, it is important to focus on the circumstances known to the justices. They affirmed the criminal conviction of Fred Korematsu for refusing to report to a prison camp to serve an indefinite sentence imposed by General DeWitt based only on Korematsu's ancestry.

The majority opinion in *Korematsu v. United States* (1944)[11] was written by Justice Hugo Black, an Alabaman who later joined the liberal majority in the 1960s and is most remembered for his opinions advocating absolute protection for speech and championing civil liberties even in the repressive McCarthy era. Black started by noting that no one doubted Korematsu's loyalty and that "restrictions which curtail the civil rights of a single racial group are immediately suspect." However, we were at war: there was "apprehension . . . of the gravest imminent danger, [and the detentions had] a definite and close relationship to the prevention of espionage and sabotage." The imprisonments were unfortunate, but "[c]itizenship has its responsibilities as well as privileges, and in times of war the burden is always heavier." Korematsu's burden was imprisonment without guilt or trial because the government had established, according to Black, a "[p]ressing public necessity."

None of the justices doubted that unusual or extraordinary measures might pass constitutional muster in wartime. The question was which measures would be allowed and what justification would be required for their imposition. Black's opinion stripped Korematsu and all Japanese-Americans of essentially all their rights based only on the word of a general. There were no hearings, no congressional committee proceedings, no studies—not even a single conviction of any person of Japanese ancestry for any act of sabotage or espionage—that tended to prove the danger asserted by the government. The Court had before it, as the sole justification and documentation offered by the government, only DeWitt's "Final Report,"[12] the logic of which raised more questions than it answered.

The Final Report did not catalogue a pattern of specific acts with names and dates and descriptions of who had done what, as one might expect. There were some general claims of radio transmissions and signaling to ships offshore and a few claimed explosions (one of which occurred after all the Japanese-Americans had been imprisoned), none of which were specific, documented, or tied to particular individuals. Rather, the Final Report attempted to establish the asserted necessity with generalized, largely hypothetical statements of bad acts that could endanger the war effort, and—most critically—assumed character traits of the Japanese that purport to demonstrate a genetic or cultural propensity to do such things.

Take, for example, the asserted danger that people who live near military installations would sabotage them. The Final Report emphasized this, but there was no list of acts of sabotage of military installations by people of Japanese ancestry—because none were ever substantiated. The Final Report focused instead on supposed characteristics of the Japanese—amounting to stereotyped character deficiencies—that made it likely that they would perform such despicable acts. Even the lack of particular acts of sabotage showed, according to the Final Report, how dangerous the Japanese were: "The very fact that no sabotage has taken place to date is a disturbing and confirming indication that such action will be taken."

The Japanese-Americans were imprisoned not because of anything they or even other Japanese-Americans had done, but because of racial—and racist—stereotypes expounded by a general. The Final Report refers to the Japanese as "subversive" and "an enemy race." Their "racial strains are undiluted," DeWitt claimed, and they are an "unassimilated, tightly knit racial group, bound to an enemy nation by strong ties of race, culture, custom and religion." Such claims were surely not new to America or directed only at Asians; they should sound familiar to descendants of Italian, Irish, and Jewish immigrants. In fact, a better case could be made, and is suggested below, that the Japanese, although segregated and excluded from much of society like other immigrant groups, faced—and continue to face today—particularly intense hostility precisely because they assimilated so successfully.

Black's majority opinion upheld Korematsu's conviction based on the Final Report, which he said was "confirmed by investigations made subsequent to the exclusion." These investigations consisted of interviews by military authorities of their Japanese-American prisoners conducted in the detention camps. "Approximately five thousand American citizens of Japanese ancestry," Black stated,

> refused to swear unqualified allegiance to the United States and to renounce allegiance to the Japanese Emperor, and several thousand evacuees requested repatriation to Japan.

It is hard to imagine a different response from any racial or ethnic minority if we imprisoned them indefinitely based only on their ancestry. This was a strange time and place to ask for "unqualified allegiance," and the extraordinary result would seem to be how few—five thousand out of over a hundred thousand—expressed doubts about life in America.

Black's harshest criticism was for those who "cast this case into outlines of racial prejudice." This "merely confuses the issue," according to Black, because the government did not intend to discriminate or act out of racial animus but was only doing what was militarily necessary. Although there was purposeful discrimination in the now-usual sense that the people singled out for imprisonment were explicitly described in racial or ethnic terms, the reason or motive for the imprisonment was, according to Black, military necessity. This analysis effectively allows the government considerable latitude for even explicitly racial measures.

Black's social and constitutional vision, although not spelled out like Jackson's in *Barnette,* was deference to the executive branch and, specifically, the military's self-assessment of the needs of national security. President Dwight Eisenhower had not yet warned us about or named the "military-industrial complex," but it was beginning to play a dominant role in social and constitutional thought as well as economics. Individual rights—particularly those of a despised minority —paled next to the needs and discretion of a military apparatus that was keeping us from destruction.

Justice Frankfurter concurred, despite the fact that a racial group was singled out and the government's action therefore lacked the general applicability that he had so emphasized in his *Barnette* dissent. It was again, for Frankfurter, a matter of judicial restraint: the government's detention scheme, approved by the legislative and executive branches, "is their business, not ours." There were three dissenters, however.

Justice Frank Murphy saw DeWitt's statements and Final Report as racist and questioned the military's knowledge and expertise to gauge or predict the propensities of racial groups. Such racial stereotypes were the basis for "the abhorrent and despicable treatment of minority groups by the dictatorial tyrannies which this nation is now pledged to destroy." He emphasized the lack of any proof or basis for believing that the FBI and military authorities could not handle any real dangers of sabotage and espionage or that guilty individuals could not be distinguished from innocent ones by the usual judicial processes. And he worried about "open[ing] the door to discriminatory actions against other minority groups in the passions of tomorrow."

Justice Jackson, now in dissent, found another star: "If any fundamental assumption underlies our system, it is that guilt is personal and not inheritable." General DeWitt's pronouncements were "unsworn, self-serving statement[s], untested by any cross-examination." The majority had "validated the principle of racial discrimination in criminal procedure" and skewed the constitutional scheme. He condemned the new subservience to claims of military necessity and national security: "We may as well say that any military order will be constitutional and have done with it."

The dissenters' insights and criticisms of the government and the Court's majority have stood the test of time. In 1980 Congress appointed the bipartisan Commission on Wartime Relocation and Internment of Civilians to investigate the entire matter thoroughly, which issued a definitive report, *Personal Justice Denied*.[13] The commission concluded that "not a single documented act of espionage, sabotage or fifth column activity was committed by an American citizen of Japanese ancestry or by a resident Japanese alien on the West Coast." Instead, the commission found at the root of the matter long-standing racial and economic hostility toward the Japanese, who by 1942 owned a substantial portion of the richest agricultural land in California and were producing 30 to 40 percent of that state's truck crops. They had accomplished this in a relatively short period by hard work and wise business decisions. Like other minorities, a combination of exclusion and choice led them generally to live and socialize among themselves. DeWitt's explicit racism was evident to anyone who wished to look carefully at the Final Report and his public comments.

The commission contrasted the treatment of German- and Italian-Americans on the East Coast.[14] German submarines fought an active war right off the East Coast, sinking almost a hundred tankers and commercial vessels in the first half of 1942 (by mid-1942, we developed effective defenses). These sinkings could sometimes be seen from the shore; some were "in full view of bathers and picnickers at Virginia Beach" and Florida resorts. There were also "visible, active pro-Nazi" groups, the most well known of which, the Bund, claimed a membership of over 200,000; and authorities the commission found "responsible" believed that the German submarines were actively aided by German-Americans. Yet, although military and civilian officials considered detaining or excluding from the coast at least some categories or groups of Germans, no such action was taken. A "small number" of German- and Italian-Americans were excluded from the coast, and some were interned. However, this was done only after individualized investigations and prompt, individualized loyalty hearings, at which the accused was often cleared. Guilt was personal, not inherited.

Political-science professor Peter Irons added another, startling dimension to the matter in his 1983 book, *Justice at War*.[15] Using the Freedom of Information Act, Irons obtained the internal government documents detailing the government's development of its *Korematsu* brief and argument before the Supreme Court. He discovered reports by the FBI, the Navy, and other government agencies concluding that there was no espionage or sabotage and that DeWitt had known there was no substantiated danger. The Final Report was a fraud.

A War Department lawyer in what was called the Alien Enemy Control Unit summed it up in a memo to Solicitor General Charles Fahy, whose job was to brief and argue the case:

> We are now therefore in possession of substantially incontrovertible evidence that the most important statements of fact advanced by General DeWitt to justify the evacuation and detention were incorrect, and furthermore that General DeWitt had cause to know, and in all probability did know, that they were incorrect at the time he embodied them in his [F]inal [R]eport. . . .

An intense conflict ensued among the government's highest-ranking officials. Some felt it their duty to inform the Court that the Final Report—which provided the entire basis for the government's extraordinary action—was inaccurate and fabricated. A footnote to this effect was inserted in a draft of the brief; but after an often-acrimonious debate and shifting positions (including twice stopping the presses printing the brief), the footnote was so watered down that it no longer alerted the Court, or the public.

Congress recently provided a small payment for reparations to those imprisoned who were still alive at that time. Based on the discovery of proof that the government misled the courts and failed to provide the defense with exculpatory evidence, Korematsu was able to overturn his conviction in 1984.[16] But neither action overturned or disturbed the constitutional force of the *Korematsu* decision, which has never been overruled. It was cited authoritatively by the Reagan administration in a recent case.[17] They viewed it as authority for the notion that the power of the government, particularly the executive branch, is extensive. It is surely authority for at least that.

CONSTITUTIONAL CHOICES

In the midst of world war almost fifty years ago, the Court issued both its most and least libertarian and egalitarian decisions of the modern era. Before turning to the basic choices that confront us in our own time, it is worth considering why the Court, without any change in personnel, did this in the period of just over one year.

One can find distinctions between *Barnette* and *Korematsu* in the different facts and specific issues, but there is a more-important difference in constitutional and social approach and vision. Thus, the dangers at issue, whether real, imagined, or fabricated, were certainly more substantial in *Korematsu* than in *Barnette*.

29

Espionage and sabotage are more serious, and more concrete, threats to the war effort than disturbed unity. On the other hand, *Korematsu* also involved far more serious individual harm and an explicitly racial classification—a race of Americans was imprisoned without trial or even allegations of individual guilt. The differing factual and legal issues might explain the results, but not the fundamental difference in reasoning or the sharply divergent constitutional and social visions.

There were two ingredients among the mix of factual, legal, and social concerns in *Korematsu* that were different from anything involved in *Barnette* and that have particular importance for us today. First, whereas *Barnette* posed a conflict between a claim of individual right and the mandate of a local school and state law, in *Korematsu* the individual right conflicted with explicit assertions of military necessity and national security by the military and the president, with the backing of Congress. The Court responded with extreme deference. Here we see the military economy and national security state gaining a foothold not only in the nation's culture but in its constitutional doctrine and social vision.

This example should be particularly instructive for us. We have recently witnessed the dissolution of the Soviet Union and with it the only credible self-defense justification for the militarization of American life. And we have learned that the most compelling argument in modern times for deference to military necessity and national security was not only exaggerated but fabricated.

Second, despite Justice Black's disclaimer, *Korematsu* is very much about what Studs Terkel recently called the "American obsession"—race. There was a basic failure of the majority to see the humanity of—and the injustice, degradation, economic harm (most lost their land and businesses) and terror imposed on—these people of color. This does not have to stem from purposeful or even conscious racism; blindness to even the most serious harm—essentially a lack of minimal human empathy—has always been a fundamental aspect of racism. Black's reasoning reflected this blindness, accepted the Final Report without question, and shifted the focus to the responses of Japanese-Americans imprisoned for their ancestry who were asked to affirm "unqualified allegiance" to the government that unjustly imprisoned them. His harshest criticism was for those who "confuse" the matter by suggesting that race had something to do with it. The *Korematsu* decision elevated two enduring themes from the American popular discourse on race to the level of constitutional justifications: blame the victim and attack the messenger.[18]

Korematsu also leaves some challenging unanswered questions. What if there had been solid proof—perhaps including numerous criminal convictions—of sabotage and espionage by Japanese-Americans? Surely Jackson's principle would be unaffected: guilt should be "personal and not inheritable." If there is an extreme breakdown of the usual processes of government, including those judicial processes that separate the guilty from the innocent, martial law may be necessary, but that need not and should not be aimed at or limited to people of a particular race or ancestry. In any event, such proof would certainly enhance the majority's position and draw into question an approach that so easily lends itself to notions of racial guilt and conviction and imprisonment without trial.

And what if the war with Japan had gone badly for the U.S., and, with defeat a real possibility and the economy in shambles, the likes of General DeWitt were entrusted with the fate of 112,000 imprisoned Japanese-Americans? His oft-stated goal, quoted in *Personal Justice Denied,* was to "wipe [them] off the map." I would like to think we could not do what the Germans did, and we have some immunity to the ethnic, racial, and religious violence that now engulfs Europe and a large portion of the world. We have traditions of freedom and equality, but there was only acquiescence and support as we imprisoned a race of Americans.

Our own history is not unblemished in this regard. As the Vietnam War went badly for our side, we increasingly turned to a campaign of terrorism and indiscriminate bombing that resulted in enormous civilian casualties. If this recent history is somewhat ambiguous, our earlier campaign against American Indians raised the clear specter of racial extermination.[19]

But whatever the underlying reasons and the unanswered questions, the legacy of *Barnette* and *Korematsu* is two contradictory constitutional approaches and social visions. The *Barnette* approach emphasizes individual liberty and equality. The government, even when it is expressing the will of a popular majority, cannot control or compel individual choice in matters of belief, expression, religion, culture, or life-style unless the individual's conduct directly and concretely harms others or undercuts a government interest of the highest order of importance that cannot be realized without infringing on the individual. Nor can the government imprison anyone without proof of individual guilt and a fair process. The individual is protected in these matters from government as a matter of basic human dignity and respect and because such individual freedom and liberty, without prior restriction or fear of punishment, are essential to democracy and self-government. Uniformity achieved by coercion is not permissible or desirable. This is not just a matter of tolerance or acquiescence in differences. Our strength, and the very core of our nation, is "our rich cultural diversities."

The institutional mechanism for this protection is the courts and what has come to be called the "strict scrutiny" standard of judicial review. Any government action that infringes on or burdens individual constitutional rights in the areas just outlined is subjected to a detailed, probing two-step analysis by courts. First, courts will determine whether it directly furthers a "compelling"—as opposed to merely legitimate and important—government interest. Second, even if the interest is compelling, courts will determine whether there is another means of furthering that interest that is "less restrictive" of constitutional rights. If the government's action infringing on or burdening these rights falls short in terms of either of these requirements—both of which amount to a very high level of necessity—it is invalid.

The strict-scrutiny standard provides a framework and approach that tend to favor individual freedom, liberty, and equality over conflicting or competing government concerns and actions. For example, in the race-discrimination cases over the fifty years in which the strict-scrutiny analysis has been available, the government's action has been sustained in only one case in which strict-scrutiny was applied (*Korematsu*). (This has lent increasing importance to the arguments and analyses that are used to determine whether strict scrutiny will be applied in a particular case, because they have a frequently decisive effect on outcomes.) The approach and analysis best set out in *Barnette*, however, have been applied by the Supreme Court in only two periods in our history, the mid-1930s to mid-1940s and the 1960s and early 1970s.

The *Korematsu* approach places government action and discretion above individual freedom, liberty, or equality in these matters. The government expresses the will of the people, and its measures are valid if they have some reasonable relation to a legitimate government interest. The hallmark of this approach is deference to government. When the government asserts interests of the highest order, like military necessity and national security, its assertions, even if only generally stated, should not be scrutinized. Even imprisonment of a race without any proof of individual guilt is permissible. The role of the courts is to defer to the other, more popular branches of government. The doctrinal formulation embodying this approach is called the "rational basis" standard (although the *Korematsu* majority used some strict scrutiny language). Courts will defer, examining the validity of government actions only superficially to determine whether there is any rational basis or rational relationship to some legitimate government interest. If there is—and there almost always is—the government's action is valid. Invalidation of government action based on rational-basis judicial review has been extremely rare. This authoritarian tradition has characterized most of our legal and social history and was particularly strong from about 1896 to 1932.[20]

The *Korematsu* approach and example is particularly important for us today because it is the approach of the current, very conservative Supreme Court. We do not know with certainty whether the result would be the same if such a situation were to recur. I believe it would, but that is speculation. Of more certainty is the approach and social vision.

As we enter the twenty-first century, *Barnette* and *Korematsu* present these two contradictory visions and approaches from among many available to us. After over a decade of conservative political hegemony, it seems appropriate to assume nothing and start with the basic question: Do we still believe that some individual rights of expression, participation in the political process, religion, equality, privacy, and/or due process should be protected from government action at all? (This is separate from the question of which rights or the scope and content of each.)

Frankfurter's judicial restraint is very different from Rehnquist's and Reagan's in this regard. Frankfurter opposed judicially imposed protections, but he favored the same protections and shared the social vision of the *Barnette* majority if implemented by more popular means. The conservatives of today tend not to address this directly, but, unlike Frankfurter, they have a clear record of opposing such protections by any branch of government or any institution. Rehnquist and Reagan were longtime opponents of civil rights, including active opposition not just to affirmative action but to all the civil-rights legislation of the 1960s.

As a law clerk to Justice Jackson (a barely noticed irony) in 1952, Rehnquist wrote a memo opposing what would, two years

later, become the basic American pronouncement of equality—
Brown v. Board of Education, which integrated the public schools.
He wrote that *Plessy v. Ferguson* and its "separate but equal" principle were "right and should be reaffirmed." Jackson disagreed,
and so did a unanimous court in *Brown.* Another Rehnquist
memo to Jackson urged approval of the all-white Democratic primary system in Texas: "It is about time the Court faced the fact
that the white people of the South don't like the colored people."
Jackson voted, with an eight-to-one majority, to invalidate the all-
white primary.[21]

As a young attorney and Republican activist in Phoenix, Rehnquist actively opposed that city's public accommodations law.
Phoenix had been embarrassed in the early 1960s when during a
national meeting of lawyers, one of its top hotels refused to admit
Jewish guests. Rehnquist, in a letter to the local newspaper,
favored the freedom of a property owner "to choose his own customers." In his active opposition to public accommodations laws,
Rehnquist showed no apparent concern for African-Americans,
who often could not find a restaurant, gas station, or even hospital
that was open to them in that era. This was not an unusual conservative position at that time. The federal public accommodations
law (in the Civil Rights Act of 1964) was also opposed by an up-
and-coming "moderate" Republican in Texas, George Bush.

Rehnquist was an organizer of a "poll watching team" accused
of obstructing voting in African-American and Hispanic neighborhoods. He responded to a school-integration proposal by the
Phoenix school superintendent with a newspaper piece that
argued: "We are no more dedicated to an 'integrated' society than
we are to a 'segregated' society." Later, in an internal memo as an
aide to President Nixon, Rehnquist vehemently opposed the proposed constitutional amendment guaranteeing equality for
women. He was overruled and told to present testimony for the
administration before Congress supporting the amendment. With

remarkable duplicity, at his 1986 confirmation hearing—before his internal memo opposing the amendment was revealed—Rehnquist said his Nixon-administration testimony favoring equal rights for women showed he favors civil rights.

, The conservatives who now dominate the Court are judicial activists on a range of issues; they simply do not share Jackson's or Frankfurter's vision of personal freedom or diversity, whether implemented by courts or any other means. The popular will on this basic issue is harder to gauge, particularly because it is so seldom discussed in the media. Polls show that despite most people preferring to label themselves "conservative" rather than "liberal," on many constitutional issues, like free expression, they strongly favor some form of individual protection. For example, although the Court's protection of flag burning spawned a lot of demagoguery and negative public reaction, after a little time to reflect, most Americans thought free speech was more important than stopping flag burning. Similarly, most people favor conservative judicial restraint in the abstract, but an overwhelming majority recoiled at Judge Robert Bork's articulation of what it could concretely mean—no protection for basic rights such as privacy—and urged their senators to reject his nomination to the Court.[22]

My premise, throughout this book, is that there must be safeguards: mechanisms and institutions that vigorously protect human integrity, dignity, freedom, and equality, as well as a citizenry that is informed and conscious of history and the potential for tyranny among the best of nations and peoples. This is the inherent message of the Bill of Rights as well as the best social vision.

If we value and wish to guarantee these protections, the next question is the mechanism for their implementation. There would seem to be four basic options: the people themselves (or some decentralized institutions for popular participation), the legislative

and executive branches of the federal government, state governments, or the courts. I will explore these options in the conclusion.
For now, it is important to recognize that conservatives have
tended to reject judicial protection while simultaneously rejecting
protection implemented by any alternative mechanism. We have
adopted, in a fundamental sense, the worst of combinations: the
courts now reject the role of protector of personal freedom, and
the legislatures and people still defer such matters to the courts.

◆ 2 ◆

EXPRESSION

The basic principle that individuals and groups have the ability to express different and unpopular views without prior restraint or punishment is a necessary element of any free and democratic society. It is indispensable to both the individual and society generally. Without freedom of expression, the individual is not truly free and cannot be an active participant or maintain self-respect and dignity while functioning with others as part of society. Expression is not just something people do; it is, in the deepest sense, an integral part of what people are. Society cannot effectively resolve conflict or competing demands and interests, generate new ideas, function democratically, or maintain stability unless individuals are free to express themselves. The downside of free speech is that on occasion people are exposed to ideas that they find stupid, upsetting, or disgusting, but this is a minimal price—and sometimes those stupid, upsetting, or disgusting ideas later gain majority acceptance.

The free-speech principle has gained a unique acceptance in the United States, for which we are rightly proud. However, free speech means much more than this in American politics and culture. Free speech is often discussed as if it defined an economic or political system, or even a religion, rather than a series of rules prohibiting governmental limits on individual expression. It is what makes us good, and better (than other countries and people). Freedom of speech is at the core of our national identity.

Yet, the American celebration of free speech is unsettling, contradictory, and quite complex. The invocation of free speech gains wide acceptance when formulated generally and abstracted from current controversies, or when aimed at specific repressive practices in other countries. But specific applications in the United States are regularly greeted with contempt, evident in the recurring controversies over flag burning and demonstrations by Nazis. There is considerably less than a consensus about or a widespread understanding of the basic aspects of American speech law that truly distinguish it from more restrictive laws and practices prevalent almost everywhere else in the world. The rejection of limits on unfettered dissent and criticism, expression in a variety of places and a variety of ways, the primacy of expression over competing concerns, the content barrier—all are controversial on the home field of free speech and may not any longer command a majority of the population.

Simultaneously, there is a widespread recognition, across the political spectrum, that the American people lack the effective means to be heard or to translate their wishes into reality through the political process. Despite all the rhetoric about free speech and our democratic political process, a very large proportion of us—perhaps most—feel silenced and disenfranchised. One very evident indication of this is the small proportion of eligible voters who vote. There is, and has been for some time, a fundamental crisis of democracy and freedom that has been ignored by public officials and the media (see chapter 3).

The widespread perception of disempowerment and the questioning of free-speech guarantees are perhaps connected. People who feel that they have lost their voice and are being ignored may understandably find it difficult to tolerate the media attention and constitutional importance accorded, say, a flag burner or Nazi demonstrator. The "downside" of free speech referred to above can appear less acceptable and provide an easy outlet for people who (rightly) feel themselves effectively silenced and disenfranchised. This is unfortunate, because the remedy for disempowerment is empowerment, which requires more speech, more dialogue, and a more democratic political process. It also separates potential allies who could transcend the usual political categories with a program of basic changes regarding free speech and the political process.

What is needed is a substantial expansion of the means accessible to ordinary people for expressing their views effectively and for effective participation in the political process. I will present some suggestions here and in the next chapter, but the conservative-dominated Supreme Court has moved decisively in the opposite direction in a series of decisions essentially ignored by the media (whose First Amendment rights have so far remained intact). These recent cases, and the fundamental challenge that we face in the twenty-first century, are difficult to understand without some appreciation of the history of free speech and the fundamental change in speech law that occurred in the twentieth century. This is summarized first, then the remainder of this chapter focuses on the recent speech cases. Voting, elections, and access to the media are discussed in the next chapter.

THE SURPRISING HISTORY OF
FREE SPEECH IN THE UNITED STATES

Despite persistent but nonspecific references to "our traditions" in legal and popular literature, no right of free speech as we know it existed, either in law or practice, until a basic transformation of the law governing speech in the period from about 1919 to 1940. It is commonly assumed in the courts and law reviews that there were no significant court decisions on freedom of speech before World War I, and that shortly thereafter speech was legally protected by

the Supreme Court and has remained so ever since. Popular literature extends these views posited in the legal literature to embrace
the idea that freedom of speech is a cornerstone of the Constitution and the basis of our country. However, before the transformation about fifty years ago, one spoke publicly only at the discretion
of local, and sometimes federal, authorities, who often prohibited
what they, the local business establishment, or other powerful segments of the community did not want to hear.

For all that has been written about freedom of speech, there
is little that acknowledges the pre–World War I history or recog-
nizes the profound change in the law in the twentieth century, and
even less that attempts to analyze the change. A particular aspect
of speech—speaking, gathering, and distributing literature in
public places—has been emphasized because it is the subject of
the Supreme Court cases that best illustrate the transformation in
the law and because this aspect played a major role in the events
leading to the transformation.[1]

Public Parks and Private Houses

In 1894, the Reverend William F. Davis, an evangelist and longtime active opponent of slavery and racism, attempted to preach
the Gospel on Boston Common, an open, public park. For his first
attempt, Davis was incarcerated for a few weeks in the Charles
Street Jail; the second time, he was fined and appealed the sentence. The hostility of the Boston authorities toward Davis probably stemmed from his espousal of the Social Gospel, a popular
religious trend of the time that emphasized social responsibility
and often condemned the corruption of city officials. In any event,
Davis believed that there was a "constitutional right of citizens to
the use of public grounds and places without let or hindrance by
the City authorities."[2]

The Supreme Court of Massachusetts disagreed. In an opinion
by Oliver Wendell Holmes—later a justice of the Supreme Court

of the United States known for his decisions protecting freedom of speech—the court upheld Davis's conviction based on a city ordinance that prohibited "any public address" on public grounds without a permit from the mayor. Holmes, like almost all state and lower federal-court judges, viewed such an ordinance as simply a city regulation of the use of its park, which was within the city's rights as owner of the property. Davis had no basis, in the Constitution or elsewhere, to claim any limits on this property right:

> That such an ordinance is constitutional . . . does not appear to us open to doubt. . . . For the Legislature absolutely or conditionally to forbid public speaking in a highway or public park is no more an infringement of the rights of a member of the public than for the owner of a private house to forbid it in his house.[3]

The Supreme Court of the United States unanimously affirmed in *Davis v. Massachusetts* (1897),[4] quoting Holmes's analogy to a private house. In the only reference to the Constitution, the Court said that it "does not have the effect of creating a particular and personal right in the citizen to use public property in defiance of the Constitution and laws of the State." Nor did the Court find any constitutional or other limit on the mayor's authority to deny permission selectively or for any reason: "The right to absolutely exclude all right to use, necessarily includes the authority to determine under what circumstances such use may be availed of, as the greater power contains the lesser."

From the adoption of the First Amendment (1791) to the beginning of the basic legal transformation (1919), a variety of social and religious activists demanded recognition of freedom of speech. The most significant of these—the abolitionists, the anarchists, the Industrial Workers of the World, the Socialist party, and the early labor and women's movements—were sometimes successful in speaking, gathering, and distributing literature publicly.

Federal and state courts, however, repeatedly refused to protect any form of speech. The change came in the 1930s (after a series of dissenting opinions starting in 1919), exemplified by a decision arising from the labor movement's attempt to organize workers in Jersey City, New Jersey.

In Trust for the Use of the Public

The labor movement of the 1930s, like Reverend Davis, believed that the government should hold and maintain public streets, sidewalks, and parks for the use of the people. Labor organizers had regularly been denied freedom of speech, which they generally saw as inseparable from the right to organize unions, except in cities with progressive or socialist mayors. After Congress passed the National Labor Relations Act (NLRA) in 1935, the Congress of Industrial Organizations (CIO) sought to explain its provisions and the benefits of unions and collective bargaining to working people throughout the country. Nowhere was their reception more hostile than on the Jersey City turf of political boss Frank Hague.

The CIO planned to distribute literature on the streets and host outdoor meetings, but permits for these activities were denied by Hague. Hague was an early supporter of the less-militant American Federation of Labor and of the New Deal, which provided him with resources for distribution to local communities and political allies. But by the mid-1930s he had firmly allied himself with the manufacturing and commercial establishments. He made it clear that labor organizers were not welcome in Jersey City, and many were cast out of town, usually by being put on a ferry to New York. Local businesses were promised that they would have no labor troubles while he was mayor; his response to the CIO was: "I am the law."[5]

The CIO took Hague to court, resulting in the *Hague v. CIO* decision in 1939,[6] in which the Court said:

Wherever the title of streets and parks may rest, they have immemorially been held in trust for the use of the public and, time out of mind, have been used for purposes of assembly, communicating thoughts between citizens, and discussing public questions. Such use of the streets and public places has, from ancient times, been a part of the privileges, immunities, rights, and liberties of citizens.

This was a direct repudiation of both the doctrinal basis and the result in *Davis*, and it first established the basic concept of free speech now taken for granted. That concept was best articulated in the famous dissents of Justices Holmes and Louis Brandeis starting in 1919, such as the following passage from a Brandeis opinion in 1927:

Those who won our independence believed that the final end of the State was to make men free to develop their faculties; and that in its government the deliberative forces should prevail over the arbitrary. They valued liberty both as an end and as a means. They believed liberty to be the secret of happiness and courage to be the secret of liberty. They believed that freedom to think as you will and to speak as you think are means indispensable to the discovery and spread of political truth; that without free speech and assembly discussion would be futile; that with them, discussion affords ordinarily adequate protection against the dissemination of noxious doctrine; that the greatest menace to freedom is an inert people; that public discussion is a political duty; and that this should be a fundamental principle of the American government. They recognized the risks to which all human institutions are subject. But they knew that order cannot be secured merely through fear of punishment for its infraction; that it is hazardous to discourage thought, hope and imagination; that fear breeds repression; that repression breeds hate; that hate menaces stable government; that the path of safety lies in the opportunity to discuss freely supposed grievances and proposed remedies; and that the fitting remedy for evil counsels is good ones. Believing in the power of reason as applied through public discussion, they eschewed silence coerced by law—the argument of force in its worst form. Recognizing the occasional tyrannies of governing majorities, they amended the Constitution so that free speech and assembly should be guaranteed.[7]

However, the *Hague* Court did not explicitly overrule *Davis,* discuss the lack of free speech prior to its decision, or even acknowledge that it had made a fundamental change in legal doctrine. Rather, the opinion was an inspiring exposition of a right to freedom of speech based on natural law and long-standing princple. Like all such conceptions, it is essentially timeless and without a social context. In the quoted passage, the streets and parks have "immemorially" been held for the people and used for speech "time out of mind," and the right of free speech stems "from ancient times." But there is no indication as to what time or place the Court was referring; it certainly had never been so in the United States—or anywhere else—before this very case, as the Court had itself ruled in *Davis.* As we shall see, it is not unusual for judges to depict even such basic changes as part of an unchanging, seamless continuum.

Davis is the only Supreme Court decision addressing these basic free-speech issues before the transformation began, but state- and lower-federal-court decisions, as well as the practice throughout the country, confirm that there was no tradition of or legally protected right to free speech as we know it prior to the transformation. The supposed existence of such a tradition and such rights is a long-standing myth.

The Constitution and the Early Popular Understanding

The Constitution, as ratified in 1787, did not mention freedom of speech, although historians and legal scholars generally agree that the Bill of Rights (see appendix), in the form of amendments adopted four years later, was promised and necessary to secure ratification. There is considerable controversy, however, about how the framers of the Constitution and the population generally viewed freedom of speech before and during the constitutional drafting and ratification process. The traditional view that freedom of speech was widely supported—which has been translated into the current popular notion that free speech was the founding principle of our country—is usually documented, if at all, by reference to eloquent but largely rhetorical writings in this century by Harvard law professor Zechariah Chafee, Jr. This view has been challenged based on convincing historical research, principally by historian Leonard Levy.[8]

The controversy has suffered from a lack of concreteness: freedom of speech as we know it consists of several specific concepts and rules guaranteeing, most basically, the ability, without restraint, punishment, or content-based limitation, to criticize government and public officials and private institutions and individuals; to express one's views in public places; and to associate with others for political purposes. Although the Constitution and the First Amendment were popularly understood to embody basic notions of political freedom, including at least a repudiation of judicial or other actions that prohibit in advance publication by the press (called prior restraints), the other aspects of free speech as we know it developed throughout our two-hundred-year history.

For example, English and American law at the time of the Constitution essentially rendered criticism of the government or its officials a criminal act. This offense, called seditious libel, was based on the conception of a monarch and government as divine and above reproach. The truth of a criticism was considered a basis for aggravation rather than mitigation of the crime because a correct criticism was more likely to create discord and contempt for the government. Although seditious libel is completely incompatible with our current conception of free speech, it was a crime in every state at the time the Constitution was adopted. Furthermore, Levy's review of the writings and speeches of the framers of the Constitution and the leaders of the revolution shows that none of them—including even Thomas Jefferson and Thomas Paine—opposed criminalization of seditious libel. Some of the framers advocated reforms of the law of seditious libel, including adoption of truth as a defense and the determination of libel by the jury, but still favored the criminalization of criticism of the government and its officials. Levy suggests, rather convincingly, that the First Amendment, alone among the provisions of the Bill of Rights in being explicitly directed at and limiting only Congress, was not viewed by its framers as changing existing law and merely constituted a reservation to the states of the power to regulate speech, press, and religion. The seeds of popular belief in free speech as we know it came later, perhaps in response to the Sedition Act of 1798.

While the ink on the First Amendment was barely dry, the Federalists, our first political party, attempted to silence their opponents with prosecutions for the common-law offense of seditious libel. The Federalists, undaunted by the First Amendment to their Constitution, became dissatisfied with the ineffectiveness of these seditious-libel prosecutions due to doubts raised about whether federal courts had common-law jurisdiction. In 1798, they pushed through Congress, by a narrow margin, the Sedition Act, which made it a crime to

> write, print, utter or publish . . . any false, scandalous and malicious writings against the government of the United States, or either House of Congress . . . or the President with the intent to defame . . . or to bring them into contempt or disrepute.

Although the act also contained two protective devices—truth was made a defense, and the jury was to decide whether the words were seditious—Federalist judges quickly negated their effect. They refused to distinguish between statements of fact and opinion, and they ruled that the defendant must prove the truth of every minute detail to establish the truth defense. Overall, they treated the First Amendment as if it only codified preexisting law and prohibited only prior censorship, which had been prohibited in England since 1695 and in the colonies since 1725. The most prominent person prosecuted under the Sedition Act was Matthew Lyon, a member of Congress critical of the Federalists. Lyon was imprisoned and his house sold to pay his fine (nevertheless he was reelected in the next election). The longest prison term, two years, was served by a laborer for erecting a sign on a post that read, in part, NO STAMP ACT, NO SEDITION . . . DOWNFALL TO THE TYRANTS OF AMERICA, PEACE AND RETIREMENT TO THE PRESIDENT. The act was "never invoked against alien enemies, or possible traitors, but solely against editors and public men whom the Federalists under President Adams desired to silence or deport in order to suppress political opposition."[9]

The act and consequent prosecutions were extremely unpopular, and convictions were difficult to obtain without manipulation of the composition of juries (which, as a result, were comprised almost entirely of Federalists) and active bias by Federalist judges. "Popular indignation at the Act and the prosecutions wrecked the Federalist Party."[10] Jefferson pardoned all those convicted, and the government repaid their fines.

The Supreme Court never reviewed any of the common-law or statutory sedition cases, but several legal doctrines that restricted expression were adopted by the lower courts and would be repeatedly resurrected later. The two foremost were the "bad-tendency" doctrine, which allowed prosecution for words that could, in however remote or indirect a fashion, contribute to disorder or unlawful conduct sometime in the future; and the "constructive-intent" doctrine, which ascribed to the speaker or writer the intent to cause such remote and indirect consequences. In addition, the public streets, sidewalks, and parks were controlled for purposes of expression by local authorities, as the Court later held in *Davis*. These were the rules governing speech until the transformation, which, as I have explained elsewhere,[11] resulted from popular demands by people at all levels of society (led most prominently by the labor movement of the 1930s) and from social and cultural changes, rather than any language in the Constitution or legal reasoning.

The Liberal Paradigm

The transformation in speech law was complete by the 1940s. However, the new speech and association rights were essentially suspended in the 1950s, when Senator Joseph McCarthy, the House Un-American Activities Committee, and many others resurrected the pretransformation tradition. Unpopular ideas and associations again became illegal; dissenters were jailed and lost jobs. The courts abdicated in the face of a reactionary conservative media blitz.[12]

The transformation-based expansion of speech rights resumed in the 1960s and early 1970s, when the civil rights and antiwar movements demanded and got heightened enforcement and a substantial expansion of speech rights. The result was a set of rules that are best described as the liberal paradigm—a term that I use with hesitancy because I value free speech, and the term *liberal* has become synonymous with various shades of bad. But the truth is that advocacy and protection of speech rights—the free speech that is a favorite of American political rhetoric—has been throughout our history a mainstay of liberal and progressive thought. Some conservatives have also favored it, but the main opposition has come from conservatives, starting with the Federalists and continuing to today.

The liberal paradigm can be capsulized with a few basic rules (which will then be discussed further below). Speech is first categorized as either "protected" or "unprotected" based on its subject matter. Protected speech cannot be infringed or burdened unless the government is furthering a compelling interest that cannot be furthered by means less restrictive of speech—the strict scrutiny standard discussed in chapter 1. The worst violations are government prohibitions of speech (prior restraints) and restrictions on the content of speech (piercing the "content barrier"), which together are what we call and condemn as censorship.

The categories of unprotected speech usually referred to are obscenity, child pornography, defamation, fraud, incitement to imminent lawless action ("clear and present danger"), and "fighting words." All other speech is protected, although there is a hierarchy among the various protected categories. Political speech is the most protected because it has the highest social value by furthering society's interest in free and open debate as well as the individual's interest in expression. Commercial speech (speech by corporations or individuals in pursuit of their business interests) is less protected.

The way in which protected speech is communicated—the mode of speech—is subject to the strict-scrutiny standard and also to reasonable regulation of the time, place, and manner. It can be direct or symbolic and verbal, written, or graphic (and technological advances may well add more to the list)—including a book or leaflet, a speech, a demonstration, picketing, door-to-door canvasing, burning a flag—as long as it does not conflict with a compelling government interest. But it is always subject to reasonable regulation of the time, place, and manner, which includes commonsense limits, so that a loud assembly at night in a residential neighborhood is more subject to limitation or prohibition than the same assembly in a downtown area during working hours.

The most important free-speech right for people of ordinary means has been the right to assemble, express themselves, and distribute literature in public places—the right denied Reverend

Davis but vindicated in *Hague v. CIO*. The property-based reasoning of *Davis* was firmly and repeatedly overruled in the fifty years following the transformation: government property or facilities open to the general public and not restricted to some particular, incompatible use were presumptively available for peaceable assembly, expression, and distribution of literature. The centrality of this right is recognized every time we conclude that societies in which the government suppresses such activities are authoritarian or totalitarian—their peoples are not free.

In the post-transformation period, particularly in the 1930s and the 1960s, the Court protected and extended speech rights against a wide range of proposed justifications for limiting them. The hostile reactions of passersby, or even a majority of the community, who disagree with expressed views was found insufficient to limit speech, because the basic idea is to allow and protect expression of a wide range of ideas and perspectives. If speech rights were limited on this ground, expression would be subject to the approval of the views expressed by the potential audience, the government, or popular sentiment—amounting to what has generally been called a "listener's veto." If listeners have a veto—whether they are in the audience or in the legislatures—there cannot be free speech.

The Court rejected the listener's veto and found such matters as littering associated with speech or demonstrations and the need for crowd control insufficient to limit speech. In addition, certain ancillary rights were recognized as necessary to exercise speech rights effectively, such as the right to distribute literature and to solicit funds or sell literature or goods in support of the views expressed. In a 1943 case, the Court noted that "the pamphlets of Thomas Paine were not free of charge." Speech rights were also extended to cover new and unforeseen public places as life-styles and the places people frequent changed: in 1946 speech rights were applied to "company towns" and in 1968 to privately owned shopping centers.[13]

The Court recognized and overcame the theoretical and practical impediments to free speech and enabled—for the first time in the history of the world—people of ordinary means and status to enter the social discourse and speak their minds freely and publicly. These rules—and the resulting openness and freedom of our public places—were the essence of American free speech.

FREE SPEECH ISN'T FREE
(AND NO ONE IS LISTENING)

The liberal paradigm, when enforced by judges who believe in the idea of free speech, embodied our unique system of freedom of expression. However, the shortcomings of even the most protective version of American speech law have been generally ignored, even by some of its most ardent advocates in liberal circles. The ideal is often assumed to be—or confused with—the reality.

First, the rules of the liberal paradigm are not as clear as they seem and embody basic contradictions. Almost all human activity involves some form of expression, so the real list of unprotected categories is much larger than acknowledged. Indeed, all government activity and all the fields of law, from antitrust and regulation of the stock market to torts and contracts, in some basic sense involve regulation of expression without application of strict scrutiny. Business negotiations and written contracts, stock transactions, price-fixing activities, and simple assault (defined as placing another person in reasonable fear of an unwanted touching) all consist substantially or sometimes exclusively of speech or expression. It would be easier to list the small number of protected categories rather than the very large number of unprotected ones.

Further, no principle or standards distinguish the unprotected from the protected categories, and they are both under- and over-inclusive. The unprotected categories represent expression that can be described as of minimal social value, but so can a lot of other speech that has escaped that status, such as racist speech. And the protected categories include much that is of little or no social value. The very judgment of social value or the lack thereof—and the project of distinguishing protected from unprotected speech—cannot be accomplished neutrally or objectively and collides with the core concept of free speech. We do not have free speech or open debate if anyone—whether they claim membership in a legislature or the Supreme Court—is allowed to decide what ideas have value or deserve protection.

The most-protected category, political speech, is difficult to define and seems to depend on the whimsy of what is currently (or has been) controversial. For example, an electric utility's promotional advertising was viewed as "commercial" rather than political speech because it "related solely to the economic interests of the speaker and audience," which is a fair characterization of much electoral speech routinely considered political.[14] Further, new ideas are often expressed and advocated for the purpose of persuading us that something perceived as ordinary or proper should be considered controversial and political. For example, the women's movement of the 1960s advanced the idea that much of the relationship between men and women traditionally considered "personal" should be a political issue requiring social intervention to provide protection and equality for women. It is circular and, again, contrary to the basic notion of free speech to require that such ideas be demonstrably "political" in advance of their advocacy in order for their advocacy to be fully protected.

This doctrinal puzzle is further complicated because the protected/unprotected distinction does not seem to matter when it collides with some of the other rules, such as the content barrier and the aversion to prior restraints. In those situations, even unprotected speech is often accorded strict scrutiny, depriving "unprotected" of meaning or significance.

And the content barrier is itself another long-standing myth. The unprotected categories are content based; they are defined by the disfavored content of the ideas expressed. Other content distinctions are apparent throughout speech law. There is no content barrier: some content distinctions are allowed whereas others are not, and there is no principle or set of standards defining the distinctions.

The result of this doctrinal tangle is extensive discretion for the judges and justices administering speech rules. The speaker, demonstrator, and writer are not as free as we so easily proclaim but must cope with a variety of unclear, indeterminate principles and rules, and with outcomes that depend ultimately on very political judgment calls.

The effectiveness and usefulness of our speech rights are also diminished by the reality that effective communication in modern society is expensive. People of ordinary means must rely on the Constitution for a means of communication and organization. People with power and money do not need to picket, demonstrate, or distribute leaflets on the street. The mass media continuously express their perspectives, both explicitly and implicitly, by "more respectable"—and more effective—means.

But most basically, freedom of speech has been exclusively defined by the historically and culturally specific set of speech rights developed in the transformation period (mainly the 1930s), and the scope and importance of these rights in contemporary society are regularly exaggerated. Freedom of speech as we know it simply does not provide people of ordinary means entree to society's dialogue on the issues of the day. Rather, we can engage in a variety of person-to-person speech activities; and beyond that, we are allowed to demonstrate, picket, hand out literature, gather in the streets, sing, chant, yell, and scream. The latter activities, which most people find difficult to participate in, effectively amount to *displays of displeasure or discontent,* without the means to explain why we are displeased much less to actually participate in any social dialogue. These displays of displeasure often will not even gain a spot on the local news unless some violation of the law, injury, destruction of property, or stunt accompanies them. If they do appear, they will usually be unexplained, without description of their context, and frequently misrepresented.

Our ability to communicate is haphazard, burdensome, lacking an effective means to explain or persuade; and our messages are filtered, edited, and censured by media organizations mostly interested in pleasing the public and making profits rather than in communication, education, or social dialogue. It should not be surprising that so many Americans—across the political spectrum—perceive themselves and their views as excluded from public discourse.

Essentially, the law and society have frozen the scope and nature of our speech rights at levels appropriate to the 1930s, when specific audiences were geographically centered, and speaking, gathering, and distributing literature in public places were primary means of communication. The speech rights conceived in that period do not provide access to our current means of communication. Technological, social, and cultural changes have rendered the fruits of the free-speech struggle and the transformation of speech law somewhat obsolete. Television, radio, newspapers, and direct mail now constitute the battleground, and the marketplace of ideas. In the absence of mass-based demands, we have allowed no meaningful inroads into these media for people or groups without substantial money or power. The ordinary person or group of ordinary persons has no means, based in the Constitution or elsewhere, to engage meaningfully in that dialogue on the issues of the day that the First Amendment is so often heralded as promoting and guaranteeing.

THE CONSERVATIVE RETRENCHMENT

In recent years, free-speech law has shifted drastically further from its transformation-period emphasis on enhancing the ability of ordinary people to express themselves meaningfully. Although some previous rulings protecting speech have been (narrowly) reaffirmed, the media and public officials have been inexplicably silent as the conservative-dominated Court has experimented with what already looks like a dismantling of the basic system of free speech.

The conservative speech retrenchment has three major elements: The Court has narrowed and restricted the free-speech rights available to people of ordinary means, enlarged the free-speech rights of wealthy people and corporations, and erected a free-speech barrier to public access to the media and to important electoral, economic, and social reforms. While all this has occurred, the media and government officials have drawn the public's attention almost exclusively to other free-speech issues—such as flag burning—shifting what should be a debate about the conservative retrenchment of vital speech rights to an often inflammatory discourse on whether we have allowed free speech to go too far.[15]

An Eyesore, a Safety Hazard, and Additional Cleanup Work

In 1988 the three publicly owned airports in the New York City area, Kennedy, LaGuardia, and Newark International, completely banned "distribution of flyers, brochures, pamphlets, books, and any other printed or written matter" and "solicitation and receipt of funds" in their terminals. Included in the ban were the open, public areas where access is not limited to air passengers. These areas, lined with shops and restaurants and bustling with people and activity, consist of publicly owned and operated walking passageways or thoroughfares and a marketplace (including in one terminal a branch of Bloomingdales), which the public is freely allowed and encouraged to use. They fit the classic mold of wholly open, public places where people pass through on their way somewhere, shop, or gather. In modern urban life, transportation terminals and shopping malls may be the last places where the increasingly suburban populations can be reached, by other than the mass media, for purposes of speech.

The airport ban on leafletting and solicitation of funds came before the Court in 1992 in *International Society of Krishna Consciousness v. Lee,*[16] where it was challenged by Hare Krishnas who wished to distribute literature and solicit funds in support of their religious views. By that time, the Court had already overturned the 1968 case protecting exercise of speech rights in privately owned shopping malls.[17] In *Krishna* it ruled that the strict-scrutiny standard does not apply to airport terminals (and, presumably, other public-transportation terminals). Using the "reasonableness" standard, the Court upheld the ban on solicitation; the ban on distribution of literature was narrowly overturned, by a five-to-four vote.

Chief Justice Rehnquist wrote the majority opinion upholding the solicitation ban and the four-vote dissent on the distribution ban. He emphasized the new doctrinal approach of the conservatives. Instead of determining whether the speech is protected and, if so, whether there is a compelling government interest in banning it—the liberal paradigm, which should lead to invalidation of both bans—his analysis started with a determination of whether the airport terminals are "public forums." If they are not public forums, the infringement on speech, even if it is the most protected speech traditionally, is not strictly scrutinized. Any "reasonable" restriction or limitation is constitutionally allowable.

The "public forum" doctrine has been at the forefront of the Court's speech rulings over the last fifteen years that systematically restrict the range of places and contexts in which speech is protected. Yet, the First Amendment contains no language explicitly or implicitly limiting its application to places or contexts that the Court decides are "public forums." This is an elaborate, often complicated set of speech-limiting rules made up by conservative justices, who call themselves strict-constructionists when criticizing liberals. (Of course, the strict scrutiny standard and the liberal paradigm are also judge made. The formulation of such rules is typical in our system for judges of all stripes, although conservatives have managed to convince the media and public that only liberals do this.)

Rehnquist's majority opinion defines a public forum as government property that has either (1) "traditionally been available for public expression" and has "as a principal purpose . . . free exchange of ideas" (traditional public forum), or (2) been specifically designated by the government as a public forum (designated public forum).

The government had not designated these terminals as public forums; they were designated for any and all lawful public access and activity *except* exercise of speech rights. The air passengers, shoppers, and passersby at airport terminals are subjected to considerable noise, crowds and activities that communicate a broad range of verbal, written, and symbolic messages whose contents include cultural, intellectual, religious, sexual, and political matters. These are not monasteries or facilities where the additional messages might startle or contrast with the regular activity. Only the messages of people who wish to distribute leaflets and solicit funds in support of their causes are excluded. The public-forum doctrine subordinates this reality to governmental whim: it lets the government agency challenged for infringing on speech decide for itself whether it is required to allow speech at all, amounting to what might be called a government veto.

Nor did airport terminals qualify as traditional forums, for two reasons. First, there has not been a tradition of exercise of free speech at airport terminals because "it is only in recent years [that] it has become a common practice." Of course, there were no airport terminals (or airplanes, for that matter) when the First Amendment was drafted. Rehnquist means that only very long traditions count, and, therefore, the list of public forums is basically closed, fixed—not open to new developments or changing circumstances. He quoted as support for his position the "time immemorial" passage from *Hague* discussed above, which he interpreted to mean that free speech can only include what it has always included, regardless of how society or circumstances have changed. This interpretation robs that momentous decision of its clear meaning and spirit: *Hague* offered a distorted version of the past as precedent and inspiration, but it promised, and provoked, a great expansion of speech rights.

Second, exercise of free speech is not "a principal purpose" of airport terminals. This is true enough, but neither is it a principal purpose of public streets, sidewalks, and parks. The sidewalks in small or large urban areas are meant to be used for walking from place to place, shopping, and gathering—like open airport-terminal passageways. With very few exceptions, governments do not construct or maintain public streets, sidewalks, or parks for the purpose of providing a forum for speech, nor do people use such facilities generally for the purpose of hearing speakers.

Rehnquist's analysis does not focus on—or even consider— the vital social and constitutional concerns at stake here, or even the physical or functional similarities or differences between this government property, in terms of the underlying notion of free speech, and public places where speech has been protected. The analysis is, typically these days, technical, mechanical, and unpredictable in its doctrinal twists and turns; but there is a passage that is startling to anyone familiar with the history of free speech. Rehnquist offered the following explanation (or underlying principle) of the public forum doctrine:

> Where the government is acting as a *proprietor,* managing its internal operations, rather than acting as lawmaker with the power to regulate or license, its actions will not be subjected to the heightened review. (Emphasis added.)

He did not elaborate further on this or explain why he concluded that this government action was proprietary rather than lawmaking or regulatory. But this is a return to the reasoning of the *Davis* case, repudiated since the transformation era—particularly in terms of the emphasis that the Court again places on the government's authority wholly or selectively to restrict access for the purpose of expression to governmental property and facilities that are otherwise open to the public or to government-approved speech.

The only remaining question was whether the ban is "reasonable." Rehnquist made it quite clear that almost any justification will be accepted; this standard simply does not limit the government or protect the individual's free-speech rights. Thus, as to solicitation, passengers "may have to alter their path," "traffic is impeded," and there are "risks of duress." Leafletting (on which Rehnquist's view gained four votes, only one short of a majority) can cause "congestion," and "those who accept material may often simply drop it on the floor . . . creating an eyesore, a safety hazard, and additional cleanup work." In the liberal paradigm, blocking a walkway, impeding traffic, duress, and littering can be prohibited, but leafletting and solicitation of funds in furtherance of protected speech cannot be banned unless they conflict with some government interest of considerably more importance.

The public-forum doctrine is now firmly established. Other applications have included: upholding a blanket prohibition of posting signs on any city-owned buildings, poles, or other property; approval of new limits on expression at state fairgrounds, residential neighborhoods, open portions of military facilities maintained like civilian communities, and areas near foreign embassies; limiting access for competing viewpoints to a government-sponsored fund-raising drive and an administrative communications network; and approving censorship of a high-school newspaper in which articles on divorce and teenage pregnancy had been removed by administrators.[18] The conservatives have restored the primacy of property-based notions that restrict speech, which characterized the *Davis* decision and the pretransformation history.

The scope and import of this new doctrine were perhaps best revealed in a 1990 case concerning political speech on a public sidewalk leading to and from the entrance to a post office. A sidewalk *is* the most traditional public forum, but that did not matter. Justice O'Connor, a relative moderate on this Court who has written many of the public-forum opinions, declared that "the mere physical characteristics of the property cannot dictate forum analysis."[19] One wonders, then, what does "dictate"—or what is—forum analysis? The Bush administration used the public-forum doctrine as a basis for arguing that exercise of basic free-speech rights can be prohibited on the public sidewalk on Constitution Avenue near the Vietnam Veterans' Memorial.[20] There is no principle resting on social or constitutional concerns, or any principled analysis, at the heart of this doctrine. It is simply window dressing for the conservative project of limiting speech to the mainstream media and insulating the mass of people from other messages.

Secondary Effects

Another new doctrine was announced by Justice Rehnquist in a 1986 case involving zoning of adult movie theaters, and it has since been applied by conservative justices to political and all other speech.

Because obscenity is a long-established unprotected category of speech, there has been little controversy about zoning schemes that limit the locations of adult book stores and movie theaters. However, in *Renton v. Playtime Theatres* (1986)[21] the Court faced zoning regulations that effectively banned such theaters entirely. The city of Renton, Washington, prohibited location of adult movie theaters within 1,000 feet of any residence, church, or park and within one mile of any school. This would restrict only a small portion of a large or medium sized city; but in Renton these restrictions covered 94 percent of the city, and the remaining 6 percent was already in use, unusable, or unsuited for a theater. The zoning regulation effectively constituted a total or near-total ban.

Nevertheless, Rehnquist, for the majority, treated it as a time, place, and manner regulation (the formulation of which might be: no time, no place, and no manner) and concluded that it was reasonable by analyzing its terms in the abstract rather than in the context of this particular small town. This was extraordinary enough, but he also had to deal with the content basis of the regulation because even a time, place, and manner regulation is not supposed to be content based. The result was a new conception of the "content barrier" and content neutrality.

This measure set up special, restrictive zoning rules explicitly made applicable only to theaters that show "adult motion pictures." All other movie theaters could locate more or less anywhere, but theaters that show movies with that particular content were greatly restricted or banned. Nevertheless, Rehnquist concluded that the regulation was "content neutral." This feat was accomplished with the "secondary effects" doctrine: content neutrality is satisfied as long as the "predominant" purpose of the measure was directed at "secondary effects" rather than content. Rehnquist found this measure content neutral because, even though it explicitly singled out a particular content of speech, the city was predominantly concerned with preventing crime, maintaining property values, and preserving the "quality of urban life," which, the city simply asserted and he simply accepted (no proof was offered), were undercut and threatened by adult movie theaters.

This doctrine introduces a purpose element to First Amendment law similar to the more-publicized role of intent in discrimination cases. In the liberal paradigm, a government action that infringed on or burdened protected speech triggered strict scrutiny and constituted a violation of the First Amendment unless the government demonstrated a compelling interest. The secondary-effects doctrine means that there is no violation unless it is also proved that the *government's purpose was to infringe on or burden speech.* If the government had some other purpose—directing its action at "secondary effects" rather than at speech—there is no First Amendment violation even though protected speech has in fact been infringed or burdened. Because the Court also accepts very generally stated alternative purposes and does not scrutinize the good faith or basis of an asserted alternative purpose, it is easy for governments to get away with all manner of free-speech violations. If the doctrine develops as it has in exercise and establishment of religion and equal-protection cases (chapters 4 and 5), the Court will not even require that the alternative purpose be the government's actual purpose; generally stated possible alternative purposes, thought up by lawyers or justices after the fact, will be sufficient to justify a denial of free speech. Malicious purposes can seldom be proved, of course; benign motives are available to explain malignant acts, and the Court does not even require an explanation if malice cannot be proved or a benign purpose can be imagined. This new doctrine fundamentally undercuts the whole notion of free speech, because speech can be denied based on its content as long as there is some generally stated alternative purpose.

Further, the secondary-effects analysis involves a species of reasoning that George Orwell long ago warned us about, doublethink.[22] *Renton* treated adult movies differently from other movies—banned or greatly restricted their location—because its officials believed that such movies cause serious harm. The "secondary" effects at issue were not some unanticipated or unpredictable result of a measure aimed at something else (sometimes called "incidental effects") but rather were the very harms that the city anticipated and believed would be caused by movies with the specified content, which the city wished to avoid by enacting the regulation. (This is different than, for example, the unemployment compensation regulations considered in chapter 4 that had the unanticipated effect of impeding exercise of religion by Seventh Day Adventists who do not work on Saturdays.) What Rehnquist calls "secondary effects" were the believed, anticipated or feared effects that led to, or formed the purpose or motivation for, the content-based regulation. Stated another way, the city enacted a regulation to avoid the effects of the content that the regulation was explicitly aimed at. There is nothing really "secondary" about this at all, and there are no multiple concerns or intentions among which one can be "predominate." What Rehnquist calls a "predominate concern . . . with the secondary effects" is simply the purpose and intended results of the regulation and has nothing to do with its content neutrality or lack of content neutrality. No amount of doublethink (or lawyertalk) can make the Renton theater-zoning scheme content neutral.

This fine-tuned doctrinal thicket is reminiscent of, but less honest than, Justice Black's approach to racial discrimination in *Korematsu* (chapter 1). Black said that the imprisonment of all Japanese-Americans on the West Coast did not amount to discrimination even though the persons to be imprisoned were explicitly described in the government's regulations by their race or ancestry—because the purpose or motivation was not racial but national security. This reasoning means that government can do anything it wants to individuals as long as its purported motive is benign. The secondary-effects doctrine is inconsistent with a society in which individuals have civil liberties and civil rights that must be respected by their government.

The Costs of Security

In 1912 all the African-Americans living in Forsyth County, Georgia, were forcibly driven out of the county after a white woman was allegedly raped by an African-American man, whom a mob lynched. Seventy-five years later, a commemorative parade was planned by civil-rights activists led by Hosea Williams, a DeKalb County (Atlanta) commissioner and colleague of Martin Luther King, Jr. The parade of about ninety people was stopped by counterdemonstrators led by the Ku Klux Klan and other similar groups, who shouted racial slurs and threw rocks and bottles. The next weekend, the civil-rights activists came back with twenty thousand marchers, including in their ranks U.S. senators and presidential candidates. A thousand counterdemonstrators, who again shouted slurs and threw rocks and bottles, were kept under control by state and local police and the National Guard.

In direct response to these two events, the county enacted a new permit regulation for "parades, assemblies, demonstrations . . . and other uses of public property" that required a fee in an amount, up to a maximum of $1,000, reflecting the costs of "maintenance of public order" and administration of permits. In 1992 the Court reviewed a challenge to this permit requirement, initiated by one of the groups of counterdemonstrators, in *Forsyth County v. The Nationalist Movement.* [23]

In the liberal paradigm, this is an easy case. Permit fees in a nominal amount for activities that will block or close streets are allowable, but this regulation did not specify any criteria for setting the amount of the fee, leaving local authorities broad discretion and posing what the Court long considered an unacceptable danger of censorship. The official who administered the regulation testified that he sometimes charged for his time and sometimes did not, and that he charged an administering amount of $25 to one applicant and $100 to another although the administering costs seemed the same. Further, to assess the costs, the administrator had to consider the content of the message to be communicated and the level of hostility it would likely engender. This makes the listeners' reactions a measure of the cost charged for speech. (The secondary-effects doctrine is not applicable because, so far, even the conservatives have held that listener reaction cannot provide a "secondary effect" permitting a content discrimination.) Justice Blackmun applied these principles for the Court's majority, invalidating the regulation: government officials cannot be given "unbridled discretion" over speech, and "[s]peech cannot be financially burdened, any more than it can be punished or banned, simply because it might offend a hostile mob."

However, Blackmun's ruling commanded only five votes; four justices—one short of a majority—filed a chilling dissent written by Chief Justice Rehnquist. Rehnquist did not discuss the constitutional or social concerns or the principles of free speech at issue. Rather, the author of many recent changes in the basics of speech law would uphold discretionary permit-fee amounts because a 1941 case said so: "The answer to this question seems to me quite simple, because it was authoritatively decided by this Court more than half a century ago."

The Court had upheld such a regulation in 1941, but it soon seemed to change its mind. In 1943 the Court invalidated a flat fee for door-to-door canvasing, imposed as a tax and intended to raise revenues rather than as a charge for the government's costs associated with speech.[24] In the course of that decision, the Court described the 1941 case as allowing only a "nominal" (small and fixed rather than varying) fee "to defray" the government's expenses. This rewriting of an earlier decision rather than more forthrightly overruling it is not unusual. In this area of law, we saw the Court depict even the change from *Davis* to *Hague* as no change at all.

Rehnquist, without a noticeable blink, simply dismissed the 1943 case as "mistaken" and "unfortunate." It misread the earlier case and therefore should be disregarded. He did not even pause to consider why a flat tax might be unconstitutional whereas a fee in a discretionary amount would be allowable, though both impose a financial burden and the latter has the additional potential of censorship based on content. Nor did he discuss why precedent has such potency on this issue but is, as we will see, irrelevant elsewhere. In two recent abortion cases, Rehnquist wrote that precedents have "less power in constitutional cases" than in cases involving economic interests, because "save for constitutional amendments, this Court is the only body able to make needed changes," and that constitutional precedents should be "reexamined" when they are "unsound."[25]

Rehnquist is playing the lawyer's game at its best, or worst. Precedents do not require anything. The Court could follow the 1941 case, follow the 1943 case, or rewrite, overrule, or ignore either or both. What is at stake—and the stakes are quite high—is whether the government will be allowed to censor speech and compel conformity.

Teenage Girl Students

Matthew Fraser's senior year at Bethel High School in Spanaway, Washington, had been a great success. He was an honor student and twice received the "top speaker" award in the statewide debate championship. His classmates chose him to deliver the student address at graduation. But at a school assembly to hear nomination speeches for student officers, Fraser's speech in favor of a friend's candidacy contained what the Court later called "pervasive sexual innuendo," which offended school officials.

Fraser had been a little worried about the quickly written speech himself. He showed it to three teachers, who thought it was off-color but not prohibited by school rules. Fraser thought that the speech was "amusing," would be so understood by the students at the assembly, and would thereby draw attention and votes:

> I know a man who is firm—he's firm in his pants, he's firm in his shirt, his character is firm—but most of all his belief in you, the students of Bethel is firm. [He] takes his point and pounds it in [and] will go to the very end—even the climax, for each and every one of you. So vote for Jeff as ASB vice-president—he'll never come between you and the best our high school can be.

There are many ways one could characterize this campaign speech, ranging from an uncalled-for, filthy-mouthed insult, to a very juvenile attempt at teenage humor, to a critique of the role of sex in advertising and electoral campaigns. Fraser's intent may well capture how the speech was in fact received, because no student complained about it or testified that it was offensive or insulting, and Jeff won the election by a landslide. (There are no known exit polls regarding its impact on the vote.) However, some teachers and school officials were offended; Fraser was suspended for three days and prohibited from speaking at the graduation.

In 1986 the Court rejected Fraser's free-speech claims in *Bethel School District v. Fraser*.[26] Chief Justice Warren Burger's majority opinion started with two principles that the whole Court could agree on. "[U]ndoubted[ly there is] freedom to advocate unpopular and controversial views in schools and classroom," but the government also has increased control over speech when dealing with students in school. In the 1960s and 1970s, the Court had favored free speech in trying to resolve these competing concerns. Burger distinguished a leading earlier case protecting a student's right to wear an antiwar armband in school, where the Court had said in 1969, "Undifferentiated fear or apprehension of disturbance is not enough to overcome the right to freedom of expression."[27] In the *Fraser* case, he said, the government had a sufficient interest in "teaching students the boundaries of socially appropriate behavior" because the speech was "plainly offensive . . . to any mature person" and "acutely insulting to teenage girl students."

This logic was new. Even in limiting contexts like schools, offensiveness had not previously been a basis for censorship. Fraser's use of "sexual innuendos" was not obscene even by the most conservative definition, and a school's power over students had never been held to include censorship of sexual innuendos. This is simply the listener's-veto argument long ago rejected as wholly inconsistent with free speech. Particularly regarding speech that is political and electoral—this was an election campaign, where we usually let the voters decide—the thinking has been that we cannot have free speech in any real sense if the government can censor messages that some listeners or government officials find offensive. Here the government taught censorship rather than civics.

In any event, the record in the case does not support the assumption that students were offended or insulted. There was no evidence that any students—teenage girls or otherwise—found the speech offensive. President Reagan's education secretary, William Bennett, commenting on the decision, said, "There is no constitutional right to disrupt the learning process"; but there was no evidence of disruption of the learning process or anything else. Regardless of the wishes of conservative justices and presidents, high-school students think and talk about sex. It would also be difficult not to notice by high-school age that pretty much everything—products, services, and political offices—are sold with appeals to sexuality, or to avoid the torrent of sexual messages in our culture. High-school students cannot have open ears during recess, watch television, or even study the classics of Western culture (such as Shakespeare's work) without exposure to sexual innuendo as blatant as Matthew's. One can condemn or applaud this, but the assumption and acceptance without any proof that sexual innuendos are offensive to high-school students seems, at best, debatable. In dissent, Justice Stevens remembered when Clark Gable's use of "damn" in a movie was shocking, and he berated the majority justices as "at least two generations and 3,000 miles from the scene." Two years later, the Court approved of censorship of a high-school newspaper, which administrators felt should not print articles addressing divorce or teenage pregnancy.[28] The demise of the liberal paradigm has not been merely of academic concern; there has been a return to censorship in an attempt to impose and compel conformity to a conservative vision of morality.

Not a Case of Suppressing a Dangerous Idea

Title X of the Public Health Service Act of 1970 funded family-planning counseling and pre-conception services for poor people, with the condition that funding was not to be used for abortions. In 1988, after *Roe v. Wade* and the almost two-decade furor over abortion, the Reagan administration's secretary of Health and Human Services, without any change in the act, adopted new regulations that went considerably further. The providers of Title X family-planning services, including doctors dealing with their patients, were forbidden to "provide counseling" or a "referral" about abortion, and, if asked by patients, were required to give this explicitly prescribed response: "the project does not consider abortion an appropriate method of family planning and therefore does not counsel or refer for abortion." Some doctors and Title X providers challenged this regulation in *Rust v. Sullivan* (1991).[29]

The liberal Court of the 1960s and 1970s had recognized the pervasive role of government and government funds in the modern economy and decided that free speech would not long survive if the government could condition funding on relinquishment of a recipient's First Amendment rights. This principle was applied to a range of other fundamental rights as well, including association, religion, travel and privacy.[30] Particularly where the condition was content based and singled out a specific viewpoint as well as subject matter, such conditioned fundamental rights were subjected to strict scrutiny. For example, the government could not, in the liberal paradigm, exclude people critical of government policies from eligibility for welfare (there is no supporting compelling or even legitimate interest).

The condition in *Rust* is content based and does not merely focus on the subject of abortion. Antiabortion speech is not prohibited; only the specific viewpoint that states what the law says—there is a choice—is forbidden. Indeed, the regulation goes further than that and is reminiscent of *Barnette,* by compelling expression of an antiabortion viewpoint, even if the doctor disagrees or believes that the patient should have all the relevant information and make the choices. Although the government has discretion to determine what it will fund and recipient's speech may be part of that determination, the Court had never, as Justice Blackmun said in dissent, sustained such a viewpoint based on suppression of disfavored speech or funding-based interference in the relationship between doctors and patients.

Justice Rehnquist wrote the majority opinion upholding the regulation. He thought that it was an easy case: "This is not a case of Government 'suppressing a dangerous idea'" but simply a matter of the government limiting the scope of its funding. He emphasized that the recipients could express other views outside of the Title X-funding context. This would be of little use to the patient, of course, who wants and expects from her doctor an explanation of the options available to her, so she can make an informed choice. Moreover, the doctor has ethical duties to provide patients with such information. Nevertheless, Rehnquist's opinion seemed to approve any restriction on a government employee's or funding recipient's speech as long as it is limited to the funded workplace, which Blackmun called "a dangerous proposition."

Federal and state governments now fund a vast array of activities and programs, and the recipients include a wide range of private as well as public institutions. For example, most colleges and universities receive at least some federal funding, raising the possibility that the government could condition such funding with content-based limits on what can be said, or taught. The education department might forbid, as health and human services did in *Rust,* any discussion of abortion that is not staunchly anti-choice, or any discussion of sex involving unmarried people.

Another possible application, which the justices may have had in mind, could be to the Bush administration's removal of the director of the National Endowment of the Arts and the new director's denial of NEA grants, although approved by review panels, because of sexual explicitness or other disfavored content. This is generally a difficult issue because of the subjectivity of art, but the specific series of events have made clear that the administration is applying nonartistic political-content criteria rather than the usual considerations of artistic merit.[31] They seem to have extended the "teenage girl students" standard of censorship. Nevertheless, legal challenges to such censorship will be difficult after *Rust*.

Fighting Words and Racist Speech

In 1990 a group of white teenagers burned a cross in the yard of an African-American family that had recently moved into a predominately white neighborhood in St. Paul, Minnesota. They were prosecuted and convicted under the city's bias-motivated crime ordinance, which proscribes "plac[ing] on public or private property a symbol . . . including a burning cross . . . which one knows or has reasonable grounds to know arouses anger, alarm or resentment in others on the basis of race, color, creed, religion or gender." The Court reversed the conviction in *R.A.V. v. City of St. Paul* (1992).[32]

This was another easy case under the liberal paradigm because the ordinance bases criminality on the reaction of or offensiveness to others (the listener's veto) and defines the crime very broadly, including protected as well as unprotected speech (called "overbreadth"). The Court could avoid the harder question of whether bias-motivated crime could be prohibited with a narrower, nonlistener-focused provision. That ultimate issue, if it were decided, would hinge on whether combatting bias-motivated crime is found "compelling" as a government interest and whether the restriction on speech is the "least restrictive means." Instead of any of these analyses, Justice Scalia wrote an opinion for the majority that rejected strict scrutiny and the distinction between protected and unprotected speech and, in their place, announced a fundamentally new approach.

Scalia started with the interpretation the Minnesota Supreme Court had given the ordinance, that it covered only expression that has been traditionally defined as "fighting words." This is one of the categories of unprotected speech in the liberal paradigm, which first arose in a 1942 case, *Chaplinsky v. New Hampshire*.[33] Chaplinsky, a Jehovah's Witness who got into an argument with a police officer over the reaction of a crowd of listeners to his street speech about religion, called the officer a "racketeer" and a "fascist." He was arrested for this, and the Court upheld his conviction based on a "fighting words" exception to free speech. Such words, the Court said, like speech in the other unprotected categories, "by their very utterance inflict injury or tend to incite an immediate breach of the peace" and are "of slight social value."

The basic assumption in this thinking seems to be that people, or more precisely men, have some almost involuntary, violent reaction when such words are spoken. This recalls the schoolyard scene in which boys taunt one another about such matters as the reputations of their mothers, and once in a while they fight. In my concededly limited experience, most of the participants in these dramas are looking for a way out, as in the common "Did you say my mother is a whore?" after just that is said, and the common retort "What if I did?" (If the "whore" comment seems stale, perhaps a more contemporary provocation might be "Your father is a liberal!") In any event, the constitutional legitimizing of this male phenomenon reflects an interesting view of the normality of violence and seems to misplace responsibility. This doctrine excuses the person who responds to words with violence and blames the person who has used only words. It is also based on the listener's-veto notion: The content is unprotected because others may be offended or insulted and may retaliate. Whatever legitimacy there is to this exception to free speech would seem to be covered by the clear-and-present-danger rule.

But Scalia did not get into any of these aspects of fighting words. He invalidated the ordinance because it singled out based on content only *one kind* of fighting words. This is unconstitutional content selectivity, according to Scalia, because bias-motivated fighting words are prohibited whereas other fighting words are not. This new conservative activism (they invalidated legislation based on a novel constitutional theory) forbids legislatures from recognizing and dealing with racism or bias-motivated crime as a particular problem calling for particular solutions. The Court has never before required such generality in this or any other area of law.

And it is a strange area in which to promote generality. For fifty years the Court was always careful to limit the fighting-words doctrine (as well as the other exceptions) precisely because if its listener's-veto rationale were enlarged or generalized, it would be incompatible with the whole notion of free speech. Sometimes treated as a historical oddity, the fighting-words exception had been limited to "inherently inflammatory" speech and contexts where the speech was very likely to provoke an imminent fight (rather than abstract analysis of simply the words used).[34]

The fighting-words exception was never extended to the reach of its underlying principle set out in *Chaplinsky:* words that "by their very utterance inflict injury or tend to incite an immediate breach of the peace." The broader category might be called speech that hurts—speech that causes some listeners to experience immediate, substantial pain or insult and may prompt a disruptive response. Many of the long-recognized categories of unprotected speech are forms of speech that hurts: defamation, threats of imminent violence, intentional infliction of emotional distress, and fighting words. Some speech that hurts may provoke men to retaliate immediately with violence (fighting words). Other speech that hurts causes as much or more injury and disruption but has been traditionally suffered by its victims without violent retaliation, such as sexual taunts directed by men at women. The traditional fighting-words doctrine singled out based on content only one kind of injury-inflicting, breach-inciting speech (and would itself seem to violate Scalia's new doctrine and approach).

Scalia held that *more generality*—a broader proscription of speech—was preferable and *constitutionally required*. The proscription of bias-motivated crime was insufficiently general, but he did not tell us how general is general enough. As the above makes clear, general and specific are not mutually exclusive or self-defining but form a complex continuum. He did offer this capsule description of the required generality:

> [T]he ordinance applies only to "fighting words" that insult, or provoke violence, "on the basis of race, color, creed, religion or gender." Displays containing *abusive invective,* no matter how vicious or severe, are permissible unless they are addressed to one of the disfavored topics. (Emphasis added.)

A proscription of "abusive invective" or "severe abusive invective"—or "all fighting words"—hardly seems preferable and is so general, broad and vague as to negate any meaningful notion of speech the government may not infringe on or regulate. If there is some socially or constitutionally beneficial principle or effect underlying this newly required generality in proscriptions of speech, Scalia did not explain it.

Scalia also rejected the distinction between protected and unprotected speech established over the last fifty years. The unprotected categories for Scalia are just *examples* of speech that can be "regulated because of their constitutionally proscribable content." This also raises the distinct possibility of enlargement of government regulation—and censorship—of speech.

Scalia accurately noted that, as explained above, "unprotected" speech was not always unprotected. However, the distinction between protected and unprotected speech, and particularly the tradition of limiting the range and extent of unprotected categories, served to *narrow* the scope of allowable government regulation. He has substituted an approach that purports to do away with categories and treats all speech the same, except that his approach still allows for speech with "constitutionally proscribable content," which is open-ended, undefined, and without fifty years of fine tuning.

Further, among the categories of speech that hurts, the one that seems most consistently to inflict severe pain and insult, to provoke individual or group violence, and to have the lowest social value is hostile racist or ethnic speech. The recognition of this reality has led to an international consensus, with the United States often the lone dissenter, that at least some forms of racist speech should be curtailed.[35] However, Scalia did not consider whether the principles leading to his "proscribable content" analysis (or the fighting-words exception) should, if consistently applied, result in a racist-speech exception.

Scalia further muddied the waters at his new dock by defining fighting words as "essentially a 'nonspeech' element of communication" and by establishing two baffling exceptions to his "proscribable content" doctrine. He said fighting words are "a mode of speech . . . analogous to a noisy sound truck," and government can regulate the noise of the truck but not the content of the message. This seems a baseless and confusing attempt to redefine the issue without contributing anything to an understanding or resolution of it. Fighting words are not a mode of speech but words with a particular content that is thought to provoke violence. His redefinition will prompt attempts to find "nonspeech" elements and tedious arguments that such elements, rather than content, are being regulated. This is another new opening for government censorship.

The first exception to the new proscribable-content doctrine is that content-based selectivity is allowable if "the basis of the content discrimination consists entirely of the very reason the entire class of speech at issue is proscribable." This was probably intended to deal with the reality that Scalia's new rule—which so neatly disposes of all bias-motivated crime legislation—would also dispose of much other legislation thought by him and most others to be rather necessary and uncontroversial. For example, it is now a federal crime to threaten the life of the president. This distinguishes based on content only one particular category from among the general class of threats to kill, and the new rule seems to forbid such legislative selectivity based on content. The exception, according to Scalia, cures this because the reasons for making threats to kill proscribable, protection from threats and acts of violence, "have special force when applied to the person of the President." Note that the exception had to be reformulated to be applied: "entirely consists" became "special force," so that the exception applies when the rationale for allowing regulation of speech in the broader category has "special force" regarding the narrower, selective category. As Justice White (a conservative who is the only remaining member appointed by the Democrats) pointed out, this exception "swallows the majority's rule." The rationale for fighting words has "special force" regarding racist speech.

The second exception applies and extends the "secondary effects" doctrine discussed above. Selectivity within generally proscribable speech categories is allowable if directed at the "secondary effects" rather than the content of speech. This twist seems aimed at other anomalies created by the new doctrine. For example, the doctrine seems to forbid a law prohibiting obscene performances involving minors and the federal employment-discrimination law that forbids sex harassment. In the latter instance, other forms of harassment are not prohibited. (Scalia defines this, like almost everything else in the opinion, in terms of fighting words. He characterized the sex-harassment provision as proscribing "sexually derogatory 'fighting words,'" although its intent and import are not limited to avoiding fights.) This is allowed by the exception because the law defines sex harassment as a form of employment discrimination, but a law that proscribed sex harassment itself may be invalid. This exception suffers from the logical and principled objections to the secondary-effects doctrine, introduces more uncertainty and confusion into the new doctrine, and, once again, negates the rule that it is supposed to modify. The proscription of racist speech can also be described as aimed at secondary effects rather than the content of the speech.

Not untypically these days, the abandonment in *St. Paul* of fundamental free-speech protections was depicted and accepted by the media (who basically ignored the case) as its opposite, as combating censorship and a victory for free speech. These new rules, the exceptions, and the tedious, convoluted, unpredictable doctrinal twists—with no apparent attention or concern for basic free-speech protections—open new avenues for justifying government censorship and further the tendency to focus on government purposes rather than infringements on speech. A racist speech case provided the conservative justices a unique opportunity to jettison strict scrutiny and the notion of protected speech without provoking a major reaction.

Nothing confuses liberals and the media more than racist speech, a sign of some virtue in both. Anyone who values free speech *and* equality should feel some ambivalence about racist speech, particularly because, regardless of the rhetoric, speech is regularly regulated based on content and much less offensive and socially disruptive messages are censored. The strict-scrutiny standard draws the issue uncomfortably well: if combating racist crimes and racism is held to be a compelling government interest and the harm inflicted and disruptive effects of racist speech are taken seriously, the speech involved—according to traditional *liberal* principles—might be regulated or proscribed.

This presented an opportunity for the conservative justices. The racist-speech issue has enabled conservatives to depict liberals as going too far on race and as intolerant and inconsistent, while at the same time providing some comfort to their right wing. Done with accomplished vagueness and ambiguity, the conservative critique of regulation of racist speech simultaneously ties into familiar conservative themes about affirmative action, taps white fears and prejudices, and mocks liberals as obsessed with "political correctness." But to forbid regulation of racist speech under strict scrutiny requires an analysis that rejects the continuing reality and importance of racism and racist crime, because strict scrutiny focuses on whether the government interest is compelling and whether the restriction on speech is a necessary means. This would surely provoke a firestorm, which could be avoided by reaching the result that they wanted while simultaneously overturning strict scrutiny in a case where that major development might not be (and was not) publicly noticed. It is interesting in this regard that, although the strict-scrutiny standard was rejected and there was no need to address the compelling-interest issue, Scalia went out of his way to say "[w]e do not doubt that these interests are compelling."

At the same time, however, the majority did not take seriously either the harm to the victims or the disruptive and socially divisive effects of cross burning. Although the conservatives regularly emphasize the plight of the victims of crime, there was no consideration or mention of the terror that the cross burning must have inflicted on an unnamed African-American family. Instead of focusing on the effects on or consequences for them, Scalia's opinion emphasizes the youth of the white perpetrators and the spur-of-the-moment nature of what they did, including a description of their rushed attempts to find wood to make the cross. The content, omissions, and tone of the opinion communicate more a sense of a youthful prank than anything socially or morally reprehensible.

There is no easy answer to the racist-speech or bias-motivated crime question unless one is prepared to abandon either free speech or equality. The conservatives have managed to abandon both: equality cannot be promoted with limits on racist speech, but the conservative doctrinal juggernaut has also devastated free speech. Racist speech is often most harmful and least socially valuable when it is directed at or foisted directly on another person (as opposed to being advocated more generally). Burning a cross on the lawn of an African-American family, and much face-to-face racist speech, are no different—except for their racist content—than the range of speech that hurts which has not been traditionally protected, such as assault and various threat-based crimes, torts like intentional infliction of emotional distress, and sex harassment at work. There is no reason to permit punishment and regulation of such speech except when it includes some racism, establishing what is effectively a kind of racist immunity. If the same thinking were applied to sex harassment, we might analyze it as "sexist speech," and laws prohibiting or regulating sex harassment might be invalidated. Race harassment, like sex harassment, intentional infliction of emotional distress, and assault, should not be constitutionally protected or socially legitimized. As Justice Blackmun pointed out, "First Amendment values [are not] compromised by a law that prohibits hoodlums from driving minorities out of their homes by burning crosses on their lawns." Drawing such lines is difficult, but no more so than in other speech areas where we have not abandoned the task because of the difficulty of drawing lines.

Another possibility is to abolish all the unprotected categories and all exceptions. This is attractive, because they are all based on listener reactions or judgments that achieving some important goals takes precedence over unfettered speech; it appears to be the logical anticensorship view. But life is more complicated than that. Freedom to express oneself is not the only important social value, and if we abolish all the distinctions between various subjects and contents, we effectively diminish the protection accorded the most important ones, and all of them. Expression is part of almost all human activity. When we regulate the stock market, the contracting process, or individual conduct that harms others, we are often regulating speech. One cannot objectively or neutrally separate speech from conduct, and to forbid regulation of all speech is to forbid all regulation and all government.

The "system of free expression," as the late Professor Thomas Emerson called our free-speech rules,[36] is being dismantled. In its place is a series of new rules and approaches that drastically narrow the free-speech rights of people of ordinary means and fundamentally alter the long-established limits on government's power to compel conformity and censor expression.

❧ 3 ❧

PARTICIPATION IN THE POLITICAL PROCESS

The predominant theme of our constitutional history after the adoption of the Constitution and the Bill of Rights has been a broadening inclusion of our people in the political process. It did not start that way, however. The constitutional convention was attended by representatives chosen by the various state legislatures to resolve interstate commercial rivalries that were impeding trade. The framers, who transformed their gathering into a constitutional convention on their own, were among the elite of each state, and they met in secret behind locked doors. Their fear that the people, if really empowered, would undercut the privileges of wealth and create chaos, dominated the proceedings. Although progressive for its time on many issues, the Constitution embraced slavery rather than the ringing pronouncement of equality that opens the Declaration of Independence, provided for direct popular election of only members of the House of Representatives, and left the matter of qualifications for voting to each state. At the time of the Constitution and considerably thereafter, most states allowed only white men who owned land or substantial property to vote. This excluded all women, all African-Americans and other minorities, and even most white men.[1]

The ensuing amendments to the Constitution extended the right to vote to African-Americans (Fifteenth, 1870), women (Nineteenth, 1920), and anyone eighteen years of age or older (Twenty-sixth, 1971); prohibited the "poll tax" or any other tax on voting (Twenty-fourth, 1964); and required popular direct election of senators (Seventeenth, 1913). No other issue has generated this level of amendments.

In the liberal 1960s, the Court recognized a basic right of all citizens to vote enforced with the strict-scrutiny standard. There is no such language in the Constitution, but this was rather uncontroversial activism. However, even then, the right was often subordinated to maintenance of the two-party system. In 1992, as public opinion was increasingly dissatisfied with the two parties and the political process, the conservative Court, again without significant media attention, rejected strict scrutiny and moved toward constitutional enshrinement of the two-party system and away from the tradition of inclusion of all our people in the political process.

The Integrity of the Democratic System

Alan Burdick wished to write in a vote as a protest because there was only one candidate for state representative for his district in Hawaii on the ballot, but a state law prohibited write-in voting. It is not uncommon in Hawaii and some other places for there to be only one candidate, particularly in local elections. This reminded Burdick of Soviet elections in which the choice for the voter was limited to voting for or against a single listed candidate. He did not view this as a meaningful election. His lawyers argued that the state's prohibition of write-in votes burdened his right to vote and deprived him of freedom of expression and association, and therefore should be subject to strict scrutiny and invalidated. Justice White, for a six-justice majority, disagreed in *Burdick v. Takushi* (1992).[2]

White set out a balancing test in which the severity of the restriction on voting is "weigh[ed]" against the government's interests. Although the language conveys a quantitative or at least objective method of decision-making, such matters cannot be "weighed," "balanced," or objectively resolved—two concerns conflict and choices must be made.

White found that the restriction on Burdick's rights was minimal because the process for getting on the ballot was fair. No candidate of choice for Burdick had played by the rules, and he could not expect to "wait until the eleventh hour to choose his preferred candidate." What he asked would sacrifice "political stability" for his unlimited freedom of choice. The state's interest, White said, was more substantial. The state wished to avoid "unrestrained factionalism" and "avert divisive sore-loser candidacies." The state need not record, count, or publish write-in votes, which amount to "individual protests against the electoral system or the choices presented." "No right is more precious in a free country" than the right to vote, but the state must maintain "the integrity of the democratic system."

Burdick, who wished to exercise what most would consider a traditional (if futile) right, sounds almost un-American in the overdrawn rhetoric of this decision. "Individual protests" and voter freedom of choice are hardly radical ideas, and under strict scrutiny they had precedence over these largely rhetorical state interests. Write-in voting is not the most important aspect of participation in the political process, but there is something much deeper at stake here. The conservative Court is restricting voting and electoral activity to the two-party system.

The heart of the matter is the reference to avoidance of "unrestrained factionalism." Stated another way, this is the avoidance of real political choices that has characterized our political process and fomented so much discontent in the 1992 presidential election. The two parties, vying for a narrow band of moderates that increasingly decide elections, muddle their messages and principles and turn off most of the eligible voters. Public officials and the media tend to ignore this and bestow legitimacy on the victors regardless of the deterioration of the process. For example, President Reagan's 1980 victory over former President Jimmy Carter was consistently described as a "landslide," although Reagan got only 28 percent of the eligible voters to Carter's 23 percent.[3]

This is most significantly a result of the structure of our electoral system. We have a winner-take-all presidential election that is divorced from elections of legislators. The votes for president garnered by each candidate or party do not translate into ongoing representation in Congress, so a vote for a candidate who loses is "wasted"—it bestows no power or ongoing influence. Contrast this to the parliamentary or proportional voting systems in Western Europe (where there are commonly large voter turnouts) and almost all other democratic countries. The representation of each party in the legislature is connected to its proportion of the votes in a general election, and then the legislature, so constituted, chooses the chief executive (usually prime minister).

This encourages multiple parties, principled positions, and a real choice for the voters. Compromises and coalitions among the parties (if one does not win an outright majority) are made to form a governing majority *after* the election, and that majority and its chief executive may be voted out at any time. The stalemate between the president and Congress which has become common in our system would be resolved by new compromises and coalitions and perhaps a new president. In our current system, the compromises must be made *before* the election (or you lose, and you lose all), so the two parties fear principled stands or discussion of ideas, votes for third-party candidates are "wasted" in the sense that they tend to help the major party one most disagrees with, and the voters do not get any real choice. Third parties are further hampered by burdensome requirements for ballot access.[4]

White's "unrestrained factionalism" is not something to be avoided by a systemic muzzling and muddling of political discourse and voter choice. We need more, not fewer, factions—more parties and more democracy—and the ability to make meaningful political choices. Instead of revitalizing and strengthening democracy by enhancing the ability of ordinary citizens to elect representatives and express and implement their views, the conservatives have tended to enshrine the deadening two-party monopoly, decrease the powers of Congress, and greatly increase the powers of the president and the executive agencies.

The Voices of People and Interest Groups Who Have Money to Spend

Following the Watergate scandal that led to the resignation of President Richard Nixon, there was strong public sentiment for reform of the electoral system to reduce corruption and the effects of money—particularly large amounts of money—on elections. Congress enacted and President Gerald Ford signed electoral-reform measures that placed a variety of monetary limits on campaign contributions and expenditures. In *Buckley v. Valeo* (1976)[5] an activist majority (consisting of conservatives and liberals) struck down many of those limits as violations of the free-speech rights of rich people. That case and succeeding decisions have essentially made it constitutionally impermissible for Congress or any state legislature effectively to reduce the role of money in elections.

Buckley was decided before the liberal paradigm was discarded, so the first issue was whether campaign contributions and expenditures constitute protected speech. There is certainly an important connection to the extent campaign funds are used for speech (rather than for polls, consultants, rents, etc.) because the expenditure of money is necessary for the most effective forms of protected speech. But writing a check is not speaking. In the liberal paradigm, such activities so connected or intertwined with speech enjoyed protection, but not to the same extent as "pure speech," the spoken and written word. In a leading case on this issue,[6] draft-card burning as a protest against the Vietnam War was held, surprisingly by a liberal majority, to be unprotected. The effect on speech was "incidental" to regulation of how the draft card was used. As discussed above, this has been extended to include "secondary" effects as well, and both doctrines have been used to restrict substantially the speech rights important to people of ordinary means.

Because the purpose of Congress was to improve the electoral system, stop corruption, and thereby further democracy by reducing the role of money in elections, the effect on speech would seem incidental or secondary. But the Court did not see it that way. The incidental-effects argument was discarded with the conclusory statement that "expenditure of money cannot be equated with such conduct as destruction of a draft card." (This is true in a sense not meant by the Court: one is what affluent people easily and effectively do when they wish to communicate with the public; and the other is what people of ordinary means, excluded from mainstream channels and frustrated, must sometimes do to be heard.) And no consideration at all was given to the many decisions that approve regulations that do not wholly prohibit expression but substantially reduce the quantity of, and variety of forms and places for, protected speech. In *Buckley* and its progeny, the Court has applied different rules to the speech rights of rich people.

Concluding that money is speech, the Court applied strict scrutiny and invalidated the various limits on expenditures by campaigns and individuals (while upholding the limits on contributions). For example, the limits that the act set on campaign expenditures for presidential elections ($10 million prior to nomination and $20 million in the general election, which hardly require bare-bones campaigns) and by candidates on their own behalf ($25,000, which would make it difficult for a rich candidate to buy an election) were invalidated.

The Court found these limits—and the goal of reducing the effects of money in elections—unacceptable, because they "restrict the voices of people and interest groups that have money to spend." Campaigns draw funds, and should be able to spend them, in amounts that "normally vary with the size and intensity of the candidate's support." This is the language of the marketplace, not of ideas but of campaign funds. According to the Court, campaigns draw funds in proportion to their support, and if this means the ones that draw the most funds will most often win, that's just the operation of a free market. The problem with this conception is that elections are a type of market phenomenon in which every person, not every dollar, is supposed to have equal weight. Campaigns draw funds mostly in proportion to their attractiveness to rich people.

In succeeding cases, the conservatives struck down other electoral-reform measures, including one that limited the power of political action committees (PACs). Congress limited the amount of money a PAC could independently spend ($1,000) in support of a presidential candidate who has opted to receive public financing. This created a trade-off: if the candidate took public campaign financing, then PACs' support of him or her was limited, but there was no limit if the candidate opted not to receive public funds. The reform was challenged by the National Conservative Political Action Committee, which wished to exceed the limit in support of President Reagan's reelection although he was receiving public campaign financing. Justice Rehnquist's majority opinion in *Federal Election Commission v. National Conservative Political Action Committee* (1985) stressed the rights of contributors to band together and spend what they wish (and have). In *First National Bank of Boston v. Bellotti* (1978) the Court also recognized, for the first time, free-speech rights of corporations, which have been used to invalidate local legislation aimed at reducing the influence of corporations on the outcomes of public referendums.[7]

In these cases, the conservative emphasis on judicial restraint, strict construction, original intent, and incidental and secondary effects—so important in their opinions limiting the speech rights of people of ordinary means—is nowhere to be found. The First Amendment refers to speech; money is not mentioned, nor would anyone suppose that the framers would interpret speech to include money. Because the purpose of these reforms is not to limit speech but to reduce the role of money in elections, they would seem to be valid based on the incidental-effects doctrine (and the secondary-effects doctrine at least as to cases decided after its adoption). Contributions by rich people are constitutionally protected; contributions by ordinary people solicited in public places are an inconvenience to others that justifies limiting speech rights (see *Krishna Consciousness v. Lee,* chapter 2). These legislatively enacted measures have been invalidated based on a novel constitutional theory—this is judicial activism. Without acknowledgment or any serious public attention, the conservatives have created different speech rules for the haves and the have-nots, or more precisely, for the have-a-lots and the rest of us.

The Court has forbidden Congress and local legislatures to interfere with the political privileges of wealth and established what amounts to a First Amendment right to buy elections and referenda. Not surprisingly, money has increasingly dominated elections and politics.[8] The First Amendment as interpreted by today's conservatives constitutes a constitutional barrier to political reform very much like the constitutional barrier to economic reform erected by conservative justices in the early 1900s.

Nothing to Do with Voting

In 1985, Lawrence Presley, Ed Mack, and Nathaniel Gosha were the first African-Americans elected county commissioners as far back as anyone could remember in Etowah and Russell Counties,

Alabama. They won in predominantly African-American districts, after the counties had been required, under the Voting Rights Act of 1965, to adopt a district election system instead of the at-large countywide system, which had never yielded an African-American commissioner in spite of substantial African-American populations. The other Etowah and Russell county commissioners, all of whom were white, voted to change the powers and authority of commissioners once they saw that the new system yielded African-American commissioners. Their previously exclusive authority over the roads and road work in their districts, the main function of the commissioners, was given to an administrator or taken over by each commission as a whole (both with white majorities), and they lost the power to control district funds.

Etowah and Russell Counties were required to "preclear" with federal officials any changes they made that could affect their future compliance with the act. Nevertheless, they did not preclear these changes, and Presley, Mack, and Gosha took over literally empty offices.

This was not the first, or even the most ingenious, structural shuffle enacted to avoid the Voting Rights Act or to subvert the rights of African-Americans to vote, but it was one of the more transparent of recent times. Offices have been abolished for that purpose, for example, but the federal courts consistently invalidated such measures pursuant to the act. As late as 1984, the Court reaffirmed the consensus understanding that the act was "enacted by Congress as a response to the 'unremitting and ingenious defiance' of the command of the Fifteenth Amendment for nearly a century by state officials . . . [and] 'new subterfuges will be promptly discovered and enjoined.'" In *Presley v. Etowah County Commission* (1992),[9] however, the Court abandoned a quarter-century commitment to equal voting rights.

91

Justice Kennedy's majority opinion, without doubting the discriminatory purpose that has been so elusive in recent race cases (except if the issue is affirmative action [see chapter 5]), simply concluded that the changes in the power and authority of commissioners, whatever their purpose or effect, had "nothing to do with voting" or, therefore, the voting-rights act. According to Kennedy, the commissioners changed their powers, which they have authority to do, and there is no "workable standard for distinguishing between changes in rules governing voting and changes in the routine organization and functioning of government." But workable standards seem rather easy here, as Justices Stevens, White, and Blackmun suggested in dissent. (Justice Thomas voted with the majority despite his moving testimony at his confirmation hearing about his grandfather from Pin Point, Georgia, who read the Bible nightly to prepare for voting literacy tests.) Counties subject to the act must preclear any reallocation of powers or decision-making authority regarding offices for which they have adopted a new electoral system pursuant to the act, particularly (but not only) changes that occur after the newly required system yields office-holders of the race previously underrepresented. Or: Any reallocation of powers or decision-making authority that increases the power of the majority group whose earlier domination led to a new electoral system pursuant to the act must be precleared.

The previous cases fit these standards, which seemed to work pretty well until the Court effectively repealed the Voting Rights Act in *Presley*. The conservatives have not only undercut constitutional protections of civil rights and civil liberties, including voting-rights cases where they have upheld at-large systems that regularly disenfranchise African-Americans. They have also used their extensive power as interpreters of legislation to nullify the meaning and effectiveness of this and other civil-rights laws adopted by Congress (other examples of this are discussed in chapter 5).[10]

The Function of Editors

In 1938 the Florida legislature, responding to widespread claims of electoral corruption stemming in part from false charges made on the eve of elections, enacted a "right of reply" statute, which required any newspaper that "assails" the character or record of an electoral candidate to publish the candidate's reply.[11] This has been a rather standard requirement for broadcast media, long subject to the broader access rules of the "fairness doctrine" (which is not limited to candidates), and is often required of newspapers and broadcast media in Western Europe, where reply rights are favored and defamation suits are usually disfavored. A distinction has been drawn between prohibiting expression of any viewpoint by the media —censorship—and requiring the media to include, in addition to its own views, the views of others. However, in 1974 the Court unanimously invalidated the Florida statute as a violation of freedom of the press in *Miami Herald Pub. Co. v. Tornillo.*[12]

Chief Justice Burger's opinion found no meaningful difference between censorship and compelled access and emphasized "the intrusion into the function of editors." He avoided seemingly inconsistent cases: the Court's decision five years earlier upholding the fairness doctrine and a decision rendered the same day as *Tornillo* imposing defamation liability for negligent editorial decisions were not even mentioned. (Nor was *Tornillo* discussed when the Court approved government-compelled speech and intrusion on the function of doctors in *Rust v. Sullivan* [chapter 2].) And the standard applied went beyond even strict scrutiny. There was no discussion of whether the government's interests in requiring access for replies were compelling; the right of newspapers to bar access—which resides with their owners, regardless of the rhetoric about editors' discretion—is seemingly absolute. An earlier case had also affirmed the right to refuse a paid advertisement based on content.[13]

The absolutism of these activist decisions seems to foreclose any government attempt to provide popular access at least to the print media, particularly because *Tornillo* invalidated a reply statute limited to electoral candidates, who present the strongest claim. But there does not appear to be a principled or sensible reason for allowing required access in the broadcast media and absolutely forbidding it in the print media. Newspapers have traditionally been more serious and intellectual and less focused on entertainment, but they are doing their best these days to dispel that distinction (which is far too subjective in any event). The decision upholding the fairness doctrine was largely based on the "scarcity" of available outlets, but the number of broadcast outlets has increased whereas the number of print outlets has diminished (to one in most markets), so that the print medium is now at least as monopolistic as the broadcast medium. Although newspapers have history on their side, there is not any meaningful social or constitutional difference.

Further, we should not ignore clear changes in the nature and social role of the mass media. The information and ideas available in our homes, newsstands, movie theaters, and book and video stores are increasingly controlled by a small number of multinational corporations that have no tradition, understanding, or interest in journalism or social dialogue. After World War II, 80 percent of the newspapers were independently owned. In the mid-1980s, forty-six corporations controlled most of the newspapers, magazines, television and radio stations, books, and movies in the United States. In the early 1990s, that number was reduced to twenty-three; and by the end of the 1990s, it is predicted that only "a half-dozen large corporations will own all the most powerful media outlets."[14] There are more varied forms of media and, with innovations like cable television, more choices in some segments, but the range of media is increasingly owned and controlled by a very small number of people.

This level of centralization and monopolization of the media is a phenomena usually associated with totalitarian or authoritarian countries, except that it is privately rather than governmentally controlled. That may seem preferable in a society that values private ownership, but it amounts to extremely centralized control of the information and ideas available to the public without the responsibility, accountability, or popular-selection process associated with government officials. Elected officials surely do not always live up to our expectations, but their mandate is to serve the public interest, they are not immune from replacement and public pressure, and they are selected by a democratic process. We never got to vote for (or against) Rupert Murdoch, S. I. Newhouse, or Robert Maxwell; nor was there any public debate or choice when General Electric bought RCA and NBC.

Yet, a handful of such people and corporations control the information and ideas available to us, and they all have pretty much the same social and political outlook. They are economic conservatives whose philosophy emphasizes free markets (while they typically have close alliances and relationships with big government). They are sometimes liberal on issues of personal freedom and, at least after they got into the media business, always liberal on free press issues. They entered the media business because it provided a better opportunity for profits than other businesses or investments. Their overriding concern is profits, not ideas. Some provide the managers of their media outlets more leeway than others, but those managers also hardly reflect the diversity of views or the range of people in the United States. Like all successful businesspeople, they do not antagonize their major customers (large advertisers), the sources of their raw materials (often government), or the regular consumers of their product—the people who watch, listen and read, an increasingly captive audience because there is no real competition.

This has fundamentally changed the media. We should not be surprised that in an earlier era when tobacco ads were a major source of media revenue, the media helped the tobacco industry cover up the dangers of smoking (or that the now-diversified tobacco companies still influence content).[15] Now a handful of leading media people and companies hold a near monopoly, and there is little pretense of journalism or ethical restraint. They do pretty much whatever they can to raise ratings and revenues. The content of our major media has degenerated; the corporate standard-bearers of free speech acknowledge and sometimes glorify their avoidance of ideas or controversy.

Local television news, and increasingly national news and overall television programming, has become the domain of fear, viciousness, snooping, and suffering. Decent media people, who usually sought a career in journalism or the media with the highest motives and ethics in mind, are pushed to value only ratings and profits. Last year a national show was launched that featured home videos of viciousness and suffering, and its ads—which were foisted on anyone who happened to be listening to that network in prime time—depicted a person tending his garden being attacked by a neighbor and a child being abused by a baby-sitter. In Philadelphia, my hometown, a major network's local news reporting in 1992 on escalating racial hostilities between Hispanics and whites showed repeatedly—and advertised—throughout an evening their "exclusive" video of a "drive-by shooting" by a Hispanic. The anchor's voiceover urged calm in the white neighborhood as the picture was full of violence, fear, and provocation. The station had no comment as it later appeared that the video actually showed only part of a series of complex, violent events that did not include a drive-by shooting. Such events, and maudlin interviews and intrusions on basic privacy and respect, are now commonplace. Indeed, watching the local news anchors, it's often hard to tell if you've got the news or *The Dating Game*.

In the transformation era, the Court vindicated the interests of individuals and society in free speech and open discourse that had theretofore been subject to government control and censorship. The practices of governments that closed channels of communication or selectively excluded people or messages from the marketplace of ideas were forbidden. This struggle is not over, as the principles and results of the new conservative Court make all too clear. But those newspapers earlier denied access to the marketplace of ideas, together with their successors in the modern press and mass media, *have become the marketplace of ideas.* Absolute freedom of the press now conflicts with meaningful freedom of speech, and we must seek some accommodation that preserves the best of both traditions. If we continue to define and treat the mass media as if they were just another leafleteer on a street corner who must be not only protected from government censorship but also shielded from all claims to access by others, we are, once again, excluding the mass of people from the social dialogue and the marketplace of ideas.

All media should be subject to the same access and monopolization rules, and those rules should break up excess concentrations and allow limited public access, including at least replies by anyone whose character or conduct has been criticized and statements by candidates and a range of community groups setting out—in their own words—their positions on important issues. Limited rights to access would probably improve quality and audience interest as well as enhance democracy. In any event, a much broader range of people and ideas must gain access to our media, or free speech will have lost its meaning.

❦ 4 ❧

RELIGION

The conservative rise to power has been very much about religion. Ronald Reagan's Christian fundamentalism was often explicit and never far from the surface, whether the subject was abortion, art, foreign policy, economics, or justice. However, this emphasis and reliance on religion—and the melding of religion and politics—is not uniquely conservative or unusual in our history. One need not look back very far to find, for example, the liberal civil-rights movement of the 1960s, and the Carter presidency, also steeped in religion. The issues that have distinguished conservative from liberal approaches to religion are not about religious motivation or the importance of religion in life or politics. Rather, the crucial differences concern the degree to which government should be separated from religion and the degree to which society should accommodate the freedom of believers in nonmajoritarian faiths to engage in their religious practices.

These two issues are addressed in the first clause of the First Amendment: "Congress shall make no law respecting an establishment of religion, or prohibiting the free exercise thereof." No other aspect of individual belief, and no other issue of any kind, is treated this way in the Constitution. The same amendment addresses free speech, but it does not prohibit government adoption of particular political, social, or even moral views. Although the terms are general, religion is clearly treated differently: its "exercise" is protected, and the government is forbidden to "establish" it.

This treatment of religion has historical roots, but here, as in other areas of constitutional history, the conventional version is distorted. Although there certainly was a sensitivity to the relationship between government and religion and a strong movement to disestablish religion after 1776, the First Amendment was not intended—and did not in its terms—separate religion from all government. Rather, as with freedom of speech and press (chapter 2), the specification of Congress as the entity prohibited was not accidental. A leading constitutional historian concluded that "[o]n the eve of the American Revolution most of the colonies maintained establishments of religion [and] discriminated against Roman Catholics, Jews, and even dissenting Protestants." Taxes to support particular religions were applicable to everyone, and in Virginia, for example, it was a crime to preach without being ordained as an Episcopalian. Many of the original states still had or allowed established religions. The framers intended to preserve the discretion of each state in this regard while prohibiting the federal government from establishing any religion.[1]

This was practical as well as principled, particularly because the usual form of establishment in the colonies and states consisted of preferences of and aid to religion generally rather than to any particular religion. Whereas in Europe establishment meant an explicitly established single church, in the colonies and early American states

> establishment included the churches of every denomination and sect with a sufficient number of adherents to form a church. In general, where Protestantism was established, it was synonymous with religion, because there were either no Jews and Roman Catholics or too few of them to make a dif-

ference; and where Christianity was established, as in Maryland which had many Catholics, Jews were scarcely known. . . . [N]o evidence exists to show that Jews were actually taxed to support Christianity. . . . An establishment of religion in America at the time of the framing of the Bill of Rights meant government aid and sponsorship of religion, principally by impartial tax support of the institutions of religion, the churches.[2]

Which particular religions were benefited or established varied within each state as well as among the states (although all were Christian).

The easiest way to assure that the federal government did not establish one religion over another or become a battleground and prize for the various religions was to prohibit a federal establishment of religion entirely and assure all people the freedom to practice their faiths. This helps us understand the uniqueness of religion among the various categories of belief and faith in the constitutional scheme. Politics, economics, regional pride, even sports can generate strong, emotional, and uncompromising positions. But religion almost always does so, perhaps because of its connection to personal identity and stability and to a range of basic, otherwise unanswerable and perplexing questions (such as why are we here?). It is not the only basis of conflict and violence among nations, peoples, and neighbors, but it is surely consistently at or near the top of the list. Religious liberty is an indispensable ingredient of individual freedom and integrity and social democracy and stability.

The essential assumption of the United States of America was, and probably had to be, tolerance and acceptance of a range of religious views—and the determination to live and thrive together in peace, as so many nations with established religions and diverse religious beliefs had been, and are today, unable to do. The individual states came to accept this wisdom as well, long before the

Fourteenth Amendment (1868) or the application of the religion clauses to the states through the Fourteenth Amendment (1940).[3] By 1833, all the previously established states had, without federal intervention, prohibited religious establishment.

We thus have two constitutional and social principles of fundamental proportions: Each person should be free to believe in and exercise the religion of his or her choice; and no government, federal, state or local, should establish or favor any religion. The new conservative Court has quickly taken on both principles.

FREE EXERCISE

The public controversy over religion in recent years has largely been about establishment issues like prayer in the schools and religious-holiday displays. Free exercise of religion seemed an accepted and settled aspect of American freedom. For over four decades, there was a fairly broad legal consensus about at least the importance of and rules applied in free-exercise cases. Free exercise of religion was recognized as a fundamental constitutional right that takes precedence over legitimate government interests unless they are "compelling" and cannot be accomplished by a means "less restrictive" of religious freedom. Any government action that "burdens" free exercise of religion triggered this "strict scrutiny" test (explained in chapter 1).

Thus, in *Barnette,* although the government had a legitimate interest in promoting unity in wartime, it was not a compelling interest and did not require an act by a Jehovah's Witness that would desecrate her religious beliefs. The government's action was not aimed at Jehovah's Witnesses or any particular religion; it was generally applicable to all. However, it did not justify the burden on religious exercise.

Similarly, in 1963 the Court ruled that South Carolina could not deny a member of the Seventh Day Adventist faith unemployment benefits because she refused on religious grounds to accept a job that required work on Saturdays.[4] The state's action, although generally applicable and not aimed at that religion, burdened her exercise of religion; and its interest in limiting expenditures for unemployment benefits, although legitimate, was not compelling. In 1972 the Court ruled that Amish children could not be required under Wisconsin's mandatory school-attendance law to attend school past the eighth grade. Chief Justice Warren Burger's majority opinion did not question the generally applicable law requiring school attendance until the age of sixteen. The law was not compelling or necessary as applied to the Amish, who had a literal understanding of the biblical injunction "Be not conformed to this world" and provided their children a sufficient substitute for further schooling. It impermissibly compelled them "to perform acts undeniably at odds with fundamental tenets of their religious beliefs."[5]

There are two general ways to understand and analyze these decisions. We can see them as bestowing a kind of privilege to violate the laws that others must obey. These laws were undeniably authorized and legitimate, and their application was uniform to all people. There was no singling out of a particular religion, or any known intent related to religion at all. The state is being compelled to grant an exemption to a select minority from duly authorized and passed laws.

However, if we focus on the social and historical context, it looks very different. Free exercise of majoritarian religions is regularly accommodated by government at all levels. Many states have or had Sunday closing laws because Sunday is the day of rest for their predominant religion, Christianity. Christians do not need a special accommodation to avoid having to work on their day of rest. Religiously observant Jews and Seventh Day Adventists do not work on Saturdays, but no legislature has declared Saturday a general day of rest. Federal prohibition laws contained exceptions for the use of wine in certain religious services. Christmas is a government-recognized holiday everywhere in the United States; Kwanzaa, Hanukkah, and Ramadan are not.[6] Majoritarian religions do not need special exemptions from generally applicable laws; such laws will accommodate them and facilitate the exercise of their religions. In this sense, accommodation of free exercise by nonmajoritarian religions is necessary to realize *equal* treatment— free exercise of religion for all our people.

The strict-scrutiny doctrinal framework remained in place throughout the 1980s, but the increasingly conservative Court did not invalidate any new government action as violative of free exercise of religion after the 1972 Amish case just summarized.[7] The conservative justices certainly favor religion, but they just as certainly do not have all religions—specifically, nonmainstream religions—in mind. The new Court first changed the meaning and content of the rules without changing their terms. It became harder to show that an action "burdened" religious exercise; less-important government interests were found "compelling"; available nonreligious means to claimed secular ends were no longer important; and government interests were considered on a very general level rather than requiring a precise compelling interest in the particular action that conflicted with free exercise. In 1990, the Court scrapped strict scrutiny altogether.

An Unavoidable Consequence of Democratic Government

Alfred Smith is a seventy-three-year-old Klamath Indian from Springfield, Oregon, and a member of the Native American Church, the largest American Indian religious institution. Several years ago, Smith was fired from his job as a counselor with a private drug rehabilitation program because he used peyote as part of a religious ceremony at the church. Oregon officials then denied him unemployment benefits pursuant to the usual rule that such benefits are limited to employees who lose their jobs through no fault of their own and are not available to an employee fired for work-related misconduct.[8]

Peyote is a cactus found in Mexico and the southwestern U.S. that contains the hallucinogen mescaline. Its use is extremely limited and has never posed a significant drug problem, perhaps because it tastes very bitter and often causes nausea. The U.S. Drug Enforcement Agency reported that only twenty pounds were seized in the U.S. over a seven-year period in the 1980s during which fifteen million pounds of marijuana were seized.

Use of peyote as a core sacrament in American Indian religion dates back over ten thousand years. The Native American Church uses peyote in ceremonies, sometimes lasting several days, under the close supervision of trained elders. Smith described his use of the drug as deeply religious, cultural, and therapeutic. As a child, Smith was taken from his tribal lands by the government and placed in a Christian boarding school, where he excelled in math, art, and athletics. However, he did not fare well in Portland after high school and became an alcoholic. He credits religious use of peyote and the Native American Church with his conquering alcoholism and reconstituting a fulfilling life. Smith's was an appealing case for accommodation of nonmajoritarian religious practices, particularly because peyote played a sacramental role in his religion similar to the familiar role of wine in Catholicism.

The Oregon Supreme Court, based on the strict-scrutiny test and the U.S. Supreme Court's precedents discussed above, ruled that Smith may not be denied unemployment benefits. Although he was fired for misconduct and peyote use is also a crime in Oregon, the highest state court found that ceremonial use of peyote was central to his religion and, in those circumstances, was not demonstrably dangerous. Oregon's prosecutors had customarily declined to prosecute criminal cases involving religious use of peyote by American Indians. The state's law, although generally applicable and legitimate, burdened Native Americans' free exercise of religion, and the government's refusal of an exception did not further a compelling interest.

Justice Scalia wrote the Court's majority opinion in *Employment Division v. Smith* (1990)[9] overturning the Oregon ruling and overruling the strict-scrutiny test, even though the strict-scrutiny test was not questioned in any of the briefs or oral arguments before the Court. Scalia emphasized the need for uniformity of application of laws and saw the only alternative as "anarchy"—"a system in which each conscience is a law unto itself." The strict-scrutiny test was replaced with the "incidental effect" rule now favored in most civil-rights and civil-liberties decisions:

> If prohibiting the exercise of religion (or burdening the activity of printing [referring to the First Amendment's free-press clause]) is not the object of the [law] but merely the incidental effect of a generally applicable and otherwise valid provision, the First Amendment has not been offended.

This means that nonmajoritarian religions no longer have the freedom to engage in religious practices that conflict with generally applicable laws, no matter how insignificant the law or how important the particular religious practice. The Court recognized and acknowledged this in a most memorable passage:

> It may fairly be said that leaving accommodation to the political process will place at a relative disadvantage those religious practices that are not widely engaged in; but that [is an] unavoidable consequence of democratic government. . . .

The Court's new rule is a consequence of a particular notion of democracy—one in which protection of the freedom to exercise nonmajoritarian religions has little or no importance. But this consequence is hardly "unavoidable," and there is no explanation of why this particular conception of democracy is either required or preferable. The Court in this very case overruled a long line of decisions that had avoided this consequence without any known impact on the ability of government to implement its policies and interests effectively. Neither Scalia nor any study or scholar has demonstrated any concrete negative impact resulting from occasional exceptions to general laws so that religion may be accommodated. The concrete effects of such accommodations on government's ability to function effectively are surely trivial, and strict scrutiny is not absolute (still allowing for governmental interests that are deemed compelling).

It could be argued against accommodation that people will "abuse" such rights, or that many people are upset by it, although Scalia does not explicitly raise these arguments. Some people may make insincere religious claims just to avoid some responsibility; but proof of sincerity has always been required, and being publicized as a religious minority, often depicted as deviant in the media, is usually not pleasant. This is no reason to deny religious freedom to those for whom it is a sincere necessity of life. Also, some (occasionally most) people may be upset by an unfamiliar religious practice or an accommodation, but, like the "listener's veto" discussed in chapter 2, this is the ultimate argument against freedom that, if obliged, could empower the state to abolish differences.

Scalia's opinion largely eschewed such considerations and relied on technical legal arguments and his version of the intent and history of the free-exercise clause. The technical arguments focus on Scalia's attempt to depict this momentous change of long-standing precedents—this conservative judicial activism—as no change at all by rewriting and strained interpretation of earlier cases. A leading conservative scholar and supporter of the result called Scalia's opinion a "paradigmatic example of judicial over-reaching. . . . [in which] use of precedent borders on fiction."[10]

Scalia claimed that the decisions in *Barnette* and the Amish school-attendance case were based on more than the right of free exercise of religion—on what he calls "hybrid" rights. He asserted that those cases did not apply strict scrutiny to free-exercise claims but only to claims with some additional "communicative" aspect, which means that they were supported by free-speech as well as free-exercise rights. However, those opinions do not say anything of the kind, and other cases in which strict scrutiny was not applied could be just as easily described as "hybrid." Indeed, one can describe almost every free-exercise claim as also involving a free-speech claim. He also argued that only unemployment-benefits cases have gotten strict scrutiny, without explaining why such a line would or should be drawn or why it has not been mentioned in any prior case. Finally, he argued that there has not been strict scrutiny where a state law, like the law criminalizing use of peyote, is involved; but all these cases involve a conflict with some authorized governmental rule or practice, and many have involved explicit laws, including criminal laws. The issue arises because there is a conflict between governmental rules and exercise of religion.

Scalia's arguments based on the intent and history of the free-exercise clause are more serious, but no more convincing. Scalia first noted that the "free exercise" language can be read either way; it may mean that accommodation is required, but it may refer to measures short of accommodation. However, he did not look to the historical context for guidance as to what the words would most likely have meant to the framers of the First Amendment, although he has been a leading proponent of the branch of original-intent jurisprudence that emphasizes such use of history to determine the original meaning of words used in the Constitution.[11] He simply ignored this original-meaning issue and passed off all historical consideration with the conclusory statement that accommodation "contradicts both constitutional tradition and common sense."

The preadoption history is somewhat ambiguous, but it provides a strong case for accommodation. At the time when the First

Amendment was written and adopted, nine of the states had free-exercise clauses in their constitutions that essentially embodied the strict-scrutiny, compelling-interest test. Typically, they guaranteed "free exercise . . . provided it be not repugnant to the peace and safety of the State." There were similar accommodation provisions and practices in the colonial period. Further, James Madison, who wrote the federal free-exercise clause, proposed language for the Virginia free-exercise clause that was even more accommodating than the "peace and safety" provision.[12]

The post-adoption history poses similar difficulties for Scalia's position, particularly the *Barnette* decision. He goes out of his way to repudiate the important elements of the *Barnette* constitutional and social vision while purporting not to overrule *Barnette*. Thus, as quoted above, Scalia emphasized the "unavoidable consequence[s] of democratic government," which is the antithesis of Justice Jackson's conception of fundamental rights as not "submitted to vote." Jackson's "fixed star" is not mentioned, and the variety of our religions and religious practices is, for Scalia, a basis for less, not more, freedom. The "danger increases in direct proportion to the society's diversity of religious beliefs." "[O]ur rich cultural diversities," a source of our strength in *Barnette,* have become a "danger" in *Smith.* And whereas *Barnette* is barely tolerated—limited to its narrow facts and not overruled on the slim thread of Scalia's "hybrid" analysis discussed above—the 1940 decision that *Barnette* overruled is cited twice with approval in Scalia's opinion, including Frankfurter's opinion there, which became his dissent in *Barnette.*[13]

These considerations, ignored by Scalia, leave us with a clause that by its language provides some form of extraordinary protection for exercise of religion, a preadoption history that is demonstrably accommodationist in its theory and practice, and a post-adoption tradition of accommodation, particularly in recent times extending back almost five decades. The authoritarian content and tone of the *Smith* decision is thus not required and cannot be justified by precedent, history, or any concrete negative effect on the ability of government to function effectively. This is simply compelled conformity in the face of constitutional language and a constitutional and social history that, at the very least, caution us to make room for religious toleration and freedom.

ESTABLISHMENT

When the religion clauses were first applied to the states in the 1940s, the Court announced the basic principle of a "wall of separation between church and state," drawing on a phrase used by Thomas Jefferson in a famous letter. Although its application has always been controversial, the principle was generally accepted for the last four decades and generally understood as prohibiting governmental preference or aid to any religion or religion generally. In modern times, as in the time of the framers of the Constitution, this separation was not hostile to religion; and it was generally accepted by conservatives and liberals and deeply religious people of a range of faiths. The idea was that religion should stay out of government and government should stay out of religion, for the benefit of both, and of the American people.[14]

This wall of separation—in which the Court has recently installed a large new gate—was always more complex and difficult to apply than its general acceptance would suggest. Religion is so intertwined with culture that separation of religious and secular aspects of various practices, customs, and ideas is usually elusive. For example, are Sunday closing laws secular or religious?[15] They have religious origins and accommodate a majoritarian religious practice, but they also have become a common secular tradition. They are both religious and secular, and one can make a good case that they are either. Even values or morals that we (often quite righteously) insist are secular, neutral, or objective have historical origins and substantial elements related to religion; and one can, therefore, again make a good case that they are either. Thus, the separation principle itself has secular and religious elements and can claim secular and religious origins. For example, there was a traditional Baptist concern that governmental participation in a religious activity like prayer is corrupting and a travesty of spirituality.[16]

This complexity is compounded by the frequent overlap of or conflict between the establishment and free-exercise principles. The more the separation principle is interpreted and applied as an absolute prohibition, the more every accommodation of free exercise, whether nonmajoritarian or majoritarian, looks like an establishment. If every practice incorporated into government measures that is to any substantial extent an accommodation of religion is invalid, then we could not allow, for example, Sunday closing laws or an officially recognized Christmas holiday. Similarly, an absolutist view of free exercise can consume the establishment principle: a particular majoritarian religion, including public officials of its faith, exercising such absolute rights could be no different in substance from a specifically declared establishment.

This does not mean that the task of separation should be abandoned, but we should not be surprised to see inconsistency and contradiction or a lack of clear doctrinal lines. The task, as I see it, is to maintain the essential separation of church and state—which is central to our society and culture and to the dignity of our people and our religions—without succumbing, as those on the liberal side of this conflict sometimes do, to triviality.

My understanding of this issue is significantly connected to my experience in a Baltimore public elementary school. The students were mainly Christian, but there was a substantial Jewish minority to which I was to discover I belonged. It was a discovery because, although I always identified myself as Jewish and knew Jews were a small proportion of the population, I did not define or really think of myself as part of a minority. Rather, my self-image was more 1950s middle-class white. It was startling that at the school's Christmas holiday gathering, after many Christmas carols had been sung by all (with the Jewish kids often skipping or mumbling references to Christ), the Jews were asked, or told, to sing the Christian hymn "Rock of Ages" while everyone else looked on and listened. (I came to think of "Rock of Ages" as a Jewish song because of this experience, although it was never sung at my synagogue or in my religious education. According to a Jewish religious scholar also from Baltimore, it is a Christian hymn that was probably selected by the school because its content is nondenominational.)[17]

I joined the huddled handful and duly sang this song I did not know, always with considerable fear and mixed feelings of pride and deviance. I wanted to stand up for my religion and my family, but I could just as well have hidden in the cloakroom. The power of the school and the state to define what is right and acceptable and what is different was never more evident, as was the enormity of that power when applied to something so identity and family based as religion. Even though the intent and effect was in part to confer some legitimacy on the different, my memories of these events are mostly about fear and confusion. Some will say that this has affected me too much in my approach to establishment of religion; others, I am sure, will say it has had too little effect. The next sections consider school prayers, religious displays, and aid to religion.

Jefferson Was of Course in France

Prayer in the public schools has been a major political issue since it was prohibited by the liberal Supreme Court in the early 1960s.[18] The latest decisions leave little doubt that prayer, in some form at least, will soon be back.

From 1978 to 1982, the Alabama legislature enacted, respectively, three laws authorizing a one-minute period of silence for "meditation," the same period of silence for "meditation or voluntary prayer," and a teacher-led prayer for "willing students" to "Almighty God . . . the Creator and Supreme Judge of the world." In *Wallace v. Jaffree* (1985)[19] the Court only considered the "meditation or voluntary prayer" law, which was struck down by a narrow five-to-four vote.

Justice Stevens's majority opinion rests most heavily on the acknowledgment by the sponsor of the law in the Alabama legislature that it was an "effort to return voluntary prayer to our public schools." This made it an easy case under the long-established wall of separation decisions. The law purposely endorses and promotes religion, and, although not directly coercive, it has a coercive effect particularly on children. Many children will take the school's suggestion of prayer as at least an encouragement to pray, and it is difficult for them to make contrary independent choices in the school context. This effect was emphasized in an early opinion by Justice Frankfurter,[20] who was something of an activist on this issue, and the Court had long applied the strictest separation where children were exposed to governmental religious activity. Thus, whereas prayer in schools was prohibited, opening a legislative session with a prayer was not.[21] Stevens reviewed the Court's long-standing principles, quoted Jackson's "fixed star" passage from *Barnette,* and reaffirmed the now-slim majority's commitment to the wall of separation.

Justice Rehnquist, dissenting, directly challenged the wall-of-separation principle. His focus, however, was not so much on whether there should be a wall of separation but on the history of the establishment clause, which he believes has been distorted. Rehnquist argued that the framers intended to prohibit only "the designation of a national church" and "preference for one religious denomination or sect over others." Preference or promotion of religion generally as well as nondiscriminatory direct aid to religion, according to Rehnquist, were allowable to the framers and

therefore must be allowable today. He condemned "[a]ny devia-
tion from their intentions."

The original-intent argument that was a favorite in conservative opinions and scholarship in the mid-1980s has more recently
been openly criticized and less frequently utilized. It purports to
limit discretion and legally require particular rules and results, but
it opens more questions and resolves none: Who were the
framers? Which framers and which historians do we credit when
they conflict? Are we looking for their specific purpose or intent or
the likely meaning of their words?, etc. History is, of course,
important—crucial, I believe—but it cannot be converted into a
determinate decision-making mechanism.

Further, because we do not have a tradition of frequent or
periodic updating of the Constitution by amendments, a focus on
original intent also means that today's problems and conflicts will
be resolved with very dated and limited knowledge and perspec-
tive. In our system, constitutional amendments are extremely difficult and time-consuming to accomplish; they occur only
occasionally and haphazardly, with no mechanism for or assurance
that they will even address the most important contemporary concerns. This means that the framers' perspectives would be influential or definitive on a problem, like prayer in public schools,
about which they had no experience or opportunity to contemplate or address. They could not know how or why our public-
school system developed or understand its role in modern society,
nor could they be expected to anticipate it in formulating their
constitution. Original intent leads us to ask questions like what
would the framers rule on prayer in the public schools, when a
more sensible question and approach is to focus on how the general principles established by the framers should be applied by us
to current issues.

Rehnquist's establishment-clause history focused on whether
Jefferson's wall-of-separation metaphor represented the view of

the framers or was, as Rehnquist concluded, "misleading." Rehnquist first noted that "Jefferson was of course in France" at the time when the First Amendment was adopted, and that he wrote the "wall of separation" language well after the amendment was ratified. Jefferson is, therefore, a "less than ideal source," and with no further explanation, Rehnquist dismissed Jefferson and turned to Madison.

Lawyers are perhaps too accustomed to sweeping dismissals of this kind to notice, but this is a strange way to examine history. The Bill of Rights was adopted in the First Congress with little debate or discussion, so the available historical evidence is sparse. But there is a consensus among historians that Jefferson's views and proposals on religious and other freedom were quite influential in Virginia, the nation, and throughout the world. Jefferson was the main author of the Virginia Statute for Religious Freedom (1779), from which Madison drew some of the language for the First Amendment religion clauses. Jefferson was also the author of the Declaration of Independence and one of the most prominent and influential leaders in the constitutional drafting process and the whole formative period of American history. His role as an integral participant and leader is indisputable. Jefferson's assessment of what was intended, whether contemporaneous or after the fact (and even though he was out of town when the religion clauses were adopted), should be seriously considered in any credible historical account.

Further, Rehnquist has not consistently applied this reasoning by which absence from drafting or adoption of a provision renders one's evaluation or interpretation of it irrelevant, or deprives even a leading, influential figure of legitimacy as a "framer." Although John Jay was of course in England during the constitutional convention (negotiating what became known as the Jay Treaty), Rehnquist has referred without qualification to his views as important to an understanding of the Constitution.[22]

After dismissing Jefferson, Rehnquist quoted from a series of drafts, in which Madison was a major participant, that are, at best, ambiguous on the issue of what kind of establishment was being prohibited. Many of them place emphasis, as one would expect, on establishment of a national religion and preference of a particular religion, without stating explicitly any view on preferences to religion generally or nondiscriminatory aid to religion.

In any event, the framers did not adopt these drafts but chose, instead, the general language "respecting an establishment of religion." Moreover, the establishments of religion known in the United States, as noted above, consisted of preferences of and aid to religion generally (without each state preferring a specific religion or denomination from among those practiced in the state). And there is little doubt that all the framers, including Madison, viewed Congress (irrespective of any amendments) as lacking any power to legislate at all regarding religion and viewed the First Amendment as a limit on—not an extension of—Congress's powers. A prominent historian of the establishment clause has described Rehnquist's analysis as "fiction . . . passed off as history."[23]

The framers' intent and the language that they adopted seem clearly to prohibit, at the very least, federal governmental preference of or aid to any religion or religion generally. Pursuant to the usual rules governing the incorporation principle, this same prohibition would then be applied to the states through the Fourteenth Amendment (which Rehnquist did not challenge, although other conservatives have[24]). In 1992 the Court reaffirmed this approach, invalidating prayer as part of official public school graduation ceremonies, but again by the narrowest of margins, a five-to-four vote.[25]

A Secular Purpose

Governmental religious displays had long been invalidated pursuant to the wall-of-separation principle, although there was considerable divergence regarding the appropriate standard to be applied. In 1984 the Court in *Lynch v. Donnelly*[26] approved a city display of a crèche in Pawtucket, Rhode Island, questioned the principle, and announced a new standard.

The Pawtucket crèche, depicting the birth of Christ, was part of a larger city Christmas display that included a Christmas tree, Santa Claus's house, reindeer, carolers, cutouts of a clown and an elephant, and a large banner saying "Seasons Greetings." Chief Justice Burger's majority opinion emphasized that the crèche was only one part of the entire city display. The other parts are or have become clearly secular in his view. He did not consider them in any detail, although I believe that the display as a whole, as well as most of its parts, would be viewed as essentially religious and sectarian by most non-Christians. We deal here with an area in which experience is overwhelmingly vital to perception and familiarity can easily lead to blindness.

In any event, the crèche is, as Justice William Brennan emphasized in dissent, "a mystical re-creation of an event that lies at the heart of Christian faith." Nevertheless, Burger ruled that, in the absence of "a purposeful or surreptitious effort to express some kind of subtle governmental advocacy of a particular religious message"—although the Pawtucket crèche seemed just that, without any subtlety—the overall display is constitutional if "there is a secular purpose." The city's secular purpose, held to be sufficient, was "to celebrate the [Christmas] Holiday and to depict the origins of that Holiday."

Because the government need show no more than a generally stated secular purpose, there is no longer any effective prohibition of governmental celebration of and participation in a particular (majoritarian) religion, even involving its most intensely religious rituals, symbols, and beliefs. The only limit appears to be the blending of the purely religious element with other elements that can be religious but also have obtained, by usage or the passage of time, a secular aspect. Subsequent to *Lynch*, the Court invalidated a lone crèche but approved of a Menorah in mixed company.[27]

I inserted the parenthetical "majoritarian" into this summary of the Court's ruling because that is surely its unstated assumption. What if, for example, a group of Buddhists somehow were elected to govern a rural county government, left the county's usual crèche display in storage at Christmas time, and, instead, installed a winter seasonal display at the county seat featuring Buddhist symbols and sacred Buddhist religious events, such as what Buddhists call the enlightenment under the Bodhi Tree in the Sarnath Deer Park? The conservatives would surely recognize—and presumably invalidate—this as an establishment of religion as soon as they saw it. They cannot or do not want to see the establishment of their own religion that they have authorized.

A Plausible Secular Purpose

Government aid to religion and to religious or sectarian schools had long been prohibited by numerous decisions through the 1970s.[28] However, these decisions, considered together, often seemed contradictory to their supporters and opponents alike. Distinctions were sometimes drawn between the religious and secular functions of religious schools, and aid directed at the latter was sometimes allowed, although any aid would defer expenses that the religious schools would otherwise have to incur to further their religious missions. For example, whereas state-paid bus transportation for field trips was disapproved, state-paid bus transportation to and from schools was allowed. However, a new approach adopted in 1983 in *Mueller v. Allen*[29] rendered the earlier disputes moot.

A Minnesota law provided a state tax deduction up to a specified maximum amount for "tuition, textbooks, and transportation" costs of a taxpayer's dependents attending primary or secondary schools. This tax deduction was available for costs incurred at any and all schools; the law did not single out or mention religious schools. However, the Minnesota legislature and governor—and the justices of the Supreme Court—knew that almost all of this aid would go to support the costs of religious education. There were little or no costs for books or transportation in public schools, and tuition, the largest deductible cost, was not charged at all by public schools. Another Minnesota law forbade public schools from charging any tuition (except in very narrow circumstances not relevant here). This tax deduction constitutes a government subsidy to religious schools and amounts to a transfer of funds collected from all taxpayers to families who send children to religious schools.

In 1973 the Court had invalidated a similar scheme as impermissible government aid to religion.[30] But in *Mueller,* Justice Rehnquist, for the majority, again changed the rules, this time facilitating government aid to religion. Rehnquist ruled that such measures, even though they clearly aid religion, are constitutional if they are "facially neutral" (i.e., by their explicit terms apply to all) and have "a plausible secular purpose." Here, the deduction was available to "all parents," not just those with children in religious schools. And the majority found "a plausible secular purpose"—whether or not it was the actual purpose or motive—to "defray the costs of educational expenses." This "plausible purpose" is always available as a justification for such measures. The Court's new standard means that aid to religious schools, at least in the form of tax benefits for tuition, is no longer prohibited as long as it applies generally, or is framed to appear as if it applies generally, to all schools. If Rehnquist's revisionist historical analysis in *Wallace v. Jaffree* is adopted by a majority, direct aid to religious schools would be permissible as long as it applies, or appears to apply, to all religious schools (so there is no preference or discrimination among religions).

Rehnquist insisted that the *Mueller* standard for establishment cases did not change the law at all. He referred to the earlier standards, but he reinterpreted them with new meanings as he purported to follow and be bound by them. Thus, he referred to earlier cases emphasizing whether the "primary effect" of a law is secular or religious, but he refused to consider any breakdown "of the type of persons claiming the deduction"—which showed, as everybody knew, that the deduction almost exclusively aided religious, not secular, schools. The 1973 case invalidating a similar scheme was distinguished, with the formalism so characteristic of the new conservative Court, because it involved a tax credit rather than a tax deduction and because the benefit was specifically available for private school costs by its explicit terms, rather than by its only possible and clearly intended effect.

The substance and context of the matter—government aid to religious schools—was essentially avoided by the majority. Justice Thurgood Marshall's dissenting opinion, on behalf of four justices (two of whom are no longer on the Court), interpreted the establishment clause to prohibit "any tax benefit . . . which subsidizes tuition payments to sectarian schools." He closed his opinion with the clear statement of the Court in 1947 as it first applied the establishment clause to the states:

> No tax in any amount, large or small, can be levied to support any religious activities or institutions, whatever they may be called, or whatever form they may adopt to teach or practice religion.[31]

RELIGIOUS FREEDOM
AND THE WALL OF SEPARATION

The conservative Court's approach to establishment and free exercise of religion is moving society in a seldom discussed direction: toward individual conformity to governmentally established norms of religious behavior, rather than accommodation for those of nonmajoritarian faiths; and toward greatly increased governmental religious activity and use of taxpayer funds to aid religious schools and institutions, rather than separation of church and state. This seems a return to, or a modern version of, the religious establishments of the colonies and states prior to the First or Fourteenth Amendments. Tolerance for religious minorities was at the whim of government officials, who may or may not have reflected the will of the people but were least likely to protect religious minorities in periods of popular religious repression, when they most needed protection. Local governments were involved in religious celebrations and activities and financially aided religious institutions.

The effect of the Court's new approach and new standards — which the justices are surely aware of—is not greater government allegiance and support for religion generally, but for Christianity. Non-Christian religions may welcome the aid to their religious schools and institutions; but this may prove to be shortsighted because tolerance and protection of them (and perhaps nonmainstream Christian faiths) is now more a matter of discretion or whim rather than basic principle or legal mandate, and the government funds may not be available to all and could be accompanied by government meddling. Recent decisions have denied Mormons and Scientologists tax benefits for religious activities similar to those of more mainstream religions for which the same benefits have been allowed, and allowed the military to forbid Jewish soldiers from wearing a yarmulke (the traditional Jewish skull cap) although it does not seem incompatible with a soldier's duties or performance.[32]

With all our diversity of peoples and religions, our population and political leaders are still overwhelmingly Christian, and non-Christians and disestablishmentarians of all stripes should not lose sight of or disrespect that reality. However, the Court has combined greatly relaxed disestablishment standards with a flat rejection of accommodation of nonmajoritarian religious exercise. This belies any generalized support or invigoration of religion or spirituality among our people. The Court is moving toward a modern establishment of Christianity, which, like the pre-Constitution American establishments, will not have to take the form of a European-style declared national or state religion.

This is a dangerous development, and it has been undertaken without significant public debate or awareness. However, for those who oppose it, there is a need for a reconceptualization of religious freedom and the wall of separation. The unique treatment of religion in the Constitution is as good a starting point today as it was 200 years ago, but the complexity of drawing lines and the contradictory liberal principles and results over the last four decades should be acknowledged, and a better social and constitutional approach sought.

Religion is a particular area where individual autonomy should be recognized and protected unless it directly and concretely collides with some extraordinarily important collective need. And although government is not prohibited from establishing positions and adopting viewpoints on a range of issues about which there is considerable disagreement, government should not adopt, prefer, or aid any religion or religion generally. Moreover, the two principles should be understood and interpreted together: if accommodation of majoritarian religious practices is not prohibited as an establishment of religion, then accommodation of nonmajoritarian religious practices is all the more appropriate as an element of free exercise.

On the other hand, disestablishment does not have to, nor should it, undercut or delegitimate the role of religion in anyone's life or invalidate government positions, actions, or programs because they comport with or were motivated by religion. For example—and here I part company with many civil libertarians—I do not find a moment of silence at the beginning of the school day for meditation—or for "meditation or voluntary prayer"—an establishment of religion or otherwise offensive.

Children (and adults) benefit from silent contemplation of their lives and the world about them, and there is surely no harm in a period of silence in which they alternatively, as they well might, contemplate music, sex, or anything else. A moment of silence (which a majority in *Wallace v. Jaffree* agreed is constitutional) is a good way to start a day in any event. Of course, some will pray and some will feel encouraged to pray, but they get that message all the time in this society. If the suggestion of a range of options is made without preference and there is truly silence and therefore no monitoring, coercion, or even implied differentiation or exclusion, there is no reason to interfere with each child's personal preference about how to use such a moment of silence. Indeed, the salient feature of this scheme is that "meditation" is on an equal footing with "voluntary prayer," and it is mentioned first!

Nor should it matter that the sponsor or all of the legislators intended the measure as a way to reintroduce prayer. The sponsor in *Mueller* was, presumably, very religious and did not place a high value on disestablishment. His or her goal or expectation of the consequences may prove correct or incorrect, but mostly it should be of little or no relevance. There is nothing to be gained by invalidating a benign measure because we do not like the motivation of its sponsor, or by approving a measure because the sponsor's intention is benign although the impact and effects are not. The government's action should stand or fall based on what it *does,* its *effects,* viewed and understood contextually. This measure emphasizes silence and individual choice, and thereby insulates the individual's choice and conduct from official view or action and from pressure to conform. It suggests or encourages prayer as one option only and conveys as strongly the message that a diversity of religious views, including meditation that can be nonreligious, is acceptable and legitimate. If it is used as a way to reintroduce prayer—say, by teachers referring to silent meditation or voluntary prayer and then leading classes in group prayer—that would still be prohibited, but not because of anyone's intentions.

One cannot ban religion from government consciousness or discourse, nor is that a laudable goal. Religion and religious ideas and values are inextricably tied to our culture, discourse, and governmental as well as personal choices. Extreme attempts at separation only succeed in obstructing and distorting discussion of ideas and values, which is crucial to child development and adult social discourse. Such attempts can also appear hostile to religion and unnecessarily polarize public sentiments.

This is not a retreat. The disestablishment principle would be strengthened if it were more focused on particular actions in which government prefers, participates in, or aids religion and less concerned with motivations or the impossible task of removing all religion from government. This would emphasize the primary concerns and avoid some of the quibbling, but it does not (nor can it) transcend or avoid the inherent complexity of many of these issues.

Prayer in public schools is government participation in a clearly religious activity, and it is performed in a context where a captive audience of children is drawn and pressured to join in. It should be prohibited. Accommodation of majoritarian religious practices without accommodation of nonmajoritarian practices that do not collide with compelling government interests is a preference of a particular religion. And except for the general range of public services that the government provides to all individuals and institutions, such as police and fire protection, government aid to any religion or religion generally, including religious schools, should be prohibited as an establishment of religion.

If one applies this principle on aid to religion consistently across the board, a long-standing and probably overwhelmingly popular practice is drawn into question: religious exemption from taxation. This is, quite simply, a government subsidy of religion, and it takes the same form as our colonial and pre–First Amendment state establishments. Nevertheless, the Court approved a state property tax exemption in 1970 with an unconvincing majority opinion by Chief Justice Burger. The Court's focus was almost entirely on the purpose of the legislature; the tax exemption was allowable because the Court did not find a legislative purpose to establish religion. It was of no import that the legislature had established religion.[33]

The extent of religious exemption from taxation is not widely discussed or understood. Religions pay no property taxes, and their religious activities are immune from the taxes that generally apply to the same transactions conducted by others. This amounts to a multi-billion-dollar yearly subsidy, revenue that is lost to government and is made up by the taxpayers. Clergy also receive particularly generous treatment under the federal tax laws. They do not pay any Social Security tax, which amounts to 7.5 percent of income up to a specified maximum. They are immune from taxation for housing provided by their employers, which is generally taxed as income for nonclergy, and the immunity extends even to money payments to them by their religious institutions in lieu of housing. And they can deduct mortgage interest and state property taxes for their homes although they receive these tax-free allowances.[34]

These tax benefits may be opposed by a substantial proportion of Americans, but another exemption from the Social Security tax—for members of Congress and the president and vice president—would probably be more controversial in the current political environment. My assumption is that a clear majority favor tax exemption for religion, even if some excesses may be controversial, and that abolishing religious tax exemption, by whatever means, would be politically difficult and, unless stretched over a substantial period, would threaten the economic viability of religious institutions long used to government subsidies. Any wise social or constitutional policy would have to consider all this as well as the purity and consistency of the separation principle.

Religious displays also present a difficult problem, whether or not they are mixed with secular or less-religious symbols. A religious display by government at a central location constitutes government participation, preference, and adoption of the religion(s) displayed. For example, a crèche displayed in front of the speaker's dais in a state legislative chamber would be prohibited even pursuant to Rehnquist's analysis. The difficulty arises when the location, although on government property, is not so central or symbolic or the display is not governmental.

Suppose a crèche is displayed on federal government property in Lafayette Park, across the street from the White House, at Christmas time by a Christian religious group or at any time by antiabortion or pro-choice groups. Suppose further that, in all these situations, the groups have duly obtained all required permits and are using the crèche to express their views. The usual rule in free-speech cases has been that use of public property for private speech does not constitute a government endorsement or adoption of the views expressed; the government is merely providing a public facility available for expression of all viewpoints. This has been diluted by the new conservative Court, which sometimes tends to see the government as endorsing the unpopular views expressed on government facilities (but not the mainstream ones).[35] In the area of religion, free exercise can be analogized to free expression regarding political and other issues, but there is also the disestablishment principle. Disestablishment could mean keeping religion, whether from a governmental or private source, off of government facilities entirely. Expression of a religious viewpoint could be distinguished from exercise of religion, but what if the gathered individuals pray—exercise their religion—to make their point? There is a conflict between free exercise and disestablishment here, and no easy line to draw. I would favor free exercise over disestablishment, unless the activity constitutes or conveys actual government endorsement.

These are some of the difficult issues, and my analysis provides no more a determinate set of rules than the formulations that I have criticized. My original intent (which will become dated) is to remove the focus from every government mention of religion or adoption of positions seen as religiously based and toward contextual consideration of particular actions or activities in which government prefers, participates in, or aids any religion or religion generally. But I may be out of town when this book is published.

⁍ 5 ⁍

EQUALITY

I n the conventional wisdom, at least the systemic, institutional forms of racism have largely been eradicated, and whatever might remain has been prohibited by law since at least the 1960s. Governmental racism—that ugly array of measures that enforced and legitimized slavery, segregation, and discrimination—is usually viewed as unconstitutional and the most clearly and completely eradicated form of discrimination. Incorporating this view, many Americans see the racial problem as a matter of the African-American community's alleged disruptions of an otherwise innocent and orderly white America: from affirmative action to drugs, crime, AIDS, and whatever else upsets them. The corollary set of villains in the Reagan version of the racial problem are the African-Americans and whites who still carry on about racism—liberals—and have supposedly stacked the deck so that African-Americans now have it better than whites.

Liberals counter that this indictment amounts to rejection of the core social and constitutional value of integration and to blaming the victims, an American tradition that has made racism socially palatable and become a staple of conservative political strategies in the national electoral arena.[1] The liberal response has been, at times, too quick to dismiss deeply felt and legitimate concerns about crime and other problems, and has tended to further isolate liberals from mainstream political debate.

But few across the political spectrum even question the basic assumption that governmental discrimination—whether against racial or ethnic minorities, women or other groups—has actually been prohibited. Recent rulings from the Court tolerate and even facilitate active governmental racism against African-Americans and discrimination against women and other minorities while simultaneously striking down attempts to remedy past discrimination. The conventional wisdom has already been incorporated into the Supreme Court's decisions, which have negated its central premise, as well as overturned the fundamental mandate for equality in the Fourteenth Amendment. In other words, the basic assumption that governmental discrimination against minorities or women has been prohibited by the courts is now simply mistaken.

Undesirable Traffic

In the early 1980s, the residents of the Hein Park neighborhood asked the Memphis, Tennessee, city council to close off West Drive to all traffic. The Hein Park residential neighborhood is all white, and West Drive is a thoroughfare running from a nearby African-American neighborhood through Hein Park to the zoo, a park, and other attractions. The council conducted hearings on the proposal during which race was not specifically mentioned by proponents of closure. There was later testimony about keeping out "undesirable traffic" and some procedural irregularity regarding participation of the nearby African-American residents in the hearings. The council voted to close West Drive with a traffic barrier at a cross street that marks the boundary between the white and African-American neighborhoods.

In *Memphis v. Greene* (1981),[2] the Court simply accepted the city's general explanation that the street was closed for "safety" related to traffic and to preserve the residential character of the neighborhood. The possibility of less-extreme traffic measures was of no import in Justice Stevens's majority opinion, although speed limits could have been lowered or traffic-control bumps installed. On the claimed violation of equal protection under the law, the African-American neighborhood did not prove "purposeful discrimination" and therefore, the Court reasoned, Memphis did not have to explain the street closing in any detail, and its action would not be seriously questioned or scrutinized.

The purposeful-discrimination doctrine is a hallmark of the conservative judicial approach. Starting from the premise that the most serious social and institutional forms of racism have been overcome, the proper role of the courts is seen as one of deference to local legislative authority and the exercise of judicial restraint. Legal relief will be considered if—and only if—it can be proved that an action harmful to a racial minority was undertaken for the specific purpose of discriminating rather than for some other, legitimate purpose.

Most significantly, this proof of purposeful discrimination must be presented before any serious questioning or scrutiny of the government's action. Thus, if purposeful discrimination is not proved, the courts will not seriously examine the government action at all: any legitimate-sounding, generally stated purpose—such as traffic safety—will simply be accepted. Even measures that have a clearly harmful effect on minorities are now assumed to be not at all influenced by racial considerations, no matter how extensive or unnecessary the harm may be, or how closely the circumstances and context may fit historical patterns of racism. In the *Memphis* case, the city never had to explain the street closing in any detail because the African-American neighborhood could not prove at the outset that the action's conscious purpose or motivation was racist.

Of course, some general, legitimate-sounding purpose often accompanies such actions or is available as a justification after the fact. Unless there is a written confession of racist motivation, racist institutions are now allowed to adopt measures that harm minorities without running into any legal obstacles. This rule not only undercuts the constitutional prohibition of discrimination, which was faithfully enforced for, at most, only two or three decades. It has in fact made purposeful discrimination quite easy, as the *Memphis* case demonstrates.

Consider first what is missing from the text of the decision. Many of my students, assigned an edited casebook version of the opinion, focused on the expressed government concern for "safety," which they usually took as a reference to problems of crime, violence, and drug addiction presumably stemming from the nearby African-American community. They saw traffic problems as, at most, secondary concerns. Students then focused on whether or not the street closing was an overreaction to crime problems. But the text of the opinion does not contain any mention of crime or any explicit or coded racial references, except possibly the mention of "undesirable traffic" in Hein Park. And the Court dismissed this reference on the grounds that its meaning is uncertain and it does not necessarily reflect the intentions of the city council. The white community and the city council claimed— and the Court accepted without any serious scrutiny—that the sole concern was traffic.

The absence of the clear or coded rhetoric of race that is so abundant in contemporary culture—especially in an entirely white neighborhood within a city that is about half African-American and a city government with a long history of resisting integration—suggests a darker side to the purposeful-discrimination rule. The *Memphis* case may be a triumph of well-honed legal advice effectively carried out. The advice might have been (here I am speculating): "Talk traffic, only traffic, and don't mention anything that the liberals can call a code word for race. Not crime, drugs, poverty, AIDS, homelessness—just traffic!" In granting such strategies an unobstructed day in court, the purposeful-discrimination rule allows—and facilitates—conscious, planned racial discrimination.

The lack of racial rhetoric should not, of course, condemn an action. Nor should measures that harm minorities be automatically deemed unconstitutional. However, the minimum that this nation should require from its courts and government at all levels is that they carefully question and scrutinize any governmental measures that harm minorities, that they reject implausible or phony justifications, and that they refrain from covering up racism. It is this minimal requirement of basic equality—perhaps the greatest achievement of the Warren Court in the 1960s—that the current Court, without much popular or legal attention, has managed to bury.

Finally, as we have seen in previous chapters, it is a mistake to view law as always, or even usually, defined or understood only by the rules and principles of legal doctrine. If one looks beyond the general terms of the purposeful-discrimination rule to its application in particular cases, a much fuller picture emerges. The *Memphis* case's "appendix"—the official court record of the case printed and presented to each justice—casts a different light on the Court's conclusion that "there is no evidence that the closing was motivated by any racially exclusionary desire." Judges have enormous discretion in interpreting rules and evaluating and crediting evidence and the arguments presented by attorneys, and in this case they ignored much of the evidence in the appendix:

- Memphis, like many cities throughout the country, has a history of actively resisting integration. In 1963 a unanimous Supreme Court invalidated Memphis's exclusion of African-Americans from its parks and recreation facilities, finding "an unmistakable and pervasive pattern of local segregation, which, in fact, the city makes no attempt to deny."[3] Indeed, their closure of West Drive impeded African-American access to one of the parks ordered integrated in this earlier case.

- Hein Park was developed before World War II as an exclusively white residential neighborhood. N. T. Greene, the resident of the African-American neighborhood who initially challenged the street closing, testified that African-Americans were often beaten by police if they walked into Hein Park. The Hein Park Civic Association had initially sought closure of all four streets to and from the African-American neighborhood. And some of the Hein Park residents had expressed their views far less elegantly than the one who testified about the incursions of "undesirable traffic." A white resident who opposed the closure of West Drive testified before the council that his neighbors were upset by his stand—and by his association with "niggers." "That," he testified, "is the issue here."

- The original petition did not meet the city's usual requirement that all property owners whose residences abut a thoroughfare slated for closure must sign the petition, because one white owner opposed the closing and refused to sign. No notice of the planning commission hearing was provided to residents of the African-American neighborhood. Opponents were given a total of fifteen minutes, and a subsequent petition with more than seven hundred signatures opposing the closure was initially not accepted. White Hein Park residents, also given fifteen minutes at the hearing, had been working closely with the commission and other city officials for more than five years to secure the closure.

- The street closing was a striking departure for the city of Memphis. Never before had the commission and council closed any other thoroughfare for traffic reasons. And the record suggests that the council may have been eager to keep Hein Park clear from more than just "undesirable traffic." It sold a twenty-five-foot-wide strip across West Drive at the point of closure to the two white landowners on either side, and passed a resolution declaring this strip "closed to the public." Even the Court admitted that there was some question of "[w]hether the closing will have the effect of barring pedestrians."

Such matters, even though they were uncontested entries in the case's appendix, went without any serious acknowledgment from the Court's majority, or any explanation of why they were deemed insignificant. Justices Marshall, Brennan, and Blackmun, two of whom are no longer on the Court, dissented, concluding that the city was seeking to "carve out racial enclaves." The Sixth Circuit Court of Appeals had earlier ruled (by a vote of two to one) that the closing was "one more of the many humiliations which society has historically visited" on African-Americans.

In disregarding this body of evidence, the Court adopted the same strategy of social evasion that has increasingly shaped political debate on questions of race. Issues such as safety and crime have been separated out from the conditions in which they take root—deprivation, degradation, and severed social connection—and reconceived as hopelessly insolvable racial problems. For many in our society, material deprivation, isolation, vulnerability, fear, and a chronic sense of inferiority are facts of life—facts that we should not and cannot afford to ignore. But instead of seeking solutions, mainstream culture has developed a dangerous racial edge: White people being reduced to such a state is seen as unfortunate though increasingly tolerable, but for African-Americans this fate is seen as largely deserved and unchangeable.

The *Memphis* case lacks common, contextual, or historical sense. At a time when we seem to have abandoned the hope that we can improve things and move forward together, this decision also has another, more ominous quality. Our budget decisions and our social discourse have made it clear that we feel free to abandon those at or near the bottom of the social order. But now the Court has allowed, without serious examination and with an apparently conscious blindness, an all-white, historically segregated community to demand and obtain from its local government erection of a physical barrier between white and African-American communities, so symbolic of apartheid.

Best Presented to the Legislative Bodies

Warren McCleskey was sentenced to death in 1979 by a Georgia jury for his participation in a robbery during which a police officer was killed. He challenged his death penalty based on a study of more than 2,000 murder cases in Georgia that utilized sophisticated multiple regression statistical methods to determine the effects of more than 230 different variables on the decision to impose death. The study, conducted by a research team headed by David Baldus, is widely viewed as authoritative and was not seriously challenged in the case. Baldus concluded that the most significant factor is the race of the victim. The death penalty was 4.3 times more likely when the victim was white rather than African-American. The death penalty was somewhat more likely still when the murderer was African-American. The bottom line was, with all other circumstances the same (premeditation, viciousness of the crime, etc.), an African-American like McCleskey, convicted of killing a white person, was four to five times more likely to receive the death penalty than a white person convicted of killing an African-American. Stated another way, if McCleskey had killed an African-American rather than a white, he would most likely not have received the death penalty.

In *McCleskey v. Kemp* (1987),[4] the Court rejected McCleskey's appeal: he had not proved purposeful discrimination.

The results of the Baldus study, which surprised many, seemed to reflect judgments, first, about the value of the life lost and, second, about the perpetrator. The jurors were saying, with their votes, that they view a white life as much more important than an African-American life. If you ask people who should live and who should die, they will, of necessity, resort to deep-seated moral and religious judgments about whether death is deserved. The study that served as the foundation of the *McCleskey* case showed that these judgments were deeply influenced by racial considerations, and perhaps could not be otherwise, no matter what instructions juries might receive from judges.

Without challenging the study, Justice Lewis Powell's majority opinion focused on the difficulty of determining the purpose of the actual jury that imposed the death penalty on McCleskey. The jurors, the Court said, should not be questioned about their decision; neither should prosecutors be second-guessed about the pattern of their decisions to seek the death penalty in particular cases—another pattern covered by the study. The Court had previously questioned and overturned discriminatory prosecutorial patterns regarding the less crucial issue of jury selection, and earlier cases covering a range of discrimination issues emphasized the importance or necessity of proving a discriminatory pattern rather than discrimination in a particular instance. Once a pattern of discrimination was established, the usual rule and practice was to infer discrimination in particular instances that fit the pattern and then place the burden on the government to disprove it.[5] But the compelling evidence of the study was considered essentially irrelevant. And judicial restraint was raised to a new level: the Court ruled that jury discretion was not to be disturbed, and "McCleskey's arguments are best presented to the legislative bodies." This was, of course, difficult for McCleskey to do from death row, and he had an inordinately short time in which to do it. His appeals exhausted, McCleskey was executed in September 1991.

Smoke Out Racism

In 1983, after years of debate, the Richmond, Virginia, city council adopted an affirmative-action plan for city construction projects modeled on a federal plan approved by the Supreme Court. In Richmond and other cities, the construction industry had proved a particularly difficult segment of the economy to integrate. Richmond was more than 50 percent African-American, but fewer than 1 percent of the city's construction contracts had gone to African-American contractors. The plan that the council adopted required that, in choosing among contractors and subcontractors who are otherwise qualified (meeting skill, experience, bond, and other normal requirements), at least 30 percent of contracts should go to businesses that are over half minority owned unless qualified minority businesses were not available. In *Richmond v. Croson* (1989),[6] Justice O'Connor's majority opinion invalidated this plan, strictly scrutinizing it to "smoke out" possible racism. Remedying past and current racial discrimination against minorities was not a sufficient purpose.

The conservatives' *Richmond* decision was clearly judicial activism—based on a novel constitutional theory, it overrode the work of a multiracial city council that arrived at a difficult compromise on a tough racial issue. The Court also subjected the plan to a strict scrutiny that does not extend to measures that disadvantage African-Americans, other minorities, or women. The Court's reasoning was simple: This is purposeful discrimination because the plan itself explicitly sets up a racial distinction. Explicitly mentioning race—which any good-faith affirmative-action plan would have to do and any bad-faith racist practice could easily avoid—has been established as the only circumstance in which courts will seriously scrutinize possibly discriminatory measures.

Applying this kind of scrutiny to affirmative-action plans all but guarantees their invalidation. Under this decision, local legislatures may remedy only discrimination that occurred inside their own borders, even though their other powers are not so limited— for example, they may act to resolve environmental or economic problems stemming from outside their borders. And they must provide detailed evidence and factual findings that establish a pattern of unlawful discrimination. These rules limit affirmative action to situations in which there is sufficient evidence for establishing a specific discrimination case. Local legislatures are thus denied any authority to go beyond existing legal remedies.

The crux of the Richmond decision was its emphasis on the possibility that a remedial purpose could mask racism. This is all but a complete inversion of the logic behind the *Memphis* ruling, which accepted implausible nonracial rationales for measures enacted by predominantly white legislatures that harmed minorities and fit the historic pattern of discrimination against them. In the process, the law has reversed the social roles that have shaped the history of American racism: whites have become the presumed victims and African-Americans the presumed racists.

It is not at all clear what the Court meant by "racism" that should be "smoke[d] out." The Richmond City Council did in fact wish to help African-Americans, much as other city governments have sought—and were allowed—to provide economic and social opportunities for other disadvantaged minorities. Many of our large cities went through periods when their police or fire departments were almost all Irish- or Italian-American. But when African-Americans, even with substantial white support (as in Richmond), try to aid their own, the Court's tendency is to see racism.

Although the city council's purpose was to undo some of the damage of centuries of racism, the Court's decision in the *Richmond* case goes beyond that. The Richmond plan was founded on the principle of simply eliminating, where possible, a long-standing unfair advantage for whites. Unless we assume the improbable—that there were no qualified African-American contractors or subcontractors although they constituted over half of the population—African-Americans were not given an unfair advantage or preference. Rather, white contractors were denied some of the preferential treatment that they had long enjoyed at the expense of their African-American competitors. Undoing current unfair racial advantages for whites, or the legacy of racism, is hardly an illegitimate purpose.

Such plans surely involve some unfairness, particularly toward whites who have not themselves discriminated and are sometimes no better off economically than minorities. But this negative impact on whites does not, as it is usually supposed, distinguish affirmative action from the other goals of the civil-rights movement. All racial progress has meant imposing limits on the freedom and interests of the majority. When African-Americans won the freedom to use public accommodations, white people lost the right to eat in segregated restaurants; when African-Americans won the right to attend integrated public schools, whites lost the right to go to segregated all-white public schools. These may seem like easy choices now, but at the time, even with much better economic conditions, the white interests were felt as dearly and defended at least as vigilantly as they are now over affirmative action. We are more interconnected than we realize; there is not unlimited freedom any more than there are unlimited jobs.

The stakes involved in affirmative action may seem very different from those in other civil-rights measures—jobs as opposed to freedom of association, for example. But the public accommodation laws also altered economic opportunities and property rights that whites had long been accustomed to. Further, the stakes, be they big or small, are felt both ways: the status quo in Richmond meant that African-Americans got almost none of the city's construction contracts because of an active and/or traditional racial preference for whites. The best solution to this dilemma would be enough jobs for everyone, but if that is not accomplished, traditional white racial preferences—whether specifically intended or merely customary—should be eliminated. In this sense, much of what we now call "affirmative action" is misnamed or misunderstood. It is, quite simply, elimination of racial preference.

Nor can the problem be resolved by affirmative action aimed at poor people generally as long as the resources committed to such initiatives remain severely limited. Income-based affirmative action will still raise the question of who among the disadvantaged will receive an opportunity when it cannot be made available to all. We cannot deny that a substantial proportion of our population deserves affirmative action, regardless of race. But we also cannot deny that the conditions under which many of our African-American and other minority communities exist are particularly deplorable and bear the distinctive mark of American racism. If we use such criteria as the "most deserving" or "best educated," most minorities will again fall through the net. A universal approach, if adequately funded, is preferable, particularly because it avoids placing people at the bottom of the economic ladder in competition for meager opportunities and resources and the political costs of preferential treatment. While we're devising aid plans for Eastern Europe and the former Soviet Union, we might consider one for African-Americans at home or, better yet, provide enough resources for all our people in need.

An Additional Risk Unique to Women

In 1974 the Court upheld a California insurance system that paid all people employed in the state benefits for absences from work due to nonwork-related temporary disabilities.[7] Work-related disabilities were covered by worker's compensation and other programs; this system paid state benefits for all other disabilities, with only one exception. The California law excluded pregnancy and "any injury or illness . . . arising in connection with pregnancy." The Court applied the rational-basis test and sustained the law on the ground that the state's interest in saving the expenses of covering pregnancy was sufficient. The majority did not perceive any discrimination, but only a financially based choice of which risks to cover.

Two years later, in *General Electric Co. v. Gilbert*,[8] the Court considered a similar disability system challenged as a violation of the sex-discrimination provision of the Equal Employment Opportunity Act of 1964 (usually called Title VII).[9] The California case involved a claim of unconstitutional denial of "equal protection" by a state government; the *Gilbert* case involved a statutory claim of "sex discrimination" by a private company, which previous cases had held to impose more stringent requirements of equality. Nevertheless, Justice Rehnquist's majority opinion reaffirmed the California case and extended it to Title VII statutory discrimination claims.

Rehnquist said the GE plan creates two groups, "pregnant women and nonpregnant persons," and pregnancy is just "an additional risk . . . unique to women." Because the distinction, as he framed it, is not *completely* along sex lines—not all women are pregnant—there is no sex discrimination. Moreover, he said, pregnancy is fairly distinguishable because it is "voluntary." Of course, the plan provides benefits for *all* temporary absences due to an inability to work *except* one that only women need in order to maintain their flow of income. Further, the plan covered many disabilities that only men could claim, including vasectomies, circumcisions, and prostectomies, and many voluntary disabilities, such as sports injuries and attempted suicides. As Justice Brennan said in dissent, "Pregnancy affords the only disability, sex-specific or otherwise, that is excluded from coverage."

Rehnquist held out the possibility that discrimination could be established by proof that the plan was a "pretext" or "subterfuge" for purposeful discrimination. But as in the *Memphis* case, he then proceeded to ignore the substantial evidence of purposeful discrimination. The original GE benefits plan in 1926 offered no benefits at all to women because "women did not recognize the responsibilities of life, for they probably were hoping to get married soon and leave the company." When women were provided benefits, they were set, quite purposely, at levels to assure that total compensation for women was two-thirds of that for men. GE forced all its women employees to take maternity leaves without pay from three months prior to six weeks after birth, regardless of whether they were able or wished to work. These forced maternity leaves were stopped only in 1973 —coinciding with the filing of this lawsuit. This is a company that had a demonstrated purposeful hostility to women employees and a pattern of purposeful sex discrimination.

Congress responded to the *Gilbert* decision with the Pregnancy Discrimination Act of 1978, which included "on the basis of pregnancy, childbirth, or related medical conditions" in the Title VII definition of sex discrimination. The Court has continued to refuse to apply strict scrutiny in constitutional or statutory sex-discrimination cases, even when sexual classifications are explicit, although the most blatant explicit forms of sexual discrimination have been invalidated. The Court has also refused to apply strict scrutiny to discrimination against the elderly, lesbians and gay men, "illegitimate" children, and the mentally retarded.[10]

In cases like *Memphis*, *McCleskey*, and *Gilbert*, the Court undercut basic equality requirements with narrow interpretations of the Constitution and antidiscrimination statutes and new procedural obstacles. Other examples include: approval of employment tests that have a discriminatory impact but no correlation to successful performance on the job, in spite of an earlier decision to the contrary written by Chief Justice Warren Burger; limiting an 1866 law prohibiting discrimination in employment and other contracts to hiring only, in spite of long-standing decisions applying it to discriminatory firing, promotion, and workplace conditions; replacing the burden on companies whose policies or practices have a discriminatory impact to show a legitimate business justification with a burden on victims of such policies or practices to show a lack of a business justification; imposing strict time limitations for filing claims on the victims of discrimination, but allowing settlements and consent decrees resolving discrimination cases to be challenged and reopened at any time. Congress has responded to some, but not all, of these decisions.[11]

An obvious alternative to the approach of these cases is to scrutinize carefully any government action that effectively harms or prefers people of a particular race, ethnicity, religion, cultural heritage, gender, sexual orientation, or any other characteristic that has historically been a source or basis of discrimination or oppression, particularly if such an action fits a pattern of historic subordination or oppression. Such actions should be found unconstitutional unless they substantially further a legitimate and compelling government purpose that cannot be achieved by less-discriminatory means. Affirmative action of the type in *Richmond* should be judged by a different, less stringent standard or considered as furthering a compelling government interest. This, or something close to it, was essentially the law for a time during the 1960s and 1970s, with an emphasis on the protection of minorities who have little opportunity to gain a fair hearing in the political process. For that brief period in our history, it could accurately be said that governmental discrimination was prohibited by law.

We have now returned to the consciously blind denial of racism that characterized the *Korematsu* decision—and the same impulse to blame the victim and condemn the messenger. African-Americans and other minorities may easily be disadvantaged by white-dominated legislatures, but predominantly African-American or multiracial legislatures will be severely scrutinized. State or local affirmative action openly aimed at correcting racial imbalance is now likely unconstitutional. It should not be surprising that most of the successful constitutional discrimination cases in the last decade or so have been won by white male plaintiffs.[12]

We have the same choice now that we have always had—at the ratification of the Constitution (which embraced slavery rather than the Declaration of Independence), after the Civil War, in 1954 (*Brown v. Board of Education*), and in the 1960s. We can continue on the path of separation and division, with its legacy of violence, degradation, and declining conditions for all; or we can again strive for equality, with the hope of unification and common purpose and an emphasis on meeting the needs of all our people.

❦ 6 ❧

PRIVACY

As long as people have tried to live together, there has been awareness and concern about interference with or intrusion on individuals by others. A leading legal scholar of privacy in the 1960s pointed out that "[a]lmost the first page of the Bible introduces us to the feeling of shame as a violation of privacy. After Adam and Eve had eaten the fruit of the tree of knowledge, 'the eyes of both were opened, and they knew that they were naked; and they sewed fig leaves together and made themselves aprons.'" Henry VIII's prosecutor asked Thomas More, "Tell your secrets." Locke said, "Every man has a 'property' in his own 'person.' This nobody has any right to but himself." The form and intensity of this concern and the range of social reactions to it have varied among peoples and cultures and seem to have a lot to do with the nature of each society's relationships among people, governing structures, and history. But widespread concern and societal measures to protect some form of what we now call privacy are not inventions of the 1960s, the United States, or modern Western societies.[1]

The framers of the Bill of Rights focused on a range of abuses of privacy with which they were familiar. No other area of concern got more attention in the Bill of Rights except the rights of criminal defendants (chapter 7), also widely but inaccurately thought

to be an invention of the 1960s. Three of the original amendments—the Third, Fourth and Fifth—explicitly protect privacy or
autonomy interests. The Third Amendment prohibits the military
from "quarter[ing]" soldiers in private homes "without the consent
of the Owner." The Fifth prohibits the government from compelling an individual to be "a witness against himself." The fourth
sets out a more general protection:

> The right of the people to be secure in their persons, houses,
> papers, and effects, against unreasonable searches and
> seizures, shall not be violated, and no Warrants shall issue,
> but upon probable cause, supported by Oath or affirmation
> and particularly describing the place to be searched, and the
> persons or things to be seized.

The preadoption history of these privacy provisions is, once
again, sparse. The framers had in mind at least a range of specific
abuses that included torture and compelled confessions reminiscent of the English Star Chamber and the "general searches" conducted by British and later state authorities in which a block or
neighborhood was searched, often house by house, for fugitives,
weapons, and subversive writings (often by authors now considered heroes, like Thomas Paine). There is little doubt that, as the
language makes clear, the home was meant to be particularly, but
not solely, protected against government intrusion. The scope of
"papers" and "effects" in the Fourth Amendment was not specified or clear.[2]

A new sense of need and urgency for privacy protections
emerged in the U.S. and elsewhere in the nineteenth century
during and after industrialization and urbanization. This is probably related to new economic and social arrangements in which
people lived and worked closer to others, had more contact with
and were more interactive and interdependent on strangers, and
first experienced (and perhaps liked) anonymity. Also, new institu-

tions and technologies developed that made possible enormous public invasions of one's private life, particularly when inexpensive, widely circulated printed media flourished.[3]

In 1890, perhaps in response to a nasty attack by a Boston newspaper on the family of Samuel Warren, he and Louis Brandeis wrote one of the most influential law-review articles (which tend to be uninfluential and unread) ever published, *The Right of Privacy*.[4] They noted that "solitude and privacy have become more essential to the individual" and advocated a "general right of the individual to be left alone." This formulation surely gets at the heart of the matter, but its generality and scope reveal the hard questions about privacy. Taken to an absolutist extreme, the right of the individual to be left alone—or to "do it my way"—would overwhelm all other rights and interests, and the only question would be which individuals would get such rights at the expense of all others. "My way" might include reneging on contracts, running red lights, or punching you in the nose. Once again, freedom is not unlimited and cannot be defined without consideration of the effects on others and on society as a whole. Our interconnection— while a source of the need for privacy—cannot be avoided in defining the scope of privacy. A viable conception of privacy must address which aspects of our lives are the subject of privacy and which interests of others and of society generally will take precedence over individual choice.

Privacy has come to include two different and important individual protections: individual autonomy in certain aspects of our lives in which the government and/or other individuals cannot intrude or interfere with individual preferences; and control over information about an individual, from their romantic pursuits to the financial, medical, and other information about each person that proliferates in modern life. In both areas, privacy limits on a range of governmental intrusions have been a major focus of the conservative attack on liberal judges. Majoritarian support for this attack has been regularly claimed by conservatives, although the public's and Senate's rejection of Judge Robert Bork's nomination to the Supreme Court was in large part a result of his insistence, with apparent draconian delight, that the Constitution does not protect privacy. In any event, privacy protections, greatly enhanced in the 1960s, have been substantially retrenched as conservatives have come to dominate the judiciary.

Penumbras and Emanations

As recently as the early 1960s, a myriad of state laws restricted a broad range of sexual practices, sometimes including practices engaged in by the majority of their citizens. It was not unusual for states to ban all oral sex, applicable to consenting adults and even married couples, all sex involving people of different races, and all or certain forms of birth control. The legislatures tended to be greatly influenced (or intimidated) by religiously motivated activists who were very upset about technological and cultural changes that allowed sex for purposes other than procreation, and who wanted the government greatly to restrict sexual activities. This was a legacy of earlier times (like the 1950s, when Elvis Presley could be shown on prime-time television only from the waist up), a legacy that was challenged on many fronts as part of the tumultuous changes of the 1960s.

In one of these restrictive measures, the Connecticut legislature simply prohibited birth control. Any person who "uses any drug, medicinal article or instrument for the purpose of preventing conception" or "assists, abets [or] counsels" such use was guilty of a crime punishable by a year in prison. A doctor committed a crime by providing information or advising even a married couple about available birth control methods.

The executive and medical directors of Planned Parenthood in Connecticut were convicted and fined under this statute for giving information and medical advice about birth control to a married couple. Their appeals resulted in *Griswold v. Connecticut,* the 1965 decision that first established a constitutional right to privacy and became a prime target of conservatives.[5]

Justice William O. Douglas's majority opinion first repudiated as authority to establish a new right the line of cases that had invalidated much of President Franklin D. Roosevelt's New Deal, which made the Court a "super-legislature." This was an attempt to distinguish the ruling from the conservative judicial activism of the early 1900s that had been condemned by liberals (see the introduction). He then catalogued and praised, however, many instances of judicial expansion of principles in the Bill of Rights to meet particular needs and stem particular abuses as times and circumstances have changed. Mentioned were the right of association, the right to educate one's children, freedom of inquiry and thought, and academic freedom—none of which is specifically referred to in the Constitution. Douglas attempted to conceptualize this phenomenon more explicitly: "Specific guarantees in the Bill of Rights have penumbras, formed by emanations from those guarantees that help give them life and substance."

Based on the First, Third, Fourth, and Fifth Amendments, and their penumbras, Douglas found a "zone of privacy" that includes at least associational and privacy rights "surrounding the marriage relationship," rights that he described as "older than the Bill of Rights." Justice Arthur Goldberg, concurring, emphasized the Ninth Amendment, which provides constitutional language that invites expansion of the Bill of Rights: "The enumeration . . . of certain rights, shall not be construed to deny or disparage others retained by the people." The preadoption history of the Bill of Rights suggests quite clearly that the Ninth Amendment was intended to address the widely held concern that the framers may not adopt a broad enough list in their enumeration of rights and that, therefore, the enumerated list should not be viewed as exclusive.[6] Pursuant to both of these analyses, the Connecticut criminal statute was an unconstitutional intrusion into a protected zone of privacy.

Although Douglas was stating the obvious—from the time judicial review was established in 1803, conservative and liberal judges had been expanding and contracting the meaning of constitutional clauses and phrases with rules and language not mentioned in the Constitution—his and Goldberg's analyses drew, and continue to draw, the wrath of many conservatives. Nevertheless, in a similarly creative deregulation decision, Chief Justice Rehnquist established a "state sovereignty" right nowhere mentioned in the Constitution based on the Tenth Amendment, which reserves to the states powers not specifically granted to the federal government.[7] As I emphasized in the introduction, both conservatives and liberals have cyclically, selectively, and cynically criticized each other (typically when the other side has gained a majority) for a judicial creativity and activism that has frequently characterized American judicial review, rather than acknowledging the value basis of judicial decisions or the nature or extent of judicial power in our society.

For the next several years after the *Griswold* decision, the liberal Court started to define and expand this new right to privacy along the lines suggested in *Barnette* (chapter 1). Privacy was a fundamental right that protected individual choice or autonomy from government-imposed norms, and infringements on it were subject to strict scrutiny and could only be justified by an extraordinary or compelling government interest. Laws banning interracial marriage were invalidated, possession in the home of even unprotected obscene materials was protected, and *Griswold* was extended to unmarried people.[8] In the last case, the Court moved toward a more general right to sexual intimacy of one's own choosing for consenting adults:

If the right of privacy means anything, it is the right of the individual, married or single, to be free from unwarranted governmental intrusion into matters so fundamentally affecting a person as the decision whether to bear or beget a child.

A majority of the population may have favored compelled conformity to some or all of these norms, but, as in *Barnette*, they were not subject to votes or government-imposed conformity. But now the conservative Court is in hasty retreat from that commitment to personal freedom in sexual matters.

What Are You Doing in My Bedroom?

On a summer day in 1982, Michael Hardwick was at his Atlanta home making love when a police officer entered his bedroom. Officer Torick, who had arrested Hardwick for possessing a bottle of beer outside a gay bar a few weeks before, later said he came to serve a warrant related to that arrest, although Hardwick had paid a small fine and the case was over. According to Torick, a friend of Hardwick's let him in the house, and the bedroom door was open. He watched for some time before making his presence known, as Hardwick and his gay lover engaged in oral sex. Hardwick looked up, saw and recognized the officer, and said, "What are you doing in my bedroom?"[9]

Hardwick and his lover were charged with the crime of sodomy, a felony in Georgia, punishable by up to twenty-years imprisonment, which consists of "any sexual act involving the sex organs of one person and the mouth or anus of another." This sodomy statute, like those in many states, does not specify any sexual preference or make any exceptions regarding the location of the act, the marital status of the actors, or anything else; it applies to, for example, a married heterosexual couple making love in the bedroom of their home. Oral and anal sex are simply criminal, by anyone and in any circumstances.

For reasons that have not been publicly explained, the prosecutor declined to prosecute the case. Hardwick then joined with a married heterosexual couple as plaintiffs in a civil-rights suit challenging the constitutionality of the Georgia sodomy law. The married couple was dismissed from the case for lack of "standing," although the statute clearly applied to them and made oral sex between them—a practice engaged in by the overwhelming majority of heterosexual as well as gay people—a serious crime. Hardwick proceeded alone, winning in the lower courts based on the privacy cases just discussed, but the Supreme Court reversed in *Bowers v. Hardwick* (1986).[10]

Hardwick's case raised basic social and constitutional issues: Should consensual sexual activities by adults in their own homes be protected from government intrusion, and is policing the bedrooms of America for correct sex allowable? However, Justice White's majority opinion framed the issue in a way that avoided the general applicability of the statute and these basic questions. White defined the issue as "whether the Federal Constitution confers a fundamental right upon homosexuals to engage in sodomy." White and the Court's majority—not the Georgia legislature—directed the crime specifically at gay people and shifted the focus from consensual sexual activity in one's home to "homosexual . . . sodomy."

White's opinion rejected strict scrutiny and claimed that none of the earlier decisions "bears any resemblance" to this case because Hardwick is gay and the history of the United States and Western culture reveals regular discrimination against, and often hatred of, gay people. His history is debatable; there were times and places in Western history where gay sex was tolerated and even exalted. In any event, interracial marriage had been long condemned and segregated public schools long approved when the Court recognized fundamental rights that protected the former and forbade the latter. White's analysis reduces to a sorry logic: we have a history of prejudice and oppression of gay people, so new principles of individual liberty and protection should not apply to them, and the courts should single them out for punishment even when a legislature has chosen not to do so.

The Court placed lesbians and gay men outside the law—as literally outlaws whose sexuality defines and encompasses their identity and is itself criminal. The sweep and stereotyping of the decision and the explicit approval of criminal measures that can be directed at a despised minority is reminiscent of *Korematsu* and the *Dred Scott* decision (which declared African-American people to be outside the law and less than human).

In the process, the Court greatly narrowed the privacy principle. White's opinion and subsequent decisions directly questioned the principle and limited privacy to, at most, three areas: "family, marriage, or procreation." Recent cases leave little doubt about what these terms mean to the conservative justices. Family means nuclear family, not the diverse array of living arrangements based on love or necessity in which probably most of our adults and children do the best they can. Marriage means exclusively heterosexual marriage, no matter how deep or lasting the commitment, or how important to the adults or children involved. Premarital (or extramarital) sex is not on this list, only procreation.[11] There is no longer any protection based on privacy—or on equality or simply human dignity, for that matter—for consensual sex between adults in their own bedrooms.

No Legitimate Expectation of Privacy

Mitch Miller, from rural Georgia, was suspected of possessing 175 gallons of whiskey upon which no taxes had been paid and of running a still. Federal agents for the Alcohol, Tobacco and Firearms Bureau investigating the matter were allowed by two banks in which Miller had accounts to inspect and copy his account statements, canceled checks, and other financial records without any court order or court-authorized subpoena. The agents filled out grand jury subpoena forms requesting "all records of accounts, i.e., savings, checking, loan or otherwise, in the name of Mr. Mitch Miller." The banks simply turned over all Miller's records and did not inform Miller of the request or their compliance.

These were not valid subpoenas, because they were signed only by a prosecutor and demanded that the records be produced at the prosecutor's office, rather than being signed or authorized by the clerk of court and returnable at a grand jury or other authorized court proceeding. Federal and state prosecutors have long sought subpoena power so that they could legally, as the ATF agents did here unlawfully, compel witnesses to appear at their offices and provide testimony and physical evidence. This power has uniformly been refused by Congress and state legislatures as unfair and too susceptible to abuse. However, the Supreme Court's review of the use of this bank account evidence at Miller's trial, where he was convicted and sentenced to three years in prison, did not focus on the prosecution's unlawful subpoena. Rather, the Court affirmed the conviction in *United States v. Miller* (1976)[12] based on the surprising announcement that there are no privacy or Fourth Amendment restrictions on federal or local police access to an individual's bank account records.

In a leading 1967 decision, the liberal Court had ruled that a telephone call from a phone booth was within the protections of privacy.[13] This did not mean that such a phone call could not be overheard or tapped for law-enforcement purposes but only that the police must meet the probable-cause and warrant requirements of the Fourth Amendment. The underlying principle of this decision was that any circumstances in which there is a "reasonable expectation of privacy" should be protected in order to provide basic privacy from government intrusion for all of us. The crux of the principle was the reasonableness of expectations of privacy. This lent a popular dimension to the matter, because current expectations were the focus of the legal standard, but it was always understood as subject to judicial interpretation rather than opinion polls or other indicia of public opinion.

This is an area in which the conservative trend started quite early. In 1971, the Court ruled that discussions with a wired police informant did not implicate any reasonable expectation of privacy.[14] When people have a one-on-one conversation, they typically believe that they are speaking to a private individual who is not wired and typically expect that the conversation is private and not being tape-recorded. But the Court ruled that this is of no import because you "consent" to speak to the other person, whether or not you know who he is or what he is doing. Justice John Harlan, a highly regarded conservative, dissented because the reasonable-expectation standard, to which he earlier subscribed, was being used to justify unrestricted electronic surveillance without warrants or probable cause. This he felt undermines the

> confidence and sense of security in dealing with one another that is characteristic of individual relationships between citizens in a free society. . . . Interposition of a warrant requirement is designed not to shield "wrongdoers," but to secure a measure of privacy and a sense of personal security throughout our society.

A similar distortion of "expectations" has been used to reject privacy protections for tapped telephone calls. As long as one of the parties consents to a tap or recording, whether or not the "consenting" party is an informer or police officer, the fact that the other party does not know of the tap or the connection of the person to whom he is speaking to the police—and typically expects that the call is private—is of no import. In another early case, the Court refused to interfere with political surveillance by the Army of people and groups that oppose government policies; even in the 1960s, no restrictions were placed on government infiltration and surveillance of groups and individuals exercising fully protected rights of expression and association.[15]

In Mitch Miller's case, the Court greatly extended this approach. People typically believe that the banks with which they have accounts will maintain their account records confidentially, and that banks have a legal as well as moral obligation to do so. But in *Miller*, the Court ruled that account records belong to the bank, not the depositor, and that we give up all privacy interests in this information, and thereby "consent," by exposing it to the bank. It is, of course, impossible to maintain a bank account— which is usually necessary to function in the modern economy— without exposing your account and all of your transactions to the bank. But the Court ruled that the information is "voluntarily conveyed to the banks and exposed to their employees." Therefore, "even if the information is revealed on the assumption that it will be used for limited purposes . . . [t]he depositor takes the risk, in revealing his affairs to another, that the information will be conveyed by that person to the Government." There is "no legitimate expectation of privacy." We have no protected privacy interest in our bank accounts, and it's our own fault. Congress responded to the decision with the Right to Financial Privacy Act of 1978, which provides some minimal (but by no means adequate) privacy protection for depositors' bank records.[16]

The Court is using the old "expectation of privacy" formulation to lend a gloss of popular will and voluntariness to judge-made decisions that have nothing to do with either. Quite simply, the Court has enhanced the power of the government to intrude without cause or justification into matters that the overwhelming majority of our people believe are and should remain private.

More Than One Should Have to Bear

The biggest surprise of the Court's 1991 term was the reaffirmation of the "essential holding of *Roe v. Wade*" in *Planned Parent-*

hood v. Casey (1992).[17] The demise of the famous abortion decision was widely predicted, and it took a switch in position by Justice Kennedy to keep it alive by a slim margin of five-to-four. The
conservative attack on the result and reasoning in *Roe v. Wade* has
been overwhelming, unmatched in modern times, and it left even
many who favor choice in abortion decisions doubting the *legal*
reasoning and legitimacy of the decision. This is a good measure of
the hegemony of conservative thinking about law and politics after
over a decade of the Reagan and Bush administrations, but there
is nothing wrong with—or even unusual about—the legal reasoning of that much-maligned majority opinion.

The *Roe v. Wade* majority started with a right (privacy in
sexual and reproductive matters) established in prior cases,
assessed its importance, considered and weighed the importance
of countervailing government interests, formulated a rule, and
applied it to the particular facts and circumstances of the case.
The right was held to be important and to encompass procreative
decisions, but "at some point" in the fetal development process
the state interests in the health of the mother and the "potential
life" of the fetus "become[] compelling." The majority drew upon
practices, analyses, and studies from a variety of biological, philosophical, and theological disciplines and perspectives and considered a range of stages at which meaningful lines might be drawn
(live birth, viability, quickening, and conception). It acknowledged
the uncertainty and arbitrariness in drawing any line, particularly
because the "disciplines of medicine, philosophy, and theology are
unable to arrive at any consensus" about the point at which life
begins. The majority drew the lines at the first trimester regarding
the interest in the health of the mother and at viability (second
trimester) regarding the interest in potential life. The trimester
analysis provided a framework for the rule that is integrally connected to the issue and the rights and interests involved. The
result was a rather ingenious compromise—rejecting both a ban

on all abortions and an unfettered right to abortion in all circumstances—on a legally and politically explosive issue.

Charles Fried, brought on as President Reagan's solicitor general to vigorously oppose *Roe v. Wade,* presented the usual conservative challenge to the legal legitimacy of *Roe v. Wade* in his
memoir. He accepted the basic constitutional protection of privacy
(*Griswold*) but argued that "abortion is different." Because a fetus
is a "potential" or "actual" human life, "whatever else is involved,
[abortion] is not a matter of privacy." And because the Constitution does not specify whether a "nonviable fetus" is a person entitled to equal protection of the laws, that question must be left to
the legislatures.

No explanation is provided of how or why this particular mode
of legal analysis is required over several others that could easily
claim legal legitimacy. For example, if a protected privacy right of
women in matters of sexuality and reproduction is recognized,
then two important concerns are in conflict—there is still a privacy
or autonomy concern. No legal methodology requires any conservative or any judge to ignore or devalue women's autonomy
regarding sexual and reproductive matters. Further, if privacy or
autonomy in such matters is a fundamental right available to
women, invalidating conflicting legislation is not unusual. Finally,
when the language of the Constitution is silent on the status of
fetuses, the question can be decided—and one can find methodological support—either way.

The unremarkability of the *Roe* methodology is also evident if
one considers other, less controversial areas in which courts have
formulated constitutional rules in terms of time-based or quantitative variables. Such rules have been adopted by conservative and
liberal majorities in a range of contexts and in regard to both criminal and noncriminal issues. Thus, for example, the maximum
allowable residency requirement for voting has been set at fifty
days, a criminal defendant has a right to a jury trial if the potential

sentence exceeds six months, and a suspect cannot be detained for more than forty-eight hours without a judicial determination of probable cause.[18]

In deciding whether and in what circumstances a state criminal defendant is entitled to a jury trial, the Court found a fundamental right and countervailing interests of the states in "speedy and inexpensive nonjury adjudications." Drawing a specific line between "serious" and "petty" offenses was an "essential if not wholly satisfactory" task. Alternative lines and a range of practices, analyses, and studies were considered, and unavoidable arbitrariness was acknowledged. The majority adopted a compromise using a time-based framework: Defendants facing more than six months' possible incarceration were entitled to a jury trial. Justices Black and Douglas, concurring, would have required a jury trial in all criminal prosecutions and criticized the majority for formulating a rule not found in the language of the Constitution. However, the decision did not generate a methodological debate, and the Court reaffirmed it in a recent case in which Solicitor General Fried praised its rule and methodology in an amicus brief.[19]

More recently, the Court faced the issue of how long a defendant may be detained without a judicial determination of probable cause.[20] Roughly the same combination of justices who have criticized *Roe v. Wade* on methodological grounds ruled that there must be a probable-cause determination within forty-eight hours. Justice O'Connor's majority opinion identified public safety and the liberty of and harm to persons detained as "important competing interests." The majority sought a specific maximum allowable period because the general standard, requiring a "prompt" determination, "has not provided sufficient guidance." The majority criticized the vagueness and uncertainty of the earlier standard because it led judges to make "legislative judgments." Yet this concern did not prevent the majority from imposing on the states its own specific and very code-like judgment.

The Court considered alternative time frames: when defendants are booked, as soon as the administrative arrest processes are completed, or "immediately" upon being placed in custody. The merits of the second alternative were acknowledged, but it was rejected because "[t]he Constitution does not compel so rigid a schedule." This typical depiction of limits and rules as compelled or legally required is particularly transparent here; surely the language of the Constitution does not mandate the majority's "48-hour" rule any more than an "immediate" rule. The former is the law and the latter is not by virtue of this very decision. Justice Scalia dissented, but his difference with the majority was not methodological; he would draw the line at twenty-four hours.

Adherents of various forms of legal determinacy (discussed in the conclusion) should at least pause in light of the methodological debate that dominates the opinions in cases like *Planned Parenthood v. Casey* and *Webster v. Reproductive Health Services* (1989).[21] In both cases, none of the justices seriously addressed the central issues: whether (and when) a fetus is a human being and the extent of women's autonomy in sexual and reproductive matters. Opponents of *Roe v. Wade* criticized the trimester framework methodologically as too specific, too general, arbitrary, not found in the language of the Constitution, code-like, and political. But most or all the same criticisms could be made of the jury-trial decision, the forty-eight-hour detention rule, the voter-residency rule, or, going beyond quantitative rules, the clear-and-present-danger rule in First Amendment doctrine or even the Court's opinion in 1803 establishing judicial review.[22]

Roughly the same combination of conservative justices making these criticisms of *Roe v. Wade* have recently created, without support in constitutional language or precedent, the specific, general, arbitrary, code-like, and political series of "public forum" rules limiting traditional free-speech rights (chapter 2). Like judicial restraint, original intent, interpretivism, strict construction, fundamental rights, and the range of other approaches, the methodological criticisms of *Roe v. Wade* are selective criticisms of the result masquerading as general principles of decision making or global theories of the role of law and courts in society.

In *Planned Parenthood v. Casey,* only two justices, Blackmun and Stevens, reaffirmed the trimester framework and strict-scrutiny standard of *Roe v. Wade.* The majority of five depended on the additional votes of Justices O'Connor, Kennedy, and Souter, who issued a "joint opinion" that rejected the trimester framework and applied a new, "undue burden" standard to regulations of abortion applicable before viability. The right of a woman to choose an abortion before viability was preserved, but the states were allowed to impose conditions and procedures as long as they do not amount to an undue burden on the right. Applying this intermediate standard, they upheld Pennsylvania regulations that required a twenty-four-hour waiting period; physician-provided information about the nature of the procedure, the risks of abortion and childbirth, and the "probable gestational age of the unborn child"; the consent of one parent for women under eighteen years of age (with the possibility of a substituted judge's determination); and a variety of record-keeping and reporting measures. They invalidated the requirement that married women notify their spouses.

The four dissenters joined in opinions by Justices Rehnquist and Scalia. Both emphasized criticism of the joint opinion's strong presumption that precedent (*Roe v. Wade*) should be followed— the leading theorists of conservative jurisprudence proclaimed that justices, according to Rehnquist, have not only discretion but a kind of activist "duty" to overrule prior decisions that "'depar[t] from a proper understanding' of the Constitution." Rehnquist here poignantly quoted from a case in which his earlier majority opinion was overruled.[23] Apparently, if the liberals did it (as they surely did), it is proper for conservatives, although this is one of the key methodology issues on which the conservatives have claimed and promised to be different. This is also of particular interest because, as we have seen throughout this book, Rehnquist, Scalia, and the other conservatives regularly claim to reach the rules and results that they do because they are *bound* by precedents to do so.

Scalia said the task is simply to "ascertain[] an objective law" and determine whether *Roe v. Wade* was "correctly decided," which, he insisted, is a matter of "reasoned"—not "value"—judgment. He did not explain how one figures out the "objective" and "correct" answer, particularly when there is not even agreement about such basics as whether or when precedents are binding. He takes refuge in being bound when he wants to but asserts the authority to determine what was "correctly decided" when he wants change. Indeed, when he wants change, he claims to be bound to change.

The guiding principle for interpreting the Constitution, according to Scalia, is "text and tradition"—the text of the Constitution and the historical traditions of American society. This principle flunks its own test: it is not itself in the text of the Constitution and does not accurately describe our constitutional history or tradition, which has been extraordinarily activist (though usually not on civil-rights issues). Nor does it require particular results or help when there is disagreement about the meaning of the text or the content of tradition, or the two seem to conflict, or there are new or changed circumstances, etc. We really know only what *he* means by an emphasis on text and tradition: a chilling return to official stigmatization of people who do things or live their lives in ways that do not meet moral standards of virtue defined by Scalia and people who agree with him. Such people are simply not entitled to even the most basic rights of freedom and liberty—the government can make it impossible for them to practice their religion if their rituals involve peyote instead of wine;

criminalize consensual adult sexual activities in the privacy of their bedrooms if they are lesbians or gay men; and compel them to carry a pregnancy to term if they are women who have had sex and gotten pregnant.

Scalia is also engaged in a particularly nasty fight with O'Connor in these cases over *stare decisis* (the principle that previous decisions should be followed) and other methodology issues. His criticisms of her abortion opinions included "cannot be taken seriously," "indecisive," "particularly perverse," "stingy," and "more than one should have to bear." These are more personal, and perhaps more telling, than the criticisms that one usually sees among the male justices. (He seems to be engaged in some sort of judicial therapy, in which he gets out often vicious personal feelings; laments the fate of conservatives of the past, such as the effect of Justice Taney's *Dred Scott* decision on his reputation [which seems thoroughly deserved]; stigmatizes segments of the population who do not meet his standards of personal virtue; and regularly ridicules those who disagree with his extreme positions. Supreme Court opinions—and the fundamental rights of others—do not seem the appropriate forum or occasion for such matters.)

Justice Blackmun, the author of the *Roe v. Wade* majority opinion and, at eighty-four, the slender thread by which abortion rights remain protected, saw the conservatives as compiling "lists of outcasts" who can now be deprived of fundamental rights based on "tradition." President Lincoln addressed the same thinking, exemplified in his time by the Know-Nothing party:

> Our progress in degeneracy appears to me to be pretty rapid. As a nation, we began by declaring that "all men are created equal." We now practically read it "all men are created equal, except negroes." When the Know-Nothings get control, it will read "all men are created equal, except negroes, and foreigners, and catholics." When it comes to this, I should prefer emigrating to some other country where they

make no pretense of loving liberty—to Russia, for instance, where despotism can be taken pure, without the base alloy of hypocrisy.[24]

Lincoln rejected the suggestion of some Republicans of his time that the party seek an alliance with the Know-Nothings to gain needed votes (unlike President Bush, who made an alliance at the 1992 Republican National Convention with the Know-Nothings of our day, led by Patrick Buchanan, Pat Robertson, and Dan and Marilyn Qualye).[25] In the modern liberal tradition, a history of oppression and scorn directed at any group in society was a reason and basis for a "more searching judicial inquiry" and protection, particularly because such groups usually do not have access and the ability to obtain relief and justice through the political process.[26] Now that status as an "outcast" is a constitutional justification for more government-imposed scorn and oppression.

◄ 7 ►

DUE PROCESS

In the conventional wisdom, constitutional protection of the rights of criminal defendants began (and went too far) in the 1960s. There certainly was an expansion of such rights in the 1960s and early 1970s, but for its origins we can look to the language of the Constitution, and to original intent. Protection of the rights of persons whom the government accuses or suspects of crime and intends to punish is the predominate concern of the Bill of Rights—the subject of five of its eight substantive amendments. These amendments limit the power of the government to search "persons, houses, papers, and effects" without probable cause and a warrant; to compel anyone "to be a witness against himself"; to deny a "speedy and public trial, by an impartial jury"; to hold an accused before trial on "excessive bail"; and, most generally and importantly, to deprive any person of "life, liberty, or property, without due process of law." This assortment of rights—along with freedom of speech, press, and religion—was the essence of the Bill of Rights, and of American freedom until the Civil War (when an end to slavery—and equality—were finally added to the list).

But these rights are now more often seen as a source of danger than protection. In an age when we have declared war on crime and drugs (one of the few wars in recent times actually to have been declared by Congress), the very pillars of our notions of freedom and limited government are being blamed for promoting crime and sacrificed to shortsighted demagoguery, even though no connection between protection of the fairness of the judicial process and increased crime has ever been demonstrated. After almost twenty years of continuous, unabashed toughness on crime and suspected or convicted criminals, the problem has gotten worse—in terms of violence, drugs, fear, or any other reasonable measure. We imprison a higher proportion of our population than any other country, more than even South Africa and the former Soviet Union. Our prison population has more than tripled since the early 1970s. The occupants of our jails and prisons are predominantly African-American and Hispanic, although they are not the predominant groups of drug users. A recent Justice Department study showed that three-quarters of "regular drug users" are white, but almost three-quarters of those imprisoned for drugs are African-Americans or Hispanics. We spend billions on prisons, police, judges, and the whole law-enforcement apparatus; and no politician seems able to oppose any further spending in these areas, while we cut back on almost everything else. Spending for "corrections" has grown faster than any other outlay by state governments, twice as fast as that for schools.[1]

This all seems quite in vain. We cannot expect people with a mainstream future limited to parking cars, washing dishes, and serving fast food—at subsistence wages with no real possibility of advancement—to reject the materialism and instant-gratification culture all around them and live lives of virtue without visible bitterness or rebellion. In many of our neighborhoods, we are producing a generation of people raised in an environment of violence and degradation who do not accept or understand middle-class limits on the American obsession with acquisitiveness. To a very large number of our people, life in the United States at the end of the twentieth century is so devoid of hope and meaningful connection to others that instant gratification and instant cash accompanied by slow (or not so slow) suicide seems as good an option as any available. The conservative experiment—funding without limit the law-enforcement apparatus and the military and eliminating or cutting almost every program that offers support, training, or an opportunity for those at the bottom—has undercut our national progress in reducing poverty and led to devastation, desperation, and increasing crime and violence. Another casualty of this war has been the basic protections of due process so vital to each of us and to the fundamental fairness of any society.

Watch for These Subjects

Edward Charles Davis III was a photographer for a leading newspaper in Louisville, Kentucky, when he was accused of shoplifting by a security guard in a store. Davis, whose only scrape with the law had been a speeding ticket, was greatly relieved when the local court cleared him of wrongdoing, but his troubles had just begun. A few days before the charges were dismissed, the police chiefs of Louisville and Jefferson County distributed a flier to hundreds of local businesses that contained the names and "mug shot" photos of "active shoplifters." The flier said that the chiefs "approved" the list "of subjects known to be active in this criminal field" and urged merchants to "watch for these subjects."

The chiefs conceded that they did not limit their flier to the worst or multiple offenders, or even to people convicted of shoplifting. All that was necessary was a charge, even if, as in Davis's case, it was not lodged by the police and the police were not witnesses and did not make the arrest. Davis's employer found out about the flier, limited his assignments so that he would not be photographing stores, and warned him not to "find himself in a similar situation" again. His picture was displayed, like a wanted poster, at a variety of shops. Davis brought a civil-rights lawsuit in federal court against the city and the chiefs claiming that his right to due process of law had been violated. Part of the relief that he requested was circulation of a statement by the chiefs to the same stores saying that he was not an active shoplifter and had not been convicted of shoplifting, which the chiefs refused to do.

Earlier cases had prohibited the government from officially branding a person a criminal who had not been convicted of a crime. The police and government officials can announce an arrest, identify the accused, and discuss the circumstances and the charges. However, the "badge of infamy" is supposed to be applied by government only to persons convicted after a process that includes a trial and an opportunity for them to defend themselves. This seemed a basic and rather uncontroversial aspect of due process. Only five years before Davis's case, the Court invalidated a Wisconsin town's practice of "posting" suspected but uncon-victed "excessive drinkers":

> Where a person's good name, reputation, honor, or integrity is at stake because of what the government is doing to him, notice and an opportunity to be heard are essential. . . . [This is] a principle basic to our society.[2]

Justice Rehnquist's majority opinion thought and ruled otherwise in Davis's case, *Paul v. Davis* (1976).[3]

Rehnquist did not focus on or even discuss the unfairness of a government that acts in this way, or the danger that a government with such powers would be oppressive and functioning in a way that is inconsistent with individual freedom and dignity. He lim-ited himself to what he described as the requirements of earlier cases, and then he proceeded to rewrite those cases. For example, the Wisconsin case, Rehnquist said, rested entirely on the state's also prohibiting sale of liquor to those posted, although the Court in that case did not say so or even emphasize that fact. Rehnquist concluded that reputation is not protected as "liberty or property," although he conceded that they include "a variety of interests which are difficult of definition," and therefore Davis was not entitled to due process at all. He could have been picked by the police at random—without even an arrest—and there would be no constitutional protection.

Unfortunate Encounters

Adolph Lyons was pulled over to the curb by two Los Angeles police officers because one of his taillights was burned out. The officers' guns were drawn as they approached Lyons's car, and he exited. They ordered him to face the car, spread his legs, and clasp his hands on top of his head, which Lyons immediately did. After a pat-down search was completed, Lyons lowered his hands, but one of the officers grabbed them and forcefully put them back on his head. Lyons complained that the ring of keys in his hand had become painful, and the officer began to choke Lyons with the "choke hold" that would make the Los Angeles police and police chief Darryl Gates famous long before the nation had heard of Rodney King. The officer continued the choke hold until Lyons fell unconscious. When he regained consciousness, Lyons was handcuffed lying on the ground, gasping for air, and spitting up blood. He soon noticed that he had urinated and defecated. The police removed the handcuffs, issued him a traffic ticket, and left.

Lyons's account of these events and the police practice and policy regarding the choke hold were uncontradicted in the federal civil rights lawsuit that he brought seeking to prohibit use of the choke hold. The choke hold is performed from behind the subject, by placing an arm across the front of the subject's neck and holding the wrist of that arm with the other hand. Enormous pressure can be applied to the carotid arteries at the sides of the lower neck or to the throat and air passage, both of which cause severe pain, unconsciousness, and sometimes death. It often also causes what was referred to by a Los Angeles officer as "doing the chicken": spasmodic convulsions, eye rolling, and wild feet and arm movements—like a chicken whose neck is wrung.

Over a period of several years, the Los Angeles police had killed sixteen people with the choke hold, three-quarters of whom, like Lyons, were African-Americans. Yet, the department did not consider the choke hold as involving deadly force and authorized and encouraged its use even when a subject presented no danger of seriously harming another person or an officer. Its use was encouraged whenever a subject was resistant or insufficiently compliant. Further, the officers were instructed that the choke hold can be safely used for three or four minutes and should be maintained until the subject goes limp, as in the case of Lyons. They were not told that, as uncontradicted evidence showed, it can cause death in just two seconds. The average choke hold time regarding the deaths for which there was evidence was only forty seconds.

Lyons sought and was granted a preliminary injunction by the federal district court which prohibited police use of the choke hold where there was no danger of death or serious bodily injury. The court of appeals stayed the injunction pending appeal, resulting in five more choke hold deaths. Meanwhile, perhaps bowing to public pressure, Chief Gates declared a temporary moratorium on choke holds before the Supreme Court reached a decision. But none of this mattered much to the conservative justices, who used *Los Angeles v. Lyons* (1983)[4] as an occasion to impede access to the federal courts and meaningful remedies for people wrongfully injured by a widespread, unlawful police practice.

Justice White's majority opinion for the first time denied civil-rights plaintiffs "standing" to seek an injunction unless they could show that the claimed unconstitutional governmental conduct would likely be imposed on them personally in the future. Of course, Lyons had already been choked and left gasping for breath, bleeding, soiled, and terrified for having a burned out taillight and complaining about the discomfort of maintaining his hands clasped over his head. But this did not matter at all: "Five months elapsed between [Lyons' being choked] and the filing of the complaint, yet there was no allegation of further unfortunate encounters between Lyons and the police." Lyons was no more likely than everyone else to be stopped and choked in the future, and therefore, the Court ruled, he did not have standing to seek an injunction. If it happened to him again, he could seek damages (or his family could if he did not survive), but although the choke hold was being used unconstitutionally and was causing deaths and serious injuries, it could not be stopped.

Standing has long been required to ensure that litigants have important interests in the outcome of litigation, so there is a real "case and controversy" as required by the Constitution, and to place some limit on federal lawsuits, which might otherwise be brought by anyone with a purely academic or fleeting interest in an issue. The long-standing rule was that a plaintiff must have a "personal stake in the outcome of the controversy," which was satisfied if he or she "suffered some actual or threatened injury." In cases challenging a police practice like the Los Angeles choke hold, someone like Lyons, who had been subjected to it, would have standing whereas someone who merely objected to it in the abstract may not. Whether a plaintiff with standing and a meritorious claim should get particular relief, such as an injunction, was another matter, determined later based on other standards that Lyons seemingly satisfied.[5]

The Court ruled that Lyons could not seek to prohibit the unconstitutional use of the choke hold. Nor could anyone else. The injunction, so useful in business and other litigation, is unavailable to civil-rights plaintiffs seeking to prohibit a widespread unconstitutional—and even deadly—practice. The Court sent a message to Chief Gates and the Los Angeles police that seems implicated in the Rodney King affair: Fight the war on crime your way, and the courts will not intervene even when you use unjustifiable deadly force. Another case in 1987 announced that police are no longer liable for violating constitutional rights, no matter how serious the violation or the injury, if they acted in "good faith" and "reasonably" believed that their conduct was lawful.[6] Constitutional violations are no longer constitutional violations, and the more widespread an even deadly unconstitutional practice, the harder it is to obtain meaningful legal relief.

Harmless Error

Oreste Fulminante was convicted by an Arizona jury of the rape and murder of his eleven-year-old stepdaughter. His conviction was reversed by Arizona's highest court because the evidence against him included a coerced, involuntary confession. This would not mean that Fulminante would go free, although most of the public apparently believes that defendants in cases like Fulminante's—or Miranda's[7]—go free; he would be tried again without admission of the coerced confession. Coerced confessions have been the most frowned-upon evidence since the tortures of the English Star Chamber were used to extract admissions of guilt. They are inherently unreliable and the product of unacceptable police conduct—completely incompatible with due process. In *Arizona v. Fulminante* (1991),[8] the Supreme Court for the first time ruled that a conviction could stand although a coerced, involuntary confession had been admitted as evidence and considered by the jury.

Five conservative justices joined Chief Justice Rehnquist's opinion expanding the "harmless error" doctrine to include coerced confessions. This is a strange doctrine for jurists who claim to be strict constructionists: it holds that violations of the Constitution in the criminal-law process—even direct violations of its explicit provisions—are excused and considered meaningless if the justices find sufficient evidence of guilt such that the "error" seems "harmless." It is as if the Constitution were amended to read, after the Bill of Rights and succeeding amendments, "but no violation of the foregoing rights of persons accused of crime matters if a majority of the Supreme Court is convinced that the defendant was guilty and the violation is no big deal!"

The harmless-error doctrine was first adopted in 1967 with very limited applicability and the caveat that certain constitutional violations—specifically including admission of coerced confessions—are "so basic to a fair trial that the[y] can never be treated as harmless error." This was repeatedly reaffirmed until *Fulminante*, which Justice White characterized as "dislodg[ing] one of the fundamental tenets of our criminal justice system."[9] Nevertheless, Rehnquist claimed that his application of harmless error to coerced confessions was consistent with these cases because they meant to establish a distinction he suggested for the first time, between "structural" and "trial" errors. The underlying reasons and source for this difference were not clear, but there is no doubt that this doctrinal shuffle fundamentally alters and undercuts the fairness and integrity of the criminal-law process.

Fulminante's conviction was reversed because one of the five justices applying the harmless-error doctrine, Justice Kennedy, was not convinced that the error was harmless in this case, particularly because of "the indelible impact" of a confession on the jury. (This case was decided before Justice Marshall was replaced by Justice Thomas, and Marshall provided the indispensable fifth vote for a new trial.) In any event, now almost all violations of the constitutional rights of people accused of crime are subject to the harmless-error doctrine.

A Policeman Perched on the Top of a Truck or a Two-Level Bus

The unique privacy that American law and culture accord to homes and to activities associated with the home included the

175

yards, patios, gardens, and other areas immediately adjacent to a house under the Court's Fourth Amendment decisions, and even under an old common law doctrine (called "curtilage"). However, this was changed in 1986, when the conservatives denied fourth amendment protection from police aerial surveillance of areas around the home visible from above.

Dante Carlo Ciraolo's suburban Santa Clara, California, home had a ten-foot-high fence around the whole property. Inside, there was a small garden plot next to the house, in which he was growing marijuana plants. The police got an anonymous call about the marijuana, but this is not sufficient grounds for probable cause or a warrant to search the premises. The police rented an airplane and flew over the Ciraolo home for the specific purpose of observing whether marijuana was growing in the garden. They concluded that it was, got a warrant, searched the premises, and arrested Ciraolo. The Court ruled in *California v. Ciraolo* (1986)[10] that the aerial search, although without probable cause or a warrant, was allowable, affirming Ciraolo's conviction and altering the privacy rights available to all Americans.

The Fourth Amendment has never been interpreted to prohibit searches entirely but only to limit them to situations in which the police have a substantial basis for believing that a crime has been committed and to require, in appropriate circumstances, a warrant approving the search signed by a judge. The pivotal question as to whether probable cause or a warrant is required has usually been whether there is a "reasonable expectation of privacy" (discussed in chapter 6 with respect to bank records). This standard seems to emphasize popular understandings of privacy, but the conservatives have imposed their very restrictive view.

The California courts had concluded that Ciraolo's erecting a ten-foot fence showed that he wanted and expected privacy, and that it was reasonable in contemporary society to expect that one's yard is private and not subject to police aerial surveillance without constitutional safeguards, particularly aerial surveillance aimed at a specific home. Chief Justice Burger, for the majority, disagreed. The ten-foot fence "might not shield these plants from the eyes of . . . a policeman perched on the top of a truck or a two-level bus." This is not, he said, "an expectation that society is prepared to honor," although he never bothered to ask society or assess the popular understanding of privacy. As long as the police do not physically break in or intrude, apparently nothing is protected by privacy unless completely shielded from all possible observation.

A Basis for Exonerating the Defendant

A ten-year-old boy was abducted by a stranger at a carnival in Pima County, Arizona, and then repeatedly molested and raped in a car and a nearby building. Police found semen in the boy's rectum and on his T-shirt and underpants, and some samples were immediately taken with a "sexual assault kit." Nine days later the boy was shown a series of pictures and asked if he could identify the assailant. At one point he said he was "pretty sure" it was Larry Youngblood, a local maintenance man, although there were discrepancies between his description and Youngblood's appearance; later, he said he was sure.

The preliminary semen and blood tests that the police lab performed were inconclusive, and the police did not preserve the evidence so that it could be analyzed by a defense expert. They did not perform any immediate tests on the T-shirt and underpants or refrigerate them, although that is the usual practice for preserving such evidence, and they had a refrigeration facility for that purpose. (The police also immediately had Youngblood's car picked up by a wrecker, who destroyed it, so that an identification of the car by the boy was not possible.)

At the trial, the jury convicted Youngblood based solely on the boy's identification, the only evidence incriminating him. Youngblood consistently maintained his innocence, which his lawyer maintained would have been conclusively established by routine tests on the semen samples.

Previous cases had held that the prosecution has a duty to maintain and provide to a defendant any evidence that may tend to prove his or her innocence. If potentially exculpatory evidence in the hands of the prosecution was material to guilt or innocence but no longer available, the charges were dismissed as a matter of "fundamental fairness," because it is then impossible to accord the defendant due process of law. In *Arizona v. Youngblood* (1988),[11] the conservatives changed that rule: the conviction stands unless the defendant can prove that the prosecution acted in "bad faith."

Chief Justice Rehnquist's majority opinion did not explain how a nonpurposeful or "good faith" denial of due process could or should satisfy the constitutional requirement that no one be "deprived of . . . liberty . . . without due process of law." The language of the Constitution—presumably of some importance to a strict constructionist—forbids imprisonment of anyone who was denied due process, seemingly regardless of the intentions of prosecutors or police. Nor did he make it clear what kind of "bad faith" is required, or how it could be proved. Rehnquist said that his new rule limits relief to "those cases in which the police themselves by their conduct indicate that the evidence could form a basis for exonerating the defendant." He seems to suggest that the defendant would have to prove that the police destroyed evidence for the specific purpose of wrongfully convicting him—a near-impossible burden to impose as a precondition to "fundamental fairness."

This is one of the many areas in which the conservatives have grafted onto constitutional protections a precondition of proof of malicious or wrongful purpose by government officials. If a person cannot prove that the government denied his or her rights purposely or maliciously, then those rights will not be enforced and are nullified. Other recent cases approve of preventive detention and kidnapping people in foreign countries so that they can be prosecuted here, and undercut the basic habeas-corpus protection. In the last category, the Court approved of the execution of Warren McCleskey (see chapter 5) although he had newly acquired evidence that would overturn his death sentence, because he "abused" habeas-corpus relief by not presenting the proof earlier when he raised a related issue (but did not have the new evidence).[12] In the area of criminal justice, we have reversed what Justice Blackmun, dissenting in *Lyons*, called the "fundamental value determination of our society that it is far worse to convict an innocent man than to let a guilty man go free." Now we just put them all in jail, or execute them.

Whether one condemns or applauds these new conservative decisions, it is surely not plausible to blame, as we so often hear, "handcuffing the police" or defendants' rights for the failure of the almost two-decade-long conservative obsession with imprisonment and execution. There may not be less crime or fear, but there is certainly little left of due process.

◄ CONCLUSION ►

We are moving toward a regime in which the Constitution yields substantially enlarged rights and power for wealthy individuals and corporations but provides the ordinary citizen with little meaningful or enforceable protection or empowerment. The essence will be enhanced governmental power to suppress and impose its will on the people in the areas usually identified as the domain of American freedom and justice—expression, political participation, religion, equality, privacy, and due process. The rationale and rallying cry for this new regime has been, as it was for the Reagan decade, freedom—a magnificent word and idea being steadily reduced to its opposite.

These monumental changes are being implemented by the Supreme Court, the same institution that in the 1960s and early 1970s (and briefly from about 1937 to 1944) carried the torch for civil rights and civil liberties. Looking realistically at history, however, this is a return to a well-charted course. For example, the recent race decisions are the descendants of *Dred Scott v. Sanford* (the 1857 decision declaring African-Americans less than human), *Plessy v. Ferguson* (the 1896 decision that established the "separate but equal" defense of segregation), and *Korematsu*.[1] The playing field has surely shifted, but *Brown v. Board of Education* in 1954 and the civil-rights decisions of the 1960s and early 1970s look like aberrations.

The civil-rights and civil-liberties successes throughout our history, including those of the 1960s and 1970s, have had more to do with social and cultural changes and successful movements for equality and freedom than with any legal principles or legal reasoning. People at all levels of society have played a role in this, including some judges; but, contrary to the common assumption (particularly by people who lived through the 1960s), courts have not been a primary, or usually even a significant, agent of these changes. More often, courts have actively opposed progressive change or stayed on the sidelines. This point should not escape the attention of anyone concerned with the sorry state of civil rights and civil liberties or the current crisis of democracy, and I will return to it shortly. But we should start with an understanding of the ways and means of the conservative justices.

CONSERVATIVE LEGAL THOUGHT AND PRACTICE

Conservative justices, scholars, and politicians have articulated an approach to law, described in the introduction, that emphasizes judicial restraint, strict construction of constitutional and statutory language, a return to democracy and the rule of law, and legal rather than political decision making. The central thrust of their approach and their criticism of liberal judges is that conservative rules and results are not only preferable but *legally required.* This is the accepted political wisdom of at least the last decade. All the favorite enemies are denounced—lawyers, bureaucrats, politicians, liberal judges, big government; and the goal is freedom and democracy.

The opinions of the conservative justices examined in this book make the same claims, sometimes explicitly but most often implicitly. The conservatives have adopted a new formalism that emphasizes technical legal analysis and purports to eschew political or policy concerns. They seldom discuss or offer justifications grounded in social or constitutional principles about the organization or functioning of government or society. If mentioned at all, such principles are reduced to meaningless, general platitudes.

Their free-speech opinions do not, for example, concern, or at most barely mention, the social effect or the significance in the constitutional scheme of their new limits on speech rights. Rather, the clear thrust of their opinions is that the rules and results that they are adopting are simply required by legal analysis and legal reasoning. That is the beginning and the end of their story.

We have surely seen enough to reject this explanation for their rules, results, and approaches. First, the conservative "strict constructionists" have created—without any support in the language of the Constitution—a multitude of new doctrines, presented as if they are required or have always been there, that restrict civil rights and liberties. These new doctrines restrict both the substantive content of personal freedom and the enforceability of the limited rights that remain. The "public forum" doctrine limits speech rights, and the classification of constitutional violations in the criminal trial process as "structural" or "trial" errors expands the "harmless error" doctrine (itself created by a mixture of conservatives and liberals) and limits due process. The new standing requirement for civil-rights plaintiffs seeking injunctive relief, the new "good faith" immunities for government misconduct, and the new burdens of proof and procedural hurdles for civil-rights plaintiffs deny access to the courts for relief from unconstitutional government misconduct.

The most general substantive limit is what might be called the "purpose doctrine," which excuses and legitimates all manner of constitutional violations unless a victim can prove that the government has acted maliciously and the government cannot suggest an alternative, plausibly benevolent purpose. The purpose doctrine has been applied across the board with a variety of names and terms—to rights of expression ("secondary effects" and "incidental effects"), exercise of religion ("incidental effects"), establishment of religion ("plausible secular purpose"), equality ("purposeful discrimination"), and due process ("bad faith")—and now dominates the whole field of individual constitutional rights. (The only area emphasized in this book in which it has not played a major role is privacy, where the Court has accomplished the same results by reducing the scope of activity that is protected at all rather than focusing on purposes that excuse infringements.) I use "purpose" rather than "intention," although the Court more frequently uses the latter and the two terms are often used interchangeably in law and popular discourse, because it more accurately describes the doctrine. Intention emphasizes the conscious, knowing, and voluntary doing of an act and sometimes includes or implies a conscious meaning to cause the consequences that reasonably and directly flow from it. Purpose, or motive, emphasizes the reason one acts, or what one hopes to accomplish by the action, which can include or go beyond one or more reasonable consequences. The conservatives regularly claim that they are examining intent and condemn any examination of the purpose or motive behind a government action, which further complicates and obscures their analysis.[2] But they are actually examining and focusing on purpose or motive when they excuse and ignore constitutional violations with this doctrine.

The conservative justices who have innovated and developed the purpose doctrine have not explained *why* we should ignore constitutional violations unless a victim can meet the almost-impossible burden of proving malicious governmental purposes. Nor have they explained or addressed the contradictions in their applications of this doctrine: they tend to ignore proof of wrongful purposes when it comes to governmental measures that disfavor minorities, women, or nonmajoritarian religions or groups (*Memphis, McCleskey* and *Gilbert,* purposeful discrimination rule; *Lynch* and *Mueller,* secular purpose rule); they tend to assume wrongful purposes when it comes to measures adopted by predominantly or substantially minority legislatures that disfavor whites (*Richmond,* affirmative action); and a clearly benevolent government purpose does not seem to matter at all—the doctrine is suspended—when the rights of wealthy people and institutions are at issue (*Buckley, Bellotti,* and the later electoral and referendum campaign-contribution and expenditure and corporate-speech cases, money-is-speech doctrine; *Tornillo,* no-access-to-media doctrine).

To understand the purpose doctrine, it is perhaps useful to start at the lowest level and acknowledge that young children regularly use a version of it in attempts to escape or ameliorate responsibility for their transgressions. What parent has not heard (and been at least somewhat moved by), "Mom (or Dad), I didn't *mean* to do it." This is usually accompanied by effusive apologies and an explanation that someone else may be at fault or the event had accidental or unknowable origins, but there was no purposeful harm done. "I didn't mean it" loses effectiveness with age, but we still distinguish purposeful from accidental conduct in adults; for example, "I'm sorry, I didn't see the light turn yellow" is different from "I was in a hurry, and you were in my way." And we require proof of intentional conduct before we brand someone a criminal and impose punishment.

But the purpose doctrine is not about discipline or punishment of children or adults, or individual government employees, who have acted wrongfully. The issue is our fundamental constitutional rights, and whether the government should be allowed to deprive individuals of the fundamental protections of the Bill of Rights with a "but we didn't mean it" response. The question answers itself is fairly framed: Should free speech, participation in the political process, religious freedom, equality, privacy, and due process be consistently and uniformly protected regardless of the government's claimed alternative purposes for their denial, or should they only be protected and enforced when we can prove that government officials purposely or maliciously meant to deny them?

Constitutional rights should not be absolute, but their vindication should depend on the importance and necessity of the government's specific interest in denying them, not on whether a person denied such rights can identify and prove the maliciousness of government officials involved in the denial. The purpose doctrine invites evasion—government can get away with denying constitutional protections if its purposes are covered up or muddled (*Memphis*)—and selective application of the sort that viewed affirmative action as an occasion to "smoke out" racism and traditional discriminatory practices as an occasion to suspend consciousness and ignore reality. The purpose doctrine undermines the purpose of the Bill of Rights; we simply do not have meaningful rights if they can be denied without remedy based on hair-splitting about purposes.

Nor is the purpose doctrine specified or even hinted at in the Bill of Rights, or required by legal analysis or reasoning. Because the language of the Constitution, the intent of the framers, and most prior decisions do not excuse constitutional violations based on the benign or possible alternative purposes of the governmental wrong-doers—violations occur when the Constitution's mandates have been violated—there is a contradiction for jurists who have emphasized strict construction, original intent, and restraint. We impose civil liability on individuals and corporations for all sorts of unintentional conduct without regard to alternative purposes. The conservative justices have simply erected a substantial new immunity for government conduct that violates the long-standing constitutional rights of individuals. To the conservatives, there is *no governmental wrongdoing and no violation* unless the person deprived of freedom, justice, or equality can produce the elusive proof of a malignant governmental purpose. This is a return to *Korematsu*—without even the claim of necessity based on a world war.

Second, the conservatives selectively use and abuse precedent and history in an attempt to depict even their most fundamental changes as part of a seamless tapestry of legally required rules and results. In the dispute over fees for permits to engage in speech activities (*Forsyth County*), Rehnquist claimed to be bound by a 1941 case that favored his position although a 1943 case—which had been followed for almost fifty years—contradicted it. They just choose which one to follow, and sometimes they ignore them all. Rehnquist had no problem applying the harmless-error doctrine to coerced confessions (*Fulminante*) in spite of the 1967 case establishing that doctrine—and over a dozen more since then— which explicitly said that the doctrine would not be applied to coerced confessions. He simply reinterpreted (more accurately, rewrote) the earlier case so that it embodied his distinction between "structural" and "trial" errors, which it and the intervening decisions did not mention and, implicitly at least, rejected. When an innocent man was the subject of a wanted poster for shoplifters and an earlier case granted due-process relief for "posted" drinkers who were not convicted, the Court claimed that the earlier case was based on other limits on posted drinkers, although the earlier case did not say so or emphasize the other limits (*Paul v. Davis*). Rehnquist dismissed Jefferson as a source to be considered regarding the meaning and history of the establishment clause (*Wallace v. Jaffree*) merely because he was in France when the first amendment was adopted and wrote his famous "wall of separation" passage after the amendment's adoption, as if these facts somehow nullify Jefferson's assessment and make it less significant than Rehnquist's (who also wasn't there). This is a common conservative technique, particularly for Rehnquist: reinterpret and rewrite earlier decisions and history as you claim to be bound by them.

Third, the conservatives, with apparent ease (and little visible guilt), lift a word or phrase, deprive it of meaning and context, and claim that it supports the opposite of what it clearly meant originally. The phrase "from time immemorial" from *Hague* was used in this way: We have not allowed speech in—or had—airports "from time immemorial," so, according to Rehnquist, public air terminals cannot be public forums, although that phrase from *Hague*—decided before the conservatives had invented the public-forum doctrine—was clearly used, meant, and generally understood as an explanation of the basis for a greatly expanded notion of free speech in public places.

Fourth, the conservative justices adopt, without explanation or support beyond their own predilections, selectively narrow and broad interpretations of constitutional language, statutes, and decisions. Rehnquist simply announced that reputation was not protected by the due-process clause, so there is no constitutional problem with police circulating flyers that brand a man a criminal and urge the public to watch out for him even though he was cleared of all charges (*Paul v. Davis*). Previous cases that had guaranteed each person a trial and a determination of guilt before the government imposed the "badge of infamy" were dismissed with meaningless distinctions. Discrimination against pregnant women is not sex discrimination because not all women are pregnant (*Gilbert*). The "reasonable expectation of privacy" language from early privacy decisions has been mutilated to the point that it is used to justify banks' turning over, without a subpoena or any legal compulsion, personal financial records to police or anyone who asks to see them (*Miller*) and an aerial police search of the backyard of a home without probable cause or a warrant (*Ciraolo*). When they wish, they also simply announce a broad interpretation, as in the conclusion that money is speech (*Buckley*).

Fifth, the conservatives, in the tradition of *Korematsu,* use exaggerated and fabricated appeals to necessity, emergency, fear, and prejudice to justify denial of fundamental constitutional rights. We are told that society will crumble if Alfred Smith is permitted to exercise his religion, involving the occasional use of peyote (*Smith*), or if Alan Burdick is permitted to write in a vote

(*Burdick*); sexual innuendos in a high-school student government nomination speech can be censored because "teenage girl students," none of whom complained or testified, are thought to have been insulted (*Fraser*); and the consensual sexual conduct of gay men and lesbians in their own bedrooms can be criminalized because we and other societies have traditionally oppressed gay people (*Hardwick*)—an argument that, if generalized, would have foreclosed any measure of justice or equality for minorities and women as well. Strict scrutiny and the notion of minimizing government intrusion on the individual have been abandoned.

The nomination of Robert Bork to the Supreme Court may have been defeated, but his approach and his values—which so upset and scared the nation—have won majority approval on the Court. The Court is on a moral crusade, fighting what Patrick Buchanan at the 1992 Republican Convention called a "religious war", to compel conformity and ostracize people whose life-styles, conduct, or identities stray from a particular conservative vision of virtue. It does not matter that other people are not directly or concretely harmed or affected by people on what Justice Blackmun called the Court's "lists of outcasts." Bork addressed this unequivocally in his latest book: "Knowledge that an activity is taking place is a harm to those who find it profoundly immoral."[3]

Sixth, the conservatives only selectively and inconsistently apply the principles of legal decision making and methodology that proved so effective as criticisms of liberals in the political arena. There has been no end to conservative denunciations of judicial activism aimed at liberal decisions that struck down legislation, particularly if the basis was some new constitutional interpretation or theory. But there was not even a word about judicial restraint, or any apparent hesitation, when conservative justices invalidated legislation aimed at reducing the effects of long-standing racial discrimination (*Richmond*), bias-motivated crime legislation (*St. Paul*), legislation providing access to the media

(*Tornillo*), and legislation adopting electoral reforms aimed at reducing corruption and the role of money in elections (*Buckley* and its progeny)—all justified with novel constitutional interpretations and theories. Apparently, judicial restraint does not apply where it would limit the rights of rich people or white men.

Conservative legal thought, in theory and practice, ultimately embraces most of the villains on its enemies list and fails to substantiate the claims of adherents to neutrality and reason. It favors substantial government intrusion on the individual and the imposition of government-compelled cultural, moral, and religious conformity. Lawyers turn out to be heroes worthy of almost mystical trust with controversies most democracies leave to the people or their representatives. Another archenemy—the bureaucrat—has received increased powers, including even the authority to nullify acts of Congress.[4] Judicial restraint is favored only very selectively. Government is bigger and wields more power over the individual, and there is disdain for democracy. Conservatives have captured the mantle of democracy and concern for the people in large part by inaccurately portraying their traditional preference for compelled conformity as its opposite—as a limit on the intrusiveness of government and as pro-democratic—and matters of substance and values as legal methodology issues.

Looking at the array of rules, standards of review, justifications, and results, it appears that the conservatives are using the legal system and the rule of law as opportunistically and politically as any liberal. The analyses in particular cases seem bewilderingly haphazard and unpredictable, but what emerges is surely a recognizable *conservative program:* The rights of people of ordinary means, minorities, and women are being restricted; government is being authorized to compel conformity in matters of expression, religion, life-style, and culture; and the rights of rich people and corporations are being enhanced, creating a new constitutional barrier to electoral and democratic reforms.

This resembles the familiar shell game, where someone manipulates three shells and a pea, and you bet on which shell the pea is under. It is very difficult to figure out how the pea is moved from shell to shell, but the outcome is clear and consistent: You lose. The conservatives are selectively and inconsistently using a range of legally recognized justifications, techniques, and principles to further a political program—just what they accused the liberals of doing. Their program is a perversion of freedom, a repudiation of equality and diversity, and a rebuke of our history of progress. However—and here I part company with so much recent liberal criticism of the conservative Court—it is not a perversion of the legal system or the rule of law, and I do not see how we are going to extract ourselves from our current mess or move successfully into the twenty-first century if we do not look harder and longer at the role of law and the decay of democracy in our country.

LEGAL REASONING, DEMOCRACY, AND THE RULE OF LAW

Before we conclude that the conservative justices (or the liberals before them) have perverted or seriously deviated from the legal system or the rule of law, we need some base understanding of the legal system and the rule of law and some norm or criterion for its proper operation. The common conservative (and liberal) explanation of the operation and virtue of law is now commonplace. According to Reagan solicitor general Charles Fried, law and legal analysis bring "reason" and "neutrality" and the certainty and consistency of fair rules applied to all. But he acknowledges that law lacks an "anchor"—a set of established principles and a legal methodology that determine rules and results. "The rule of law is not quite a law of rules" and "there are no criteria about criteria" are his distracting ways of conceding that there are no legally required principles or any legal methodology that yields legally required results neutrally or by reason. He tries to reassure us, however, on two grounds. The "good faith" legal mind works, somewhat mysteriously but reliably, such that "you just know." Further, results do not really matter: the legal *process* guarantees us all freedom and liberty.[5]

Such reassurances should not be very comforting. The "you" who "knows" is the lawyer, among the villains on the conservatives' enemies list. If the good-faith legal mind is William Rehnquist's or Edwin Meese's, the rules and results that it knows tend to be conservative. If it is mine, the rules and results tend to be progressive. And results, of course, matter very much.

Law is indeterminate—it does not provide *legally required* rules or results. This is so in part because of the limits of language and interpretation, which are necessarily subjective and value laden. More important, indeterminacy stems from the reality that the law usually embraces and legitimizes many or all the conflicting values and interests involved in controversial issues and a wide and conflicting array of "logical" or "reasoned" arguments, without providing any legally required hierarchy of values or arguments or any required method for determining which is most important in a particular context. Judges then make choices, and those choices are most fundamentally value based, or political.[6]

For example, in the abortion controversy, the law embraces both privacy and individual choice in sexual and reproductive matters and protection and preservation of life and health. One can find prior decisions of the Supreme Court placing great importance on each of these values or principles. However, the law does not provide any method or process for determining neutrally or objectively which of the competing values is more important. Nor does the law provide any required method or process for determining whether or when a fetus is a life, the extent of reproductive choice, or when the courts should follow one, another, or any precedent.

Often a particular rule or result can be relatively predictable and appear to be "sensible" or "correct," but this occurs when the issue or circumstances are not controversial in a specific period or context (or when one consciously or unconsciously projects one's own values as neutral and correct). A relative societal consensus or a lack of controversy regarding particular values, issues, or results can create a false sense of determinacy. In another period or context where the same issue or circumstances are controversial, the law's indeterminacy is again readily visible.

The extraordinary role of law in our society and culture presents seldom-discussed contradictions for conservatives and liberals. If law is not determinate or neutral or a function of reason and logic rather than values and politics, the rule of law reduces to rule by lawyers, and there is little justification for the broad-scale displacement of democracy. Perhaps this is why we usually prefer to debate other issues, such as legal methodology.

Fried claims "that there is a distinct method which is the legal method, that lawyers and judges can learn to deploy that method, that it can be deployed more or less well, and that it yields a distinct set of answers more or less out of itself." He attempts to demonstrate this method and his methodological criticism of liberal judges by focusing on *Roe v. Wade,* which he views as an "extreme example of judicial overreaching" and "a symptom of a mistaken approach to judging." However, the methodology of the *Roe* majority, although much maligned, is not novel or even unusual (chapter 6).

The law's variety of approaches, methods and principles of decision making are applied selectively; every justice uses some of them some of the time and has used them all at least on occasion (and once in a while some justice originates a new one). None is required in any particular case or circumstance. The justices cannot agree on the straightforward matter of how one goes about deciding an important constitutional case because there is no legally required methodology but rather many methodologies that can claim legitimacy within the legal system, from which a judge may pick and choose. The role of value choices in a case like *Roe v. Wade* is no different than in environmental, economic-regulation, or affirmative-action cases where the conservatives favor judicial activism.

The law provides only a wide and conflicting range of what I have called *stylized rationalizations,*[7] most of which correspond to nonlegal—civilian—justifications but are expressed in the style of legal discourse and have legitimacy in legal culture. For example, there is a commonly understood notion that consistency is a positive value; we should try to treat similar problems and situations similarly. In the legal world, this idea has a Latin name (*stare decisis*) and is discussed in terms of whether an earlier decision is "controlling" or "binding" and what "distinctions" can be conceived. The legal version adds rigidity, an exaggerated sense of rigor, and a false sense of outcomes required by skilled analysis and independent of anyone's values or choices. But it has the very same flexibility and ultimate dependence on judgments about how similar the two situations are, whether the earlier one was resolved well or should be rethought, and whether some other concern is in the circumstances more important than consistency.

Judges are free to pick and choose from among these stylized rationalizations in any particular case, and those choices are not neutral or objective but incorporate and depend on value or political judgments. Some rationalizations may raise eyebrows in the legal world and may be rejected by many legal scholars, jurists, and lawyers. Justice Douglas was pushing the limits acceptable to his contemporaries with his "penumbras and emanations" theory in *Griswold v. Connecticut* (chapter 6). This was probably most upsetting because it tended to expose the myth of legal determinacy. I like Douglas's opinions because they were unusually honest and tended to address underlying problems with unusual insight—

and I usually agreed with his rules and results. This potential limit on stylized rationalizations constitutes in some sense a limit on judicial discretion. However, the line between acceptable and illegitimate stylized rationalizations is not clear or fixed, leaving considerable leeway; and the available stylized rationalizations that are clearly acceptable and legitimate in legal discourse and legal culture are more than ample for reaching most any result.

The liberal justices generally provided more analysis of the social and constitutional consequences and significance of the rules and results that they reached than the conservatives now do. But their decisions and methods were as selective, inconsistent, and rooted in the false notion of legally required rules and results as the conservatives'. The legal system's emphasis on principles, ideals, and consistency and the tradition of offering at least some explanation for the results of decisions affects some outcomes and is preferable to naked or wholly unaccountable force.[8] But we do not and cannot have a "government of laws, not people," as our politicians regularly proclaim. Law is driven and determined by *people* rather than disinterested or neutral logic, reasoning, or methodology; and particularly in our system, the rule of law amounts to rule by lawyers.

Neither conservative nor liberal rules and results are legally required; the only achievable objectivity and neutrality about law requires the basic recognition that the decisions one agrees with, as well as those one opposes, are not legally required. In this sense, what the conservatives are doing now that they dominate the Court, and what the liberals did when they dominated, *is the legal system and the rule of law*.

The alternative to rule by lawyers, or to the myth that law rather than people determine legal rules and results, is not, as we so easily and fearfully assume, chaos or anarchy. Nor do I mean that we should give up the attempt to formulate and enforce principles and rules. It is simply a fact of reality and life that people have varying experience and values that affect how they perceive the world, including how they view and interpret principles and rules, and language generally. The contest or struggle over values goes on continuously; it is not over or decided because at some point there was a majority or consensus about a particular formulation of a principle or rule. The meaning of principles and rules, like the values themselves, is always potentially open for further challenge. Maintenance of a particular meaning requires continual struggle and continuous efforts to reaffirm understandings and values.

For example, in the public accommodations and voting-rights conflicts of the mid-1960s, my perception, and my memory of the events, focuses on people so long oppressed and mistreated who courageously used nonviolent methods to gain some measure of justice and dignity. There was joy on their faces that I will never forget (and, I am sure, pride on mine for being part of it). Justice Rehnquist, who viewed some of the same events, saw (according to his own contemporaneous statements quoted in chapter 1) African-Americans attaining rights that he did not believe they should have and white store owners denied the privileges of property ownership. Such differences are deep, and they are not resolved by society adopting public accommodations and voting-rights laws favoring my side. When people with Rehnquist's values and experiences gain a majority on the Supreme Court, no language in the civil rights acts has preserved the liberatory meaning or history of those events (see chapter 3). We can deplore the perversion of our progressive history of inclusion and equality, the reintroduction of inequality when the acts were meant to establish equality, and the strange meanings given words and history that seem clear. But the law does not *require* my or Rehnquist's interpretation, any more than it required a right to privacy in *Griswold* or integrated schools in *Brown v. Board of Education*.

Language can have meaning, and principles can mean just what they say, but that shared experience, particularly among large numbers of people, is not as frequent as we regularly assume it to be. If we draw realistically on our own experiences, the moments of principles and ideals deeply shared among large numbers of people—of meaningful connection with other people working, living, or acting together—are rare but among the best of our lives. (We like political candidates who can evoke that feeling and often underestimate its power as a manipulative tactic.) For me, there is the hot August day in 1963 when I marched on Washington with hundreds of thousands "for jobs and freedom" and heard (barely, from where I stood) the immortal words of Martin Luther King, Jr. We knew what that speech, and our presence that day, meant, although there were differences among us (and doubts within many of us). For a young, naive college student like me, headed at the time for a career in engineering, the truth of that day was something I thought almost every American would quickly see and embrace. But politics, and life, do not work that way. It would (with time) change the course of my life, but language was of little use in preserving and furthering the meaning that we shared. Look at what happened to one of Dr. King's most memorable passages that day.

Dr. King said: "I have a dream that my four little children will one day live in a nation where they will not be judged by the color of their skin, but the content of their character." This was both a criticism of the racism that had devastated the potential and hopes of African-Americans and an inspiring vision of a future in which race and color do not affect anyone's opportunities. Take it out of context and apply it immediately—before there has been a process that includes eliminating discrimination, making some fair measure of amends for the past, dealing with widespread racial biases, and equalizing opportunities—and it becomes a principle that forbids that very process. Instead of a clarion call for rectification of the sins of the past and restoration of a shared sense of integrity and fair play, the "color blindness" principle became a rallying cry for a return to the past. To some (including me) "color blindness" in context was a criticism of white racism and a vision or goal for the future; but to others it was an immediate imperative—irrespective of injustices of the past or a corrective process that requires time, effort, and resources—that forbids any meaningful corrective measures.[9]

We live in a diverse society with a great range of differing backgrounds, experiences, perceptions, and values. Some believe that we have already done enough and the time for color blindness has come, or they believe that the way to stop racism is to treat all distinctions based on race as equally bad; others find their own situations so precarious that it is difficult to worry about the sins of the past, particularly when they have not themselves discriminated, or feel no need to address the troubles and alienation of others when no one is addressing theirs; still others cynically manipulate the language as a conscious tactic to impede interracial harmony. As much as I feel—and know—the importance of seeing color blindness as I view it, the phrase itself *does not define or require a particular meaning*, and it can be embraced by opposing sides without resolving or ending the political struggle. Nor does it help to say (or yell) "You had to have been there."

In our law-oriented society, the debate about the meaning of principles and rules and the contest over values is engaged in principally by lawyers (in legislatures as well as courts). However, lawyers are trained, first and foremost, to distill and manipulate language and to generate and develop arguments and evidence; little or no attention is paid in their education or in their extremely competitive profession to values or the uses to which these skills will be devoted. The "adversarial" system of adjudication has its benefits, but more importantly here, the skills, training, and moral orientation of lawyers—particularly the generally accepted notion among lawyers that they will sell their skills to whoever can pay for them, regardless of the goals or consequences—do not render them particularly suited as arbiters or decision- or policymakers for the whole of society. If we were going to consciously replace democracy with governance by a trained elite core of decision- and policymakers, I do not see a good reason why we would select lawyers or educate such an elite core in language manipulation and legal advocacy rather than in history, philosophy, and archeology, to name but a few of the available aternatives.

FREEDOM, EQUALITY, AND DEMOCRACY

This brings me to the two basic questions about civil rights and civil liberties that were highlighted in chapter 1: What is the best approach and vision, and how should it be implemented and maintained?

Formulating an approach and vision—and a set of principles or rules—that protect fundamental individual liberty but do not sweep too broadly is particularly difficult in a society and culture that celebrates freedom almost as a limitless religious or life force. There are certainly historical roots for this kind of abstracted glorification and the resulting confusion when one has to deal with reality; if our nation was conceived in freedom, it was freedom with slavery. We tend to discuss freedom without any concrete understanding that we are all here together, and that what one or some of us does can very easily affect others. But if asked specifically and concretely, we all support limits on individual freedom, whether it is the freedom of others to walk down the street nude, to shout "fire" (or shout at all) in a theater, or to pursue personal financial gain in a way that pollutes the air that we breathe or the water that we drink.

Many conservatives, who tend to proclaim faith to the cause of freedom the loudest and most often, seem to limit it to doing and saying things the "right" way, which of course is not freedom at all. Their conception of privacy, for example, is limited to "family, marriage or procreation" (*Hardwick*). This is where the celebration of freedom seems most hollow; there is no freedom in conformity to limits or to rigid formulations of moral correctness determined by others. With this approach, liberty and conformity become indistinguishable.

In our society, as pointed out in the introduction, conservatives tend to reject limits on freedom in economic matters (which I called "entrepreneurial" freedom) and to favor limits on freedom in matters of expression, religion, sexuality, life-style and culture (which I called "personal" freedom). For liberals, the tendencies flip-flop: favoring extensive personal freedom but limits on entrepreneurial freedom. Neither formulates their celebration of freedom this way, however; both tend simply and generally to say that they favor freedom, and to condemn each other for simply and generally opposing freedom. And both tend to encrust and exaggerate their visions of freedom: for example, the liberals with myths about free speech that ignore its limits and often place it above all other social and individual needs; and the conservatives with myths about free enterprise that glorify deregulation (as we fall behind more highly regulated—and taxed—economies) and that ignore big business's penchant for big government and the regular abuses connected to large, unregulated accumulations of wealth.

The central focus for all civil-rights and civil-liberties issues is the tension between individual freedom and collective needs and priorities. The basic inquiry is whether in particular areas or instances we wish to permit government to dictate to the individual. Each area and particular situation boils down to a determination of whether individual autonomy will take precedence over or be subjugated to collective will. For example, if some people wish to burn a flag as a protest, others object, and the duly constituted police authorities prohibit it, there is a conflict between individual freedom and collective authority. Saying that we are for free speech does not resolve this issue unless we decide that all expressive conduct is within a zone of individual autonomy that is, in any and all circumstances, impermeable to collective infringement. Even this would not settle the matter, because we would still have to decide how to define expressive conduct. Basically, we have to determine, in the form of principles or rules or on a case-by-case basis, whether such activity is within an area in which autonomy is appropriate and desirable and, if so, whether individual autonomy or collective will takes precedence.

One can go about this in a variety of ways, including formulation of general principles or very specific rules, or on an ad hoc basis. For example, one can attempt to classify, define, and rank the importance of various areas of desired autonomy (e.g., religion, privacy, bearing arms) and various collective interests (e.g., avoiding violence, sanitation, pleasing everyone); to eliminate some autonomy areas or interests (e.g., waste disposal on public streets) and collective interests (e.g., "listener's veto," pleasing everyone) deemed illegitimate or less worthy; and to mesh it all in a series of principles or rules. But notice how quickly freedom gets complicated, because once we reject absolutes (as we must, and which also turn out to be complicated), we have to face a series of complex compromise judgments. And the more complicated it gets, the less clarity or likelihood that there will be enforceable autonomy in even the most important matters.

The *Barnette* approach and the liberal strict-scrutiny standard offer a general scheme that, for some periods at least, succeeded in implementing probably the most protective system of personal freedom in the history of the world. It embodies a strong presumption of individual autonomy by generally defining the very limited circumstances in which collective interests are given precedence over individual autonomy in selected areas. In the selected areas of autonomy, the government can infringe on or burden individual autonomy only if it is directly, concretely, and specifically necessary to implement a "compelling" interest and if there is no "less restrictive" means. The vision is of a government that cannot interfere with its people in these areas unless their conduct is directly, concretely, and imminently harming others or undercutting the most important of government functions or interests. We cannot require the interpretation or meaning that this or any other formulation will be given, but as a principle or vision, I do not think we can do better than this.

Once we arrive at this or some other favored vision, approach, and principles of civil rights and civil liberties, there is still the difficult question of how to implement, enforce, and maintain them. In chapter 1, I raised four possibilities: direct popular action, the legislative or executive branches of the federal government, state governments, or the courts.

It is important not to limit our imaginations based on our experiences with or assumptions about current political and economic arrangements or based on the difficulty of accomplishing major changes. For example, although we tend to assume that protection of freedom, equality, and democracy has been provided by courts or not at all, in modern times Congress has been as or often more protective than the Supreme Court. Many of the most important advances even in the 1960s and 1970s were embodied in acts of Congress—including equality in public accommodations, voting, employment, and housing; protection of a range of privacy interests, covering personal finances, telephone and other electronic communications, and work-related polygraph tests; and access to the media and government information.[10] The only areas in which the protection has been almost exclusively judicial are free speech, religion, and due process, which were not taken up by Congress in large part because they were thought to be up to the courts alone and the courts were performing a protective function in those areas. The series of constitutional amendments subsequent to the Bill of Rights that included everyone eighteen years and over in the political process were also accomplished by legislative rather than judicial means.

The least-fruitful alternative is the executive branch. Historically, the most dreaded form and vehicle of denial of personal freedom has been the tyranny of despotic leaders. It should be no surprise that our worst denial of personal freedom in modern times—the imprisonment of people of Japanese ancestry in World War II—was conceived and implemented in the executive branch (and subsequently approved by the president, Congress, and the institution then and currently thought to be the major guardian of our basic rights, the Supreme Court).

The courts are more removed from everyday politics than legislatures and chief executives. This can serve the purpose of calmer reflection and perception of the need to protect in spite of the passions of the day. Judges also have a tradition of publicly explaining their decisions. But the outcomes still depend on the values, experiences, and self-perceived roles of the people who wear the robes—and the results are haphazard and unreliable. We must remember that the judicial victories for freedom, equality, and justice in the 1960s and 1970s were an aberration, a departure from usual judicial practice. Some state courts are now performing the same function, but this is sporadic and localized. The distance from the political process and the longevity of judicial appointments can as easily frustrate as serve personal freedom, a prospect we now face with the Supreme Court for at least another decade. Legislatures have been at least as protective in contemporary times, and judicially adopted protective rules and results are accurately seen as less democratic.

The best vehicle for implementing and maintaining civil-rights and civil-liberties protections—or for accomplishing anything else in a democracy—is the people, either directly or through broadly participatory or representative institutions. Certainly, the people should decide on the appropriate vehicle (as well as the vision and approach), and such basic changes are impossible to envision unless the impetus comes from the people. But we must be realistic about whether the people can themselves—through votes, referenda, or other direct methods—be that vehicle.

In societies with democratic ideals, there is commonly a tension (or contradiction) between direct participatory democracy and representative democracy. The framers of the Constitution and the evolution of our system have tended very much toward the representative model, which has been rendered considerably less representative and less democratic by the unusual structure of our electoral and political system and the related two-party dominance throughout almost our entire history. Conservatives (and usually liberals) have traditionally opposed and feared enhanced democracy, whether direct or representative. The recent conservative version of this is their push for greatly increased presidential and executive-branch power, including unprecedented power for the dreaded bureaucrats. (It remains to be seen whether this position will outlive the 1992 election and their loss of control over the executive branch.) However, there are good reasons—not based on condescension, hostility, or fear directed at the people—for limiting direct democracy, particularly in the extraordinary forms in which it could soon be implemented.

Although education and a reawakened understanding and sense of pride in these protections must be encouraged if there is to be meaningful change, we cannot realistically expect constant popular vigilance or activism on this or any other issue. We need institutional arrangements that, although they will not be perfect, are most likely to provide long-term, reliable protection of personal autonomy. Moreover, the worst crises of freedom, justice, and equality have come when an aroused populace—fed by demagogues, who come in a range of political stripes—has sought retribution or solace regarding perceived problems or grievances by oppression of dissenters, minorities, or people who are just different. These are the very times when the protections of civil rights and civil liberties are most needed and will depend on an understanding that every person should have basic rights and protections regardless of a majority's antagonism to them, their lifestyles, or their beliefs.

This understanding has not characterized human history, and seems only to have touched our own history episodically. But we do have an extraordinary—probably unique—tradition of it, most of which came only with sustained popular support and struggle by people at all levels of society for freedom, justice, and equality, and with considerable sacrifice: the Civil War amendments, which finally adopted the promise of the Declaration of Independence; the free-speech rights that emerged from the political struggles of the 1930s, never before the law of any land; the understanding in 1943 that we are more free and a better nation if the Barnett sisters could go to school without having to salute the flag; *Brown v. Board of Education* and the Supreme Court's civil rights and civil liberties decisions of the 1960s, responding to a prophet's dream and mass movements for racial and sexual equality that again changed the nation; and the national legislation over the last thirty years that recognized and enforced the rights of an array of previously oppressed, scorned, or "outcast" people, including most recently the broadest protection and opportunity for full participation in society that any nation has ever accorded to disabled people.[11]

This tradition needs reinvigoration and new popular and institutional support, but it—and any hope for meaningful democracy—are endangered by the prospect of new vehicles for what will likely be deceptively billed as direct democracy: instant polling or voting with televised "town meetings" or "two-way" television devices that will soon be widespread. No meaningful dialogue or deliberation is possible by these means, and exclusion of the true range of people and beliefs and approaches is likely no matter how sophisticated the sampling techniques. This is an extension of the lack of content and context that now characterize our political and electoral process, rather than any improvement.

In a nation of our size and diversity, meaningful democracy on the national level lies in enhanced representative democracy along the lines suggested in chapter 3. The best possibility for civil rights and civil liberties—and for democracy generally—lies in a restructuring of our institutions so that the people directly participate, to the extent possible, in the decisions that affect their lives; there is meaningful political dialogue and a range of political choices; representatives in government are closely connected to their constituents (but mindful of their duties to the larger community) and have ongoing mandates, authority, and power; and government is enabled to function rather than left to suffer from "gridlock" arising from conflicts among the three branches. This requires basic alterations of our governmental and economic institutions and arrangements.

Looking realistically at the current political environment, we may have to decide most basically, and before too long, whether we really want a government at all. Antigovernment and extreme individualistic traditions run deep in American history and culture. We seem to assume that government will fail and be oppressive and that private enterprise will succeed and be liberatory regardless of substantial, repeated evidence and experience to the contrary. (Neither is working very well for us right now, but how many industries—like the savings-and-loan banks, airlines, and cable television—do we have to deregulate before we remember why they were regulated?) We celebrate government structures like checks and balances, which in their current forms and context produce gridlock and an inability to function rather than protection from oppression, and an electoral system that makes serious change or real voter choice near impossible. The changes discussed here assume a willingness to reinvigorate democracy and enable government to function that, I must concede, may not be shared by most Americans.

I briefly addressed the parliamentary or proportional-representation systems common in Western Europe, where the legislatures play a primary role and the courts are restrained. This structure promotes diversity of opinion and choice for voters in the electoral arena and produces a legislature that then forms coalitions and elects a chief executive. The chief executive serves only as long as he or she maintains a majority in the legislature, so there is no gridlock; voters have a choice and do not have to worry about "wasted" votes for parties and candidates that they believe in; and change is possible when it is needed, rather than only after long and arbitrarily chosen intervals.

This can result in a different kind of "gridlock," such as in Israel where no party or coalition has been able for some time to sustain a clear majority. However, that gridlock reflects the reality that Israeli society is politically split approximately in half; it is the reality of democratic government there that a majority is hard to come by, and so the political direction of government is not clear. Our gridlock results from a distortion or suppression of democracy: Our people do not have meaningful choices, a coalition based on popular choices cannot be formed, the leaders in power often cannot function, and more power is wielded by well-funded lobbyists than the people or their representatives.

Further, we must eliminate the barriers to voting, eliminate or greatly reduce the role of money in elections and politics, and require the media that now constitute our marketplace of information and ideas to include diverse and unedited information, opinions, and approaches. We are the only major democracy that requires voters to register and regularly strikes them off lists of eligible voters if they haven't voted recently. Most everywhere else, if you are a citizen and you show up on election day, you vote.

(These countries maintain lists of their citizens and assign each newborn or naturalized citizen a number, and they keep these lists updated by deleting names of people who have died. This rather basic governmental function has been widely opposed in the United States, but for some time Social Security numbers and lists have performed the same function.) The other major democracies regularly have voter turnouts in the range of 70 to 90 percent of eligible voters, whereas ours are about 50 percent. The turnout of 55 percent of the eligible voters in the 1992 presidential election was widely considered something of a record.[12]

Electoral campaigns should be financed exclusively with limited public funds in combination with free, unedited media time, both available in equal amounts to all candidates who can demonstrate some significant popular support. This would eliminate PACs, donations by "special interests," and all private funding of electoral campaigns. It is not uncommon for politicians to condemn the influence of special interests and to propose electoral reforms, such as term limits. This taps into a widely shared dissatisfaction with the electoral process, but reforms like term limits miss the mark. A good representative favored by his or her constituents should not be arbitrarily ineligible after gaining important experience on the job. The connection between politics and money should be severed; candidates should stand or fall based on their ideas, their character, and other attributes that the people deem important. (A revitalized legislature of this kind could also legitimately implement more participatory and collectively beneficial policies regarding research, development, investment, taxation, housing, nutrition, health care, and education, which have characterized the economies that now successfully challenge our own.)

These changes do not automatically guarantee protection of civil rights and civil liberties or any other substantive outcomes. But no structural arrangement—and no constitutional language—

will ever accomplish that, and the current one fails whenever the Court is dominated by conservatives (which has been most of the time). Some of the civil rights and liberties protected by courts in the past would, no doubt, be difficult to implement through Congress. Protection of unpopular speech, such as flag burning, and a woman's right to choice in abortion are examples of this difficulty. However, *lasting* protection in such areas has been difficult to maintain when they are imposed by courts. The opposition to these rights continues and is bolstered by the antidemocratic fashion in which they were adopted.

The best we can do—and the principled alternative—is to reinvigorate democracy with a more representative and democratic structure and the clear message that personal freedom is the work of these representatives and all of us, not the exclusive or even primary terrain of courts and lawyers. The bursting of the illusion of courts as nonpolitical, neutral enforcers of personal freedom—or nonpolitical, neutral enforcers of anything else—presents us an opportunity to reinvigorate democracy and reconceive personal freedom as a matter at the heart of democracy and government by the people.

The federal judiciary and executive branch, and state governments at all levels (as to issues within their purview), should take up this task when Congress fails to do so or itself infringes on personal freedom. *Korematsu* is a good example of such a situation: The military imprisoned a race of Americans, with the assistance of the president and Congress. An oppressive majority was punishing a minority, with Congress either joining in or deferring to the courts. Judicial intervention in the tradition of Justice Jackson's *Barnette* opinion was necessary and appropriate. But maintenance and strengthening of freedom, equality, and democracy should be primarily placed on the most democratic branch, the legislature, should not be deferred to courts or lawyers, and should be understood as a necessity of democratic government.

These proposals would likely be opposed by both of our current parties. The Democrats as well as the Republicans have opposed, for example, elimination of registration. There is a comfortable elite that would prefer to continue the system that focuses on gimmicks, personal attacks, and thirty-second spots and fears a system that is open to all and not driven by money. They prefer the current obsession with a narrow band of "middle-of-the-road" voters who now supposedly determine elections and with strategies that attempt to please the most people while displeasing the least people. After 200 years—and with democracy fueling revolts around the world—American democracy must mean more than voting every four years in elections that are devoid of content and context and the right to picket when you're really upset.

This is where the real difference between conservatives and a genuinely progressive approach lies. Rehnquist, Scalia, and Bork, and Reagan, Bush, and Buchanan, will rail against the liberal decisions and judges as antidemocratic and proclaim dedication to empowerment of the people, but their judicial restraint is not Frankfurter's and their democracy is not Jefferson's, Paine's, or Lincoln's. Frankfurter saw strength and hope for the future in diversity and protection of personal freedom, but he did not believe that this should be implemented by courts. To Jefferson, Paine, and Lincoln, the people were a source of faith and hope, not fear. For the conservatives of our day, appeals to judicial restraint, democracy, and empowerment are just tactics. They have consistently opposed personal freedom, equality, and democracy, whenever and however implemented.

A vision is, of course, a goal and a hope, and we must deal with the current realities while we seek broader changes. While courts still play such a prominent role in society, the value contest in the courts should not be ignored or diluted by progressives deferring to a vision of a more democratic system yet to be realized. Protection of personal freedom and diversity should be vigorously advocated before the federal and state courts. There are lawyers throughout the country who have made this their occupation in a variety of ways, and this tradition should be supported and reinvigorated by new generations of lawyers. But courts should not be the only terrain for this struggle; the Supreme Court does not own the Constitution. Even with our current system, in modern times Congress has played at least as protective a role as the courts, and that role should be encouraged and expanded. Congress can enact rules, standards of review, and approaches on the whole range of civil rights and civil-liberties issues. This will take—as progress has always required—an informed and mobilized populace.

❦ APPENDIX ❦

THE BILL OF RIGHTS

Amendment I

Congress shall make no law respecting an establishment of religion, or prohibiting the free exercise thereof; or abridging the freedom of speech, or of the press; or the right of the people peaceably to assemble, and to petition the Government for a redress of grievances.

Amendment II

A well regulated Militia, being necessary to the security of a free State, the right of the people to keep and bear Arms, shall not be infringed.

Amendment III

No Soldier shall, in time of peace be Quartered in any house, without the consent of the Owner, nor in time of war, but in a manner to be prescribed by law.

Amendment IV

The right of the people to be secure in their persons, houses, papers, and effects, against unreasonable searches and seizures, shall not be violated, and no Warrants shall issue, but upon probable cause, supported by Oath or affirmation and particularly describing the place to be searched, and the persons or things to be seized.

Amendment V

No person shall be held to answer for a capital, or otherwise infamous crime, unless on a presentment or indictment of a Grand Jury, except in cases arising in the land or naval forces, or in the Militia, when in actual service in time of War or public danger; nor shall any person be subject for the same offence to be twice put in jeopardy of life or limb; nor shall be compelled in any criminal case to be a witness against himself, nor be deprived of life, liberty, or property, without due process of law; nor shall private property be taken for public use, without just compensation.

Amendment VI

In all criminal prosecutions, the accused shall enjoy the right to a speedy and public trial, by an impartial jury of the State and district wherein the crime shall have been committed, which district shall have been previously ascertained by law, and to be informed of the nature and cause of the accusation; to be confronted with the witnesses against him; to have compulsory process for obtaining witnesses in his favor, and to have the Assistance of Counsel for his defence.

Amendment VII

In Suits at common law, where the value in controversy shall exceed twenty dollars, the right of trial by jury shall be preserved, and no fact tried by jury, shall be otherwise re-examined in any Court of the United States, than according to the rules of the common law.

Amendment VIII

Excessive bail shall not be required, nor excessive fines imposed, nor cruel and unusual punishments inflicted.

Amendment IX

The enumeration in the Constitution, of certain rights, shall not be construed to deny or disparage others retained by the people.

Amendment X

The powers not delegated to the United States by the Constitution, nor prohibited by it to the States, are reserved to the States respectively, or to the people.

❦ NOTES ❦

Legal citations are presented here in the accepted legal form, except that some usual abbreviations are written out for the nonlegally trained reader. Supreme Court opinions are available at any law library. The abbreviated symbol designates the collection of volumes ("U.S." is for United States Reports and "S.Ct." for Supreme Court Reporter); the number preceeding the symbol specifies the volume in which the case is found, and the number succeeding is the page number on which the case begins.

Introduction

1. See generally Charles Fried, *Order and Law; Arguing the Reagan Revolution—A Firsthand Account* (New York: Simon & Schuster, 1991); Edwin Meese III, *With Reagan* (Washington: Regnery Gateway, 1992); Robert Bork, *The Tempting of America* (New York: Free Press, 1990). Much of the introduction is drawn from my reviews of Fried's book, *Conservative Legal Thought Revisited*, 91 COLUMBIA L. REV. 1847 (1991) and "Of Politics and Conservative Legal Thought," *Philadelphia Inquirer*, 26 April 1991, p. 2G.

2. Meese, 318

3. Fried, 17, 57, 61.

4. See Fried, 135–36, 183–86; Lucas v. South Carolina Coastal Council, 112 S.Ct. 2886 (1992).

5. Fried, 118–19.

6. See, e.g., Robert L. Stern, *The Commerce Clause and the National Economy, 1933–46*, 59 HARVARD L. REV. 645, 659–72 (1946).

7. See Catherine Drinker Bowen, *Miracle at Philadelphia* (Boston: Little, Brown and Co., 1966), particularly chap. 6; *The Federalist Papers* (New York: Mentor, 1961), no. 10.

8. See Stephen L. Schecter, "Amending the United States Constitution: A New Generation on

Trial," in *Redesigning the State: The Politics of Constitutional Change,* ed. Keith G. Banting and Richard Simeon (Toronto: University of Toronto Press, 1985); Clement E. Vose, *Constitutional Change: Amendment, Politics and Supreme Court Litigation Since 1900* (Lexington, Mass.: Lexington Books, 1972).

9. Fried, 67; William Rehnquist, *Grand Inquests* (New York: William Morrow and Co., 1993), 9. On the recent rise of the executive and decline of democracy and the effects on ordinary Americans, see Donald Bartlett and James Steele, *America: What Went Wrong?* (Kansas City: Andrews & McMeel, 1992); William Greider, *Who Will Tell the People?* (New York: Simon & Schuster, 1992).

10. See Heckler v. Chaney, 470 U.S. 821 (1985); Chevron v. Natural Resources Defense Council, 467 U.S. 837 (1984). See also Gade v. National Solid Waste Mngt. Assoc., 112 S.Ct. 2374 (1992) (expanding "preemption" doctrine to invalidate state environmental regulations). Agencies that have attempted to enforce antidiscrimination laws have not been so favored. See, e.g., General Electric Co. v. Gilbert (chap. 5).

11. See Francis Fox Piven and Richard A. Cloward, *Why Americans Don't Vote* (New York: Pantheon, 1988), 17–18. This is addressed further in chapter 3 and the conclusion, pages 207–8.

12. For a good account of that progression through the 1990–1991 term, see David Savage, *Turning Right, The Making of the Rehnquist Supreme Court* (New York: John B. Wiley & Sons, 1992).

13. See *The Thomas-Hill Sex Harassment Hearings, An Interview with David Kairys,* 1 TEMPLE POLITICAL & CIVIL RIGHTS L. REV. 107 (1992).

Chapter 1

1. On the Barnett family and the details not in the Court's opinions, see "Flag Salute Rule Voided," *Charleston Gazette,* 15 June 1942, p. 1A; "Civil Liberties Gain by the Flag Decision," *New York Times,* 21 June 1943, p. 10E; "West Virginia Bans Flag Salute as Too Much Like Hitler's," *Charleston Gazette,* 1 Feb. 1942, p. 1A; "Flap Over Pledge Was Traumatic Experience," *Charleston Gazette,* 12 Sept. 1988, p. 5B; "'With Liberty and Justice for All,'" *Charleston Gazette,* 14 June 1989, p. 1D; "George Bush's Pledge of Allegiance Problem," *U.S. News and World Report,* 12 Sept. 1988, p. 16. I appreciate the assistance of Linda Miller of the Kanawha County Public Library in locating and copying the early newspaper articles.

2. 319 U.S. 624 (1943). The Barnett family name is misspelled with an "e" at the end in the name of the case due to a mistake in court records that was not corrected.

3. Minersville Sch. Dist. v. Gobitis, 310 U.S. 586, 595 (1940).

4. "Justice Jackson Dead at 62 of Heart Attack in Capital," *New York Times*, 10 Oct. 1954, p. 1; Glendon Schubert, *Dispassionate Justice, A Synthesis of the Opinions of Robert H. Jackson* (New York: Bobbs-Merrill, 1969) (noting Jackson's ability to surprise, including his vote affirming anticommunist prosecutions in the 1950s which was criticized by liberals).

5. See Ernest Barker, *Reflections on Government* (New York: Oxford University Press, 1958); Alexis de Tocqueville, *Democracy in America* (New York: Mentor, 1956).

6. Marbury v. Madison, 5 U.S. 137 (1803).

7. See Thomas Jefferson, "Draft Constitution for Virginia," in *Thomas Jefferson: Writings,* ed. Merril D. Peterson (New York: The Library of America, 1984), 344; Letter of 16 September 1819 to Judge Spencer Roane, in *Jefferson: Writings,* 1425–28; and "Draft of the Kentucky Resolutions," in *Jefferson: Writings,* 449–56.

8. David Wyman, *The Abandonment of the Jews* (New York: Pantheon, 1984).

9. Background information not in the opinions came from "Legal Legend Urges Victims to Speak Out," *New York Times,* 24 Nov. 1984, p. 25A, and authorities in notes 12–15.

10. I was honored to represent AFSC on its amicus curiae brief in Korematsu's recent challenge to his conviction, see note 16.

11. 323 U.S. 214 (1944).

12. Quotes and references to DeWitt's "Final Report" are from *Personal Justice Denied,* Report of the Commission on Wartime Relocation and Internment of Civilians (Washington: Government Printing Office, 1982).

13. Id.

14. Id. at chap. 12.

15. Peter Irons, *Justice at War* (New York: Oxford University Press, 1983).

16. Reparations were provided by H.R. Rep. No. 442, 100th Cong., 1st Sess., §1 (1988), and the recent decision is Korematsu v. United States, 584 F. Supp. 1406 (N.D.Cal. 1984).

17. Brief of the United States, at 17, United States v. Salerno, 481 U.S. 739 (1987). See also Brief for Petitioners, at 31, Kissinger v. Halpern, 452 U.S. 713 (1981); Brief for the United States, at 17, New York Times Co. v. United States 403 U.S. 714 (1971) (citing a related case, Hirabayashi v. United States,

320 U.S. 81 [1943]). Solicitor General Fried, who submitted the government's *Salerno* brief, later called the *Korematsu* decision "deplorable" and "frankly racist." "Suit on Evacuation of Japanese-Americans Is Called Too Late," *New York Times,* 21 April 1987, p. 24A.

18. See Studs Terkel, *Race: The American Obsession* (New York: New Press, 1992).

19. See Dee Brown, *Bury My Heart at Wounded Knee* (New York: Holt, Rinehart & Winston, 1970).

20. See Paul L. Murphy, *World War I and the Origins of Civil Liberties in the United States* (New York: W.W. Norton, 1979).

21. On Rehnquist's early civil rights record, see David Savage, *Turning Right: The Making of the Rehnquist Supreme Court* (New York: John Wiley & Sons, 1992), chap. 2.

22. See, e.g., "Flag Decision Sets Off Scramble in Congress," *Los Angeles Times,* 12 June 1990, p. 25A; "First Amendment put to the test," *USA Today,* 28 Dec. 1990, p. 6A; "Most Americans favor some gay rights," *Chicago Tribune,* 6 Sept. 1992, p. 25C.

Chapter 2

1. This brief historical account is drawn from my longer essay published in 1982 and revised in 1990. Kairys, "Freedom of Speech," in *The Politics of Law,* ed. Kairys, rev. ed. (New York: Pantheon, 1990; first ed., 1982). The most helpful secondary sources on the pretransformation history are Leon Whipple, *The Story of Civil Liberty in the United States* (Westport, Conn.: Greenwood Press, 1927); Leon Whipple, *Our Ancient Liberties* (New York: Da Capo Press, 1927); Zechariah Chafee, Jr., *Free Speech in the United States* (Cambridge, Mass.: Harvard University Press, 1941); Norman Dorsen, Paul Bender, and Burt Neuborne, *Emerson, Haber and Dorsen's Political and Civil Rights in the United States* (Boston: Little, Brown, 1976), 1:20–51; Thomas Emerson, *The System of Freedom of Expression* (New York: Random House, 1970); John Roche, *The Quest for the Dream* (New York: Macmillan, 1963); Jerold Auerbach, *Labor and Liberty* (New York: Bobbs-Merrill, 1966); Jerold Auerbach, "The Depression Decade," in *The Pulse of Freedom,* ed. Alan Reitman (New York: W. W. Norton, 1975); Paul Murphy, *World War I and the Origin of Civil Liberties in the United States* (New York: W. W. Norton, 1979); David Rabban, *The First Amendment in Its Forgotten Years,* 90 YALE L. J. 514 (1981).

2. *Boston Globe,* 11 May 1987.

3. Commonwealth v. Davis, 162 Mass. 510, 511 (1895).

4. 167 U.S. 43 (1897).

5. See Dayton McKean, *The Boss* (Boston: Houghton Mifflin, 1940); Irving Bernstein, *The Turbulent Years* (Boston: Houghton Mifflin, 1970); Richard Connors, *A Cycle of Power* (Metuchen, N.J.: Scarecrow Press, 1971).

6. 307 U.S. 496 (1939).

7. Whitney v. California, 274, U.S. 357, 375–76 (1927) (concurring opinion).

8. See generally note 2; Zechariah Chafee, Jr., *How Human Rights Got into the Constitution* (Boston: Boston University Press, 1952); Leonard Levy, *Emergence of a Free Press* (New York: Oxford University Press, 1985); David M. Rabban, *The Ahistorical Historian: Leonard Levy on Freedom of Expression in Early American History*, 37 STANFORD L.REV. 795 (1985).

9. Whipple, *The Story of Civil Liberty*, 21, 25–27. This historical account on the Alien and Sedition Acts (Act of June 25, 1798, 1 Stat. 570; Act of July 14, 1798, 1 Stat. 596) is drawn from Kairys, "Freedom of Speech"; Whipple, *The Story of Civil Liberty*, 21–27; James Stephens, *Digest of the Criminal Law* (New York: Macmillan, 1904), 96–99; Frank Anderson, "The Enforcement of the Alien and Sedition Laws," in *Annual Report of the American Historical Association* (1912), 113–26; Chafee, *Free Speech*, 18, 27.

10. Whipple, *The Story of Civil Liberty*, 27.

11. See Kairys, "Freedom of Speech."

12. See, e.g., Barenblatt v. United States, 360 U.S. 109 (1959); Dennis v. United States, 341 U.S. 494 (1951); Lawson v. United States and Trumbo v. United States, 176 F.2d 49 (D.C. Cir. 1949), *cert. denied,* 339 U.S. 934 (1950) (the "Hollywood 10" case). Justice Jackson was not immune to the anticommunist scare. See particularly his concurring opinion in *Dennis*. The ACLU also succumbed, including its expulsion of well known labor activist Elizabeth Gurley Flynn from its board, but rescinded and repudiated its actions in 1976.

13. Murdock v. Penna., 319 U.S. 105, 111 (1943); Marsh v. Alabama, 326 U.S. 501 (1946); Amal. Food Employees Union Local 590 v. Logan Valley Plaza, 391 U.S. 308 (1968).

14. Central Hudson Gas v. Public Services Commission, 447 U.S. 557, 561 (1980).

15. See Texas v. Johnson, 491 U.S. 397 (1989); R.A.V. v. St. Paul (discussed in this chapter).

16. 112 S.Ct. 2701 (1992).

17. Hudgens v. NLRB, 424 U.S. 507 (1976), overruling *Logan Valley Plaza*, note 14.

18. Members of the City Council v. Taxpayers for Vincent, 466 U.S. 789 (1984); Heffron v. Intern. Soc. for Krishna Consciousness, 452 U.S. 640 (1981); Frisby v. Schultz, 487 U.S. 474 (1988); Greer v. Spock, 424 U.S. 828 (1976); Boos v. Barry, 485 U.S. 312 (1988); Cornelius v. NAACP Legal Def. and Educ. Fund, 473 U.S. 788 (1985); Perry Educ. Assn. v. Perry Local Educ. Assn., 460 U.S. 37 (1983); Hazelwood Sch. Dist. v. Kuhlmeier, 484 U.S. 260 (1988).

19. United States v. Kokinda, 497 U.S. 720 (1990) (O'Connor's opinion was for a plurality of four).

20. See Henderson v. Lujan, 964 F.2d 1179 (D.C. Cir. 1992) (rejecting the administration's claim, but suggesting that similar sidewalks near important attractions may be restricted).

21. 475 U.S. 41 (1986).

22. George Orwell, *1984* (New York: Harcourt Brace & Co., 1949).

23. 112 S.Ct. 2395 (1992).

24. Cox v. New Hampshire, 32 U.S. 569 (1941); Murdock v. Pennsylvania, 319 U.S. 105 (1943).

25. Webster v. Reproductive Health Services, 492 U.S. 490, 518 (1989); Planned Parenthood of Southeastern Penna. v. Casey, 112 S.Ct. 2791, 2861 (1992).

26. 478 U.S. 675 (1986). The phrase "teenage girl students" has an odd ring that may reflect Burger's uneasiness with the whole subject. See also "Man in the Off-Color Suit," *San Jose Mercury News,* 17 Nov. 1985, p. 1L (Fraser reflected: "High school kids have filthy minds. There may have been some other humor that I could have used, but joke for joke, this was funnier."); "Political Shift on 'Vulgar' Speech," *New York Times,* 15 July 1986, p. 1-C. After Fraser's name was removed from consideration for student speaker at graduation, he was elected to speak anyway by write-in votes, and, before the Supreme Court decision, he was allowed by the lower court to speak at graduation.

27. Tinker v. Des Moines Indep. Comm. Sch. Dist., 393 U.S. 503, 508 (1969). On offensiveness as an insufficient basis for limiting speech, see Cohen v. California, 403 U.S. 15 (1971).

28. Hazelwood Sch. Dist. v. Kuhlmeier, 484 U.S. 260 (1988).

29. 111 S.Ct. 1759 (1991).

30. Wooley v. Maynard, 430 U.S. 705 (1977); Elrod v. Burns, 427 U.S. 347 (1976); Perry v. Sinderman, 408 U.S. 593 (1972); Sherbert v. Verner, 374 U.S. 398 (1963); Speiser v. Randall, 357 U.S. 513 (1958).

31. See "Art Chief Vetoes 2 Approved Grants," *New York Times,* 13 May 1992, p. C13; "NEA Head Won't Explain Reasons She

Denied Grants," *Philadelphia Inquirer*, 1 Aug. 1992, p. C1.

32. 112 S.Ct. 2538 (1992).

33. 315 U.S. 568, 572 (1942).

34. E.g., Houston v. Hill, 482 U.S. 451 (1987); Lewis v. City of New Orleans, 415 U.S. 30 (1974); Cohen v. California, 403 U.S. 15 (1971).

35. See Mari Matsuda, *Public Response to Racist Speech: Considering the Victim's Story*, 87 MICH. L. REV. 2320 (1989).

36. See Emerson, *The System of Freedom of Expression*.

Chapter 3

1. For an accessible account of the constitutional convention, see Catherine Drinker Bowen, *Miracle at Philadelphia* (Boston: Little, Brown, 1986). See also *The Federalist Papers* (New York: Mentor, 1961), nos. 10, 39, 40, 48, 52. The Declaration of Independence is often dismissed as merely rhetorical, but recent writings suggest that the framers of the Constitution excluded its egalitarian language because of slavery and that the framers of the Fourteenth Amendment viewed that amendment as finally incorporating the Declaration into the Constitution. See Robert Reinstein, *Completing the Constitution*, to be published in 1993; Garry Wills, *Lincoln at Gettysburg* (New York: Simon & Schuster, 1992).

2. 112 S.Ct. 2059 (1992).

3. Congressional Quarterly, *Presidential Elections since 1787*, 5th ed. (Washington: Congressional Quarterly, 1991), 130; Bureau of the Census, *Statistical Abstract of the United States, 1991*, 11th ed. (Washington: Government Printing Office, 1991), 268.

4. See Bradley A. Smith, *Judicial Protection of Ballot-Access Rights: Third Parties Need Not Apply*, 28 HARVARD J. ON LEGISLATION 167 (1991). A useful newsletter on ballot-access problems is published by Richard Winger, *Ballot Access News*, P. O. Box 470296, San Francisco, CA 94147.

5. 424 U.S. 1 (1976) (per curiam).

6. United States v. O'Brien, 391 U.S. 367 (1968) (where the liberal majority also held that the ban on draft-card burning was "unrelated to the suppression of expression" even though it was enacted by an amendment aimed specifically at stopping draft-card burning as a vehicle of protest).

7. Federal Election Comm. v. National Conservative Political Action Comm., 470 U.S. 480, 494 (1985); First National Bk. of Boston v. Bellotti, 435 U.S. 765 (1978). See also Federal Election Comm. v. Massachusetts Citizens for Life, 479 U.S. 238 (1986); Citizens Against Rent

Control v. Berkeley, 454 U.S. 290 (1981).

8. See Philip M. Stern, *Still the Best Congress Money Can Buy* (New York: Regnery Gateway, 1992); Donald Bartlett and James Steele, *America: What Went Wrong?* (Kansas City: Andrews & McMeel, 1992); William Greider, *Who Will Tell the People?* (New York: Simon & Schuster, 1992)

9. 112 S.Ct. 820 (1992). Voting Rights Act of 1965, 42 U.S.C. §1973c (1965; reenacted in 1970, 1975, and 1982). Earlier cases include McCain v. Lybrand, 465 U.S. 236 (1984); Allen v. Bd. of Elections, 393 U.S. 544 (1969); Bunton v. Patterson, 393 U.S. 544 (1969). On the history of the struggle to establish equal rights, see Richard Kluger, *Simple Justice: The History of Brown v. Board of Education and Black America's Struggle for Equality* (New York: Knopf, 1976); Juan Williams, *Eyes on the Prize* (New York: Penguin, 1987) (book version of the Public Broadcasting System series, which provides an excellent introduction to civil rights).

10. See, e.g., Mobile v. Bolden, 446 U.S. 55 (1980).

11. IX Florida Statutes §104.38 (1913), citing J.V. Keen, *Brief History of the Corrupt Practice Acts of Florida,* 9 FLA. L. J. 297 (1935).

12. 418 U.S. 241 (1974).

13. Red Lion Broadcasting v. FCC, 395 U.S. 367 (1969); Gertz v. Robert Welch, 418 U.S. 323 (1974); CBS v. Democratic Natl. Comm., 412 U.S. 94 (1973). See also Pittsburgh Press Co. v. The Pittsburgh Commission on Human Relations, 413 U.S. 376 (1973) (approving a commission decision that prohibited the newspaper from listing ads for jobs separately by gender, because the purpose was to combat unlawful sex discrimination, the effect on press rights was "incidental," and the speech involved was mostly "commercial"); Associated Press v. United States, 326 U.S. 1 (1946) (press subject to antitrust laws).

14. Ben H. Bagdikian, *The Media Monopoly,* 3d. ed. (Boston: Beacon Press, 1990), 3–4.

15. *Id.* at chap. 9; Kenneth E. Warner, et al., *Cigarette Advertising and Magazine Coverage of the Hazards of Smoking,* 326 NEW ENGLAND J. OF MED. 305, 307–8 (1992); "Cigarette Maker Cuts off Agency that Made Smoking-Ban TV ads," *New York Times,* 6 April 1988, p. A1.

Chapter 4

1. For a range of current views and historical materials, see generally Leonard W. Levy, *The Establishment Clause: Religion and the*

First Amendment (New York: Macmillan, 1986); Robert L. Cord, *Separation of Church and State: Historical Fact and Current Fiction* (New York: Lambeth Press, 1982); Laurence Tribe, *American Constitutional Law,* 2d. ed., chap. 14 (New York: Foundation Press, 1988); Michael W. McConnell, *Free Exercise Revisionism and the Smith Decision,* 57 U. CHI. L. REV. 1109 (1990); William P. Marshall, *In Defense of Smith and Free Exercise Revisionism,* 58 U. CHI. L. REV. 308 (1991); Michael W. McConnell, *A Response to Professor Marshall,* 58 U. CHI. L. REV. 329 (1991). The main source relied on in this chapter is Levy.

2. Levy, *The Establishment Clause,* 61.

3. See Cantwell v. Connecticut, 310 U.S. 296 (1940). Incorporation is discussed in the introduction.

4. Sherbert v. Verner, 374 U.S. 398 (1963).

5. Wisconsin v. Yoder, 406 U.S. 205, 218 (1972).

6. Kwanzaa is an African-American holiday from December 26 to January 1 celebrating unity, creativity, and faith; Hanukkah is a Jewish celebration at the winter solstice of the victory of the Maccabeans in the second century B.C. and the rededication of the Temple of Jerusalem; Ramadan is the sacred ninth month of the Mohammedan year observed with fasting from dawn to dusk.

7. See Lyng v. Northwest Indian Cemetery Protective Ass'n., 485 U.S. 439 (1988) (approving government logging on land used for sacred religious purposes); O'Lone v. Estate of Shabazz, 482 U.S. 342 (1987) (denying claim of Muslim prison inmates that prison policies prevent them from attending their Friday religious services); Bowen v. Roy, 476 U.S. 693 (1986) (rejecting claim that use of Social Security numbers in program administration violated free-exercise rights of Native Americans who saw it as interfering with their spiritual well-being); Goldman v. Weinberger, 475 U.S. 503 (1986) (rejecting claim of Jewish serviceman to wear a religiously required skullcap based on Air Force regulations that required uniformity); United States v. Lee, 455 U.S. 252 (1982) (rejecting claim of religious objection to receiving public insurance benefits as basis for refusal to pay Social Security taxes). The Court continued to uphold exercise claims for unemployment compensation covered by Sherbert v. Verner. See Frazee v. Illinois Dept. of Empl. Sec., 489 U.S. 829 (1989); Hobbie v. Unemployment Appeals Comm'n., 480 U.S. 136 (1987); Thomas v. Review Bd., Ind. Empl. Sec. Div., 450 U.S 707 (1981).

8. The details on Smith's background, peyote, and the Native American Church, largely omitted from the Court's opinions (although some are in the *Smith* appendix), were widely reported in the media after the decision. See "Constitution Doesn't Protect Peyote Use," *Oregonian*, 18 April 1990, p. A1; "Peyote Use Won't End with Court Ruling," *Arizona Business Gazette*, 20 April 1990, p. 28; "Man Defends Peyote Use," *Oregonian*, 13 May 1991, p. B3; "Roberts Signs Peyote Bill," *Oregonian*, June 25, 1991, p. A10 (reporting on the enactment of an exception to the Oregon drug laws for religious use of peyote by American Indians); "Oregon's Peyote Reform a Hollow Victory, Indians Say," *Sacramento Bee*, 5 August 1991, p. A2; Peter Mc-Swain, "Religion, Peyote, Courts and Rights," *Oregonian*, 18 August 1991, p. B7. Substantial scholarly works have long confirmed the nature and role of peyote use in American Indian religions. See generally Omar Stewart, *Peyote Religion: A History* (Norman: University of Oklahoma Press, 1987); James Slotkin, *The Peyote Religion* (Glencoe, Ill.: Free Press, 1956); David Aberle, *Peyote Religion Among the Navaho*, 2d. ed. (Chicago: University of Chicago Press, 1982).

9. 494 U.S. 872 (1990).

10. Marshall, *In Defense of Smith*, 309.

11. See Antonin Scalia, *Originalism: The Lesser Evil*, 57 U. CIN. L. REV. 849 (1989).

12. McConnell, *Free Exercise Revisionism*, 1116–19.

13. See Minersville School District v. Gobitis, 310 U.S. 586 (1940), discussed in chapter 1.

14. Cantwell v. Connecticut, 310 U.S. 296 (1940); Everson v. Bd. of Educ., 330 U.S. 1 (1947); Letter of 1 January 1802 from President Thomas Jefferson to the Baptist Association of Danbury, Connecticut, *Thomas Jefferson: Writings*, 16: 281–82. On the history of the religion clauses and modern perspectives and cases, see generally Levy, *The Establishment Clause*; Tribe, *American Constitutional Law*.

15. In the 1960s, when the wall-of-separation doctrine was strongest, the Court upheld Sunday closing laws. See McGowan v. Md., 366 U.S. 420 (1961).

16. See Mark DeWolf Howe, *The Garden and The Wilderness, Religion and Government in American Constitutional History* (Chicago: University of Chicago Press, 1965).

17. There is a Jewish song with the first line and name "Rock of Ages," but this is not the same or a related song. My religious his-

torical source is Arthur Waskow, author of *Seasons of Our Joy* (New York: Summit, 1982) and other books.

18. See Engel v. Vitale, 370 U.S. 421 (1962); Abington Sch. Dist. v. Schempp, 374 U.S. 203 (1963).

19. Wallace v. Jaffree, 472 U.S. 38 (1985).

20. See McCollum v. Bd. of Educ., 333 U.S. 203, 227 (1948). See also Wallace v. Jaffree, 472 U.S. at 81 (O'Connor, concurring).

21. Marsh v. Chambers, 463 U.S. 783 (1983).

22. See Dames & Moore v. Regan, 453 U.S. 654, 659 (1981).

23. Levy, *The Establishment Clause,* 155

24. See James McClellan, "The Making and Unmaking of the Establishment Clause," in *A Blueprint for Judicial Reform,* ed. Patrick B. McGuigan and Randall R. Rader (Washington: Free Congress Research and Educational Foundation, 1981); Robert G. McCloskey, "Principles, Powers, and Values: the Establishment Clause and the Supreme Court," in *1964 Religion and the Public Order,* ed. Donald A. Giannella (Chicago: U.M.I., 1965); comments of former Attorney General Edwin Meese, "Meese Attacks Supreme Court Religion Rulings; Scores Reaffirmation of Government Neutrality," *Los Angeles Times,* 10 July 1985, p. 1.

25. Lee v. Weisman, 112 S.Ct. 2649 (1992).

26. 465 U.S. 668 (1984).

27. Allegheny County v. Greater Pittsburgh ACLU, 492 U.S. 573 (1989). A menorah is a candle holder that plays a major religious role in the celebration of the Jewish holiday Hanukkah.

28. See, e.g., Everson v. Bd. of Educ., 330 U.S. 1 (1947) (approving state provision of bus transportation to and from religious schools); Wolman v. Walter, 433 U.S. 229 (1977) (state provision to religious schools of secular books and diagnostic, therapeutic, and remedial services allowable, but field trips and instructional materials and equipment disapproved); Board of Educ. v. Allen, 392 U.S. 236 (1968) (state lending of secular textbooks approved); Meek v. Pittenger, 421 U.S. 349 (1975) (state lending of instructional material and equipment and supplying professional staff and supportive materials disapproved); see also Wallace v. Jaffree, 472 U.S. at 110–11 (Rehnquist, dissenting; collecting some of the contradictions).

29. 463 U.S. 388 (1983).

30. Committee for Public Education v. Nyquist, 413 U.S. 756 (1973).

31. Everson v. Bd. of Educ., 330 U.S. 1, 16 (1947). The "plausible secular purpose" rule seems

also inconsistent with the analysis of constitutional rights in early cases like Yick Wo v. Hopkins, 118 U.S. 356 (1886).

32. See Hernandez v. Commissioner 490 U.S. 680 (1989) (approved IRS denial of deductibility as a contribution of Scientologists' payments to their church for which they receive religious training and practice essential to that religion, although similar payments, such as Christian "pew rentals" for guaranteed seats at services, are regularly deductible); Davis v. United States, 495 U.S. 472 (1990) (approved IRS denial of deductibility for Mormon family payments to children as an integral part of the children's missionary work); Goldman v. Weinberger.

33. Walz v. Tax Commission, 397 U.S. 664 (1970).

34. Internal Revenue Code of 1986, 26 U.S.C. §§107, 265 (a)(6), 3121(b)(8) (1992); Treasury Regulations, 31 C.F.R. §1.107–1 (1992); IRS Revenue Ruling 87–32, 1987–1 Cumulative Bulletin 131 (1987).

35. See, e.g., Hazelwood School District v. Kuhlmeier, 484 U.S. 260 (1988); Greer v. Spock, 424 U.S. 828 (1976).

Chapter 5

1. See Derrick Bell, *Faces at the Bottom of the Well: The Per-manence of Racism* (New York: Basic Books, 1992).

2. Memphis v. Greene, 451 U.S. 100 (1981). Some of this chapter is drawn from my article "Prejudicial Restraint: Race and the Supreme Court," *Tikkun*, May–June 1992: 37.

3. Watson v. Memphis, 373 U.S. 526, 534 (1963).

4. McCleskey v. Kemp, 481 U.S. 279 (1987).

5. See Batson v. Kentucky, 476 U.S. 79 (1986); Duren v. Missouri, 439 U.S. 357 (1979); Hazelwood Sch. Dist. v. United States, 433 U.S. 299 (1977).

6. 488 U.S. 469 (1989).

7. Geduldig v. Aiello, 417 U.S. 484 (1974).

8. 429 U.S. 125 (1976).

9. 42 U.S.C. §2000e, et seq. (1988). For prior cases on the difference between Title VII and equal-protection claims, see Justice Brennan's dissent in *Gilbert*.

10. 42 U.S.C. §2000(e)(k) (1988); Kirchberg v. Feenstra, 450 U.S. 455 (1981) (invalidating Louisiana law describing men as "head and master" and giving them power unilaterally to dispose of jointly owned property); Gregory v. Ashcroft, 111 S.Ct.. 2395 (1991) (approving mandatory retirement age); Bowers v. Hardwick (chapter 6); N.J. Welfare Rights Org. v. Cahill, 411 U.S. 619 (1973); Cle-

burne v. Cleburne Living Center, 473 U.S. 432 (1985).

11. Washington v. Davis, 426 U.S. 229 (1976) (the earlier Burger decision is Griggs v. Duke Power Co., 401 U.S. 424 (1971)); Patterson v. McLean Credit Union, 491 U.S. 164 (1989), overruling Runyon v. McCrary, 427 U.S. 160 (1976); Ward's Cove Packing Co. v. Antonio, 490 U.S. 642 (1989); Lorance v. AT&T Technologies, Inc., 490 U.S. 900 (1989); Martin v. Wilks, 490 U.S. 755 (1989). See Civil Rights Act of 1991, P.L. 102–166, 105 Stat. 1071 (1992); Civil Rights Restoration Act of 1987, P.L. 100–259, 102 Stat. 28 (1988).

12. See David Cole, *Strategies of Difference: Litigating for Women's Rights in a Man's World,* 2 LAW & EQUALITY 33 (1984). These developments have led to a reassessment of long-accepted approaches to race issues best exemplified by a new approach called "critical race theory," which is the focus of a forthcoming collection from The New Press edited by Kimberlé Crenshaw, Neil Gotanda, and Kendall Thomas.

Chapter 6

1. See generally Milton R. Konvitz, *Privacy and the Law: A Philosophical Prelude,* 31 LAW AND CONTEMPORARY PROBLEMS 272

(1966); Laurence Tribe, *American Constitutional Law,* 2d. ed. (New York: Foundation Press, 1988), chap. 15; Richard Turkington, George Trubow, and Anita Allen, *Privacy, Cases and Materials* (Houston: John Marshall, 1992).

2. See Anthony G. Amsterdam, *Perspectives on the Fourth Amendment,* 58 MINN. L. REV. 349 (1974); Wayne R. LaFave, *Search and Seizure: Treatise on the Fourth Amendment* (St. Paul: West, 1978).

3. See generally Edward Shils, *Privacy: Its Constitution and Vicissitudes,* 31 LAW & CONTEMPORARY PROBLEMS 281 (1966); Don Pember, *Privacy and the Press* (Seattle: University of Washington Press, 1972).

4. Louis D. Brandeis and Samuel D. Warren, *The Right of Privacy,* 4 HARVARD L. REV. 193 (1890).

5. 381 U.S. 479 (1965).

6. See Tribe, *American Constitutional Law,* §15-3.

7. See note 23.

8. Loving v. Virginia, 388 U.S. 1 (1967); Stanley v. Georgia, 394 U.S. 557 (1969); Eisenstat v. Baird, 405 U.S. 438 (1972); Roe v. Wade, 410 U.S. 113 (1973).

9. See Peter Irons, *The Courage of Their Convictions* (New York: Free Press, 1988), chap. 16; Rhonda Copelon, "A Crime Not Fit to Be Named: Sex, Lies and the Constitution," in *The Politics of Law,* ed.

David Kairys, rev. ed. (New York: Pantheon, 1990), chap. 8.

10. 478 U.S. 186 (1986).

11. See Turkington, et al., *Privacy, Cases and Materials,* chap. 4.

12. United States v. Miller, 425 U.S. 435 (1976).

13. Katz v. United States, 389 U.S. 347 (1967).

14. United States v. White, 401 U.S. 745 (1971).

15. See Turkington, et al., *Privacy, Cases and Materials,* chap. 2, noting that some state legislatures have required the consent of both parties; Laird v. Tatum, 408 U.S. 1 (1972). On political surveillance, see generally Frank J. Donner, *The Age of Surveillance* (New York: Vintage, 1981).

16. 12 U.S.C. §3401 (1978).

17. 112 S.Ct. 2791 (1992). Some of the discussion of this case is drawn from my review of Charles Fried's book, *Order and Law* (New York: Simon & Schuster, 1991), in *Conservative Legal Thought Revisited,* 91 Columbia L. Rev. 1847 (1991). Fried's analysis of the abortion issue referred to herein is from *Order and Law,* 20, 33, 77–78, 217 n. 14.

18. Burns v. Fortson, 410 U.S. 686 (1973); Baldwin v. New York, 399 U.S. 66 (1970)(plurality opinion); County of Riverside v. McLaughlin, 111 S.Ct. 1661 (1991).

19. Brief of the United States as Amicus Curiae at 9–10, Blanton

v. City of North Las Vegas, 489 U.S. 538 (1989).

20. County of Riverside v. Mc Laughlin.

21. 492 U.S. 490 (1989).

22. Marbury v. Madison, 5 U.S. (1 Cranch) 137 (1803).

23. The internal quote is from Garcia v. San Antonio Metro. Transit Auth., 469 U.S. 528, 557 (1985), which overruled National League of Cities v. Usery, 426 U.S. 833 (1976), both discussed briefly in the introduction.

24. *The Collected Works of Lincoln,* ed. Roy P. Basler (New Brunswick, N.J.: Rutgers University Press, 1953–55), 2: 323.

25. See *id.*; Don E. Frehrenbacher, *Abraham Lincoln's Speeches and Writing, 1859–1865* (New York: Literary Classics, 1989), 168, 172–73; Charles B. Strozier, *Lincoln's Quest for Union* (New York: Basic Books, 1982).

26. United States v. Carolene Products Co., 304 U.S. 144, 152–53 n. 4 (1938).

Chapter 7

1. See "U.S. Jail Rate Still Tops World," *Philadelphia Inquirer,* 11 Feb. 1992, p. A3; "Racial Imbalance Seen in War on Drugs," *Philadelphia Inquirer,* 1 Nov. 1992, p. A1; "Cost of Justice System Is Put at $39.7 Billion in U.S. Study," *New York Times,* 14 July 1987, p. B7;

"Feeling Prisons' Costs, Governors Look at Alternatives," *New York Times,* 7 Aug. 1992, p. A17. See generally Elliot Currie, *Crime, Justice and the Social Environment,* in *The Politics of Law,* rev. ed. (New York: Pantheon, 1990), chap. 13; Elliot Currie, *Confronting Crime* (New York: Pantheon, 1985).

2. Wisconsin v. Constantineau, 400 U.S 433, 437 (1971); Jenkins v. McKeithen, 395 U.S. 411 (1969); Joint Anti-Fascist Refugee Comm. v. McGrath, 341 U.S. 123 (1951).

3. 424 U.S. 693 (1976).

4. 461 U.S. 95 (1983). The decisions limiting access started with the Burger Court. See generally Burt Neuborne, "Justiciability, Remedies, and the Burger Court," in *The Burger Years,* ed. Herman Schwartz (New York: Viking, 1987).

5. Gladstone, Realtors v. Bellwood, 441 U.S. 91 (1979); Rondeau v. Mosinee Paper Co., 422 U.S. 49 (1975) ("cognizable danger of recurrent violation" standard for injunction); Brown v. Chote, 411 U.S. 452 (1973) ("abuse of discretion" standard for reviewing district court issuance of injunction); Lankford v. Gelston, 364 F.2d 197 (4th Cir. 1966), cited with approval, Allee v. Medrano, 416 U.S. 802 (1974). See generally Justice Marshall's dissent in *Lyons.*

6. Anderson v. Creighton, 483 U.S. 635 (1987).

7. See Miranda v. Arizona, 384 U.S. 436 (1966) (establishing right of suspect in custody to an attorney during questioning).

8. 111 S.Ct. 1246 (1991).

9. Chapman v. California, 386 U.S. 18 (1967); succeeding cases are collected in Justice White's opinion in *Fulminante.*

10. 476 U.S. 207 (1986). Oliver v. United States, 466 U.S. 170 (1984); United States v. United States District Court, 407 U.S. 297 (1972).

11. 109 S.Ct. 333 (1988); Brady v. Maryland, 373 U.S. 83 (1963); United States v. Agurs, 427 U.S. 97 (1976).

12. United States v. Salerno, 481 U.S. 739 (1987); United States v. Alvarez-Machain, 112 S.Ct. 2188 (1992); McCleskey v. Zant, 111 S.Ct. 1454 (1991).

Conclusion

1. 60 U.S. 393 (1856); 163 U.S. 537 (1896). Portions of the conclusion are drawn from David Kairys, *Conservative Legal Thought Revisited,* 91 COLUMBIA L. REV. 1847 (1991).

2. See, e.g., Renton v. Playtime Theatres, Inc., 475 U.S. 41, 47–48 (1986); Barenblatt v. United States, 360 U.S. 109, 132–33 (1959).

3. Robert Bork, *The Tempting of America* (New York: Simon & Schuster, 1990), 123.

4. See introduction, pages 6–8 and note 10.

5. Charles Fried, *Order and Law, Arguing the Reagan Revolution—A Firsthand Account* (New York: Simon & Schuster, 1991), 17, 59–62, 151–54.

6. See generally David Kairys, ed., *The Politics of Law, A Progressive Critique,* rev. ed. (New York: Pantheon, 1990). This view is most closely associated with critical legal studies and legal realism. See Duncan Kennedy and Karl E. Klare, *A Bibliography of Critical Legal Studies,* 94 YALE L. J. 461 (1984); Richard Bauman, *Critical Legal Studies: A Selected Bibliography* (1992) (available from Professor Bauman at University of Alberta, Faculty of Law, 111th St. and 89th Ave., Edmonton, Alberta, Canada T6G 2H5).

7. David Kairys, Introduction, *The Politics of Law.*

8. See E. P. Thompson, *Whigs and Hunters, the Origin of the Black Act* (New York: Pantheon, 1975), 258–69.

9. Dr. King's "I Have a Dream" speech is reproduced in full in Juan Williams, *Eyes on the Prize* (New York: Penguin, 1987), 203–5.

10. See Civil Rights Acts of 1960, 1964, 1965, and 1968, 42 U.S.C. §§1971, 1973, 1975, 1995, 2000, 3601 (1988); Age Discrmination Act of 1975, 42 U.S.C. §6101, et seq. (1991); Americans with Disabilities Act, 42 U.S.C. §12101, et seq. (1991); electronic communications and surveillance provisions, 18 U.S.C. §§2510–21, 2701–11, 3121–27 (1991); Employee Polygraph Protection Act of 1988, 29 U.S.C. §§2001–9 (1991); Right to Financial Privacy Act of 1978, 12 U.S.C. §3401 (1992): Freedom of Information and Privacy Acts of 1967 and 1968, 5 U.S.C. §552 (1988).

11. Civil Rights Act of 1991, 102 P.L. 166, 1991 S. 1745, 105 Stat. 1071.

12. See Francis Fox Piven and Richard A. Cloward, *Why Americans Don't Vote* (New York: Pantheon, 1988), chap. 1 (other major democratic countries either maintain complete lists or government assumes the responsibility of finding and facilitating voting by all eligible people); "Record Number Voted; Analysts Debate Long-term Trend," *Philadelphia Inquirer,* 5 Nov. 1992, p. A11.

❦ TABLE OF CASES ❦

The major cases that are the subject of sections of the book are shown in **bold.**

Abington School District v. Schempp, 374 U.S. 203 (1963), 227n

Allee v. Mendrano, 416 U.S. 802 (1974), 231n

Allegheny County v. Greater Pittsburgh ACLU, 492 U.S. 573 (1989), 227n

Allen v. Bd. of Elections, 393 U.S. 544 (1969), 224n

Amal. Food Employees Union Local 590 v. Logan Valley Plaza, 391 U.S. 308 (1968), 221n

Anderson v. Creighton, 483 U.S. 635 (1987), 231n

Arizona v. Fulminante, 111 S.Ct. 1246 (1991), 174–75, 187

Arizona v. Youngblood, 109 S.Ct. 333 (1988), 177–79

Associated Press v. United States, 326 U.S. 1 (1946), 224n

Baldwin v. New York, 399 U.S. 66 (1970), 230n

Barenblatt v. United States, 360 U.S. 109 (1959), 221n, 231n

Barnette v. West Virginia Bd. of Educ., 319 U.S. 624 (1943), 13–21, 26, 29–34, 72, 102, 107, 109, 113, 152, 153, 201, 209

Batson v. Kentucky, 476 U.S. 79 (1986), 228n

Bethel School District v. Fraser, 478 U.S. 675 (1986), 68–71, 189

Board of Educ. v. Allen, 392 U.S. 236 (1968), 227n

Boos v. Barry, 485 U.S. 312 (1988), 222n

Bowers v. Hardwick, 478 U.S. 186 (1986), 153–55, 189, 199–200, 228n

Brady v. Maryland, 373 U.S. 83 (1963), 231n

Brown v. Bd. of Educ., 347 U.S. 483 (1954), 35, 145, 181, 196, 205

Brown v. Chote, 411 U.S. 452 (1973), 231n

Buckley v. Valeo, 424 U.S. 1 (1976), 87–88, 185, 188, 190

Bunton v. Patterson, 393 U.S. 544 (1969), 224n

Burdick v. Takushi, 112 S.Ct. 2059 (1992), 84–87, 188–89

Burns v. Fortson, 410 U.S. 686 (1973), 230n

California v. Ciraolo, 476 U.S. 207 (1986), 175–77, 188

Cantwell v. Connecticut, 310 U.S. 296 (1940), 225n, 226n

CBS v. Democratic Natl. Comm., 412 U.S. 94 (1973), 224n

Central Hudson Gas v. Public Services Commission, 447 U.S. 557 (1980), 221n

Chapman v. California, 386 U.S. 18 (1967), 231n

Chevron v. Natural Resourses Defense Council, 467 U.S. 837 (1984), 218n

Citizens Against Rent Control v. Berkeley, 454 U.S. 290 (1981), 223n

Cleburne v. Cleburne Living Center, 473 U.S. 432 (1985), 229n

Cohen v. California, 403 U.S. 15 (1971), 222n, 223n

Committee for Public Education v. Nyquist, 413 U.S. 756 (1973), 227n

Commonwealth v. Davis, 162 Mass. 510 (1895), 220n

Cornelius v. NAACP Legal Def. and Educ. Fund, 473 U.S. 788 (1985), 222n

County of Riverside v. McLaughlin, 111 S.Ct. 1661 (1991), 230n

Cox v. New Hampshire, 32 U.S. 569 (1941), 222n

Dames & Moore v. Regan, 453 U.S. 654 (1981), 227n

Davis v. Massachusetts, 167 U.S. 43 (1897), 42–46, 50, 61, 62, 67

Davis v. United States, 495 U.S. 472 (1990), 228n

Dennis v. United States, 341 U.S. 494 (1951), 221n

Dred Scott v. Sanford, 60 U.S. 393 (1857), 155, 165

Duren v. Missouri, 439 U.S. 357 (1979), 228n

Elrod v. Burns, 427 U.S. 347 (1976), 222n

Employment Division v. Smith, 494 U.S. 872 (1990), 104–106, 109–110, 188

Engel v. Vitale, 370 U.S. 421 (1962), 227n

Everson v. Bd. of Educ., 330 U.S. 1 (1947), 226n, 227n

Federal Election Comm. v. Massachusetts Citizens for Life, 479 U.S. 238 (1986), 223n

Federal Election Comm. v. National Conservative Political Action Comm., 470 U.S. 480 (1985), 89, 223n

First National Bank of Boston v. Bellotti, 435 U.S. 765 (1978), 89, 185, 223n

Forsyth County v. The Nationalist Movement, 112 S.Ct. 2395 (1992), 66,187

Frazee v. Illinois Dept. of Empl. Sec., 489 U.S. 829 (1989), 225n

Frisby v. Schultz, 487 U.S. 474 (1988), 222n

Gade v. National Solid Waste Mngt. Assoc., 112 S.Ct. 2374 (1992), 218n

Garcia v. San Antonio Metro. Transit Auth., 469 U.S. 528 (1985), 230n

General Electric Co. v. Gilbert, 429 U.S. 125 (1976), 141–45, 184, 188, 218n

Gertz v. Robert Welch, 418 U.S. 323 (1974), 224n

Gladstone, Realtors v. Bellwood, 441 U.S. 91 (1979), 231n

Greer v. Spock, 424 U.S. 828 (1976), 228n

Gregory v. Ashcroft, 111 S.Ct. 2395 (1991), 228n

Griggs v. Duke Power Co., 401 U.S. 424 (1971), 229n

Griswold v. Connecticut, 381 U.S. 479 (1965), 150–53, 194, 196

Hague v. C.I.O., 307 U.S. 496 (1939), 44–46, 52, 60, 67, 187–88

Hazelwood School Dist. v. Kuhlmeier, 484 U.S. 260 (1988), 222n, 228n

Hazelwood School Dist. v. United States, 433 U.S. 299 (1977), 228n

Heckler v. Chaney, 470 U.S. 821 (1985), 218n

Heffron v. Intern. Soc. for Krishna Consciousness, 452 U.S. 640 (1981), 222n

Henderson v. Lujan, 964 F.2d 1179 (D.C. Cir. 1992), 222n

Hernandez v. Commissioner, 490 U.S. 680 (1989), 228n

Hirabayashi v. United States, 320 U.S. 81 (1943), 219n

Hobbie v. Unemployment Appeals Comm'n., 480 U.S. 136 (1987), 225n

Houston v. Hill, 482 U.S. 451 (1987), 223n

Hudgens v. NLRB, 424 U.S. 507 (1976), 221n

International Society of Krishna Consciousness v. Lee, 112 S.Ct. 2701 (1992), 57–61, 90

Jenkins v. McKeithen, 395 U.S. 411 (1969), 231n

Joint Anti-Fascist Refugee Comm. v. McGrath, 341 U.S. 123 (1951), 231n

Katz v. United States, 389 U.S. 347 (1967), 230n

Kirchberg v. Feenstra, 450 U.S. 455 (1981), 228n

Kissinger v. Halpern, 452 U.S. 713 (1981), 219n

Korematsu v. United States, 323 U.S. 214 (1944), 21–34, 65, 144, 155, 181, 186, 188, 209, 219n

Laird v. Tatum, 408 U.S. 1 (1972), 230n

Lankford v. Gelson, 364 F.2d 197 (4th Cir. 1966), 231n

Lawson v. United States, 176 F.2d 49 (D.C. Cir. 1949), 221n

Lee v. Weisman, 112 S.Ct. 2649 (1992), 227n

Lewis v. City of New Orleans, 415 U.S. 30 (1974), 223n

Lorance v. AT&T Technologies, Inc., 490 U.S. 900 (1989), 229n

Los Angeles v. Lyons, 461 U.S. 95 (1983), 171–74, 179

Lucas v. South Carolina Coastal Council, 112 S.Ct. 2886 (1992), 217n

Lynch v. Donnelly, 465 U.S. 668 (1984), 117–18, 184

McCain v. Lybrand, 465 U.S. 236 (1984), 224n

McCleskey v. Kemp, 481 U.S. 279 (1987), 136–38, 143, 184, 228n

McCleskey v. Zant, 111 S.Ct. 1454 (1991), 231n

McCollum v. Bd. of Educ., 333 U.S. 203 (1948), 227n

McGowan v. Md., 336 U.S. 420 (1961), 226n

Marbury v. Madison, 5 U.S. 137 (1803), 219n, 230n

Marsh v. Alabama, 326 U.S. 501 (1946), 221n

Marsh v. Chambers, 463 U.S. 783 (1983), 227n

Martin v. Wilks, 490 U.S. 755 (1989), 229n

Meek v. Pittenger, 421 U.S.. 349 (1975), 227n

Members of the City Council v. Taxpayers for Vincent, 466 U.S. 789 (1984), 222n

Memphis v. Greene, 451 U.S. 100 (1981), 130–36, 139, 143, 184, 186, 228n

Miami Herald Pub. Co. v. Tornillo, 418 U.S. 241 (1974), 93–94, 189–90

Minersville Sch. Dist. v. Gobitis, 310 U.S. 586 (1940), 219n, 226n

Miranda v. Arizona, 384 U.S. 436 (1966), 231n

Mobile v. Bolden, 446 U.S. 55 (1980), 224n

Mueller v. Allen, 463 U.S. 388 (1983), 118–20, 123, 184

Murdock v. Penna., 319 U.S. 105 (1943), 221n, 222n

National League of Cities v. Usery, 426 U.S. 833 (1976), 230n

N.J. Welfare Rights Org. v. Cahill, 411 U.S. 619 (1973), 228n

New York Times Co. v. United States, 403 U.S. 714 (1971), 219n

Oliver v. United States, 466 U.S. 170 (1984), 231n

Patterson v. McLean Credit Union, 491 U.S. 164 (1989), 229n

Paul v. Davis, 424 U.S. 693 (1976), 169–71, 187, 188

Perry v. Sinderman, 408 U.S. 593 (1972), 222n

Perry Educ. Assn. v. Perry Local Educ. Assn., 460 U.S. 37 (1983), 222n

Pittsburgh Press Co. v. The Pittsburgh Commission on Human Relations, 413 U.S. 376 (1973), 224n

Planned Parenthood v. Casey, 112 S.Ct. 2791 (1992), 158–66, 222n

Plessy v. Ferguson, 163 U.S. 537 (1896), 35, 181

Presley v. Etowah County Commission, 112 S.Ct. 820 (1992), 90–92

R.A.V. v. City of St. Paul, 112 S.Ct. 2701 (1992), 73–82, 189, 221n

Red Lion Broadcasting v. FCC, 395 U.S. 367 (1969), 224n

Renton v. Playtime Theatres, Inc., 475 U.S. 41 (1986), 62–65, 231n

Richmond v. Croson, 488 U.S. 469 (1989), 138–41, 144, 184, 189

Roe v. Wade, 410 U.S. 113 (1973), 71, 158–66, 193–94, 229n

Rondeau v. Mosinee Paper Co., 422 U.S. 49 (1975), 231n

Runyon v. McCrary, 427 U.S. 160 (1976), 229n

Rust v. Sullivan, 111 S.Ct. 1759 (1991), 71–73, 93

Sherbert v. Verner, 374 U.S. 398 (1963), 222n, 225n

Speiser v. Randall, 357 U.S. 513 (1958), 222n

Texas v. Johnson, 491 U.S. 397 (1989), 221n

Thomas v. Review Bd., Ind. Empl. Sec. Div., 450 U.S. 707 (1981), 225n

Tinker v. Des Moines Indep. Comm. Sch. Dist., 393 U.S. 503 (1969), 222n

Trumbo v. United States, 339 U.S. 934 (1950), 221n

United States v. Agurs, 427 U.S. 97 (1976), 231n

United States v. Alvarez-Machain, 112 S.Ct. 2188 (1992), 231n

United States v. Carolene Products Co., 304 U.S. 144 (1938), 230n

United States v. Kokinda, 497 U.S. 720 (1990), 222n

United States v. Miller, 425 U.S. 435 (1976), 155–58, 188, 230n

United States v. O'Brien, 391 U.S. 367 (1968), 223n

United States v. Salerno, 481 U.S. 739 (1987), 219n, 231n

United States v. U.S. District Court, 407 U.S. 297 (1972), 231n

United States v. White, 401 U.S. 745 (1971), 230n

Wallace v. Jaffree, 472 U.S. 38 (1985), 113, 119, 123, 187, 227n

Walz v. Tax Commission, 397 U.S. 664 (1970), 228n

Ward's Cove Packing Co v. Antonio, 490 U.S. 642 (1989), 229n

Washington v. Davis, 426 U.S. 229 (1976), 229n

Watson v. Memphis, 373 U.S. 526 (1963), 228n

Webster v. Reproductive Health Services, 492 U.S. 490 (1989), 162, 222n

Whitney v. California, 274 U.S. 357 (1927), 221

Wisconsin v. Constantineau, 400 U.S. 433, 437 (1971), 231n

Wisconsin v. Yoder, 406 U.S. 205 (1972), 225n

Wolman v. Walter, 433 U.S. 229 (1977), 227n

Wooley v. Menard, 430 U.S. 705 (1977), 222n

Yick Wo v. Hopkins, 118 U.S. 356 (1886), 228n

❦ INDEX ❧

Aberle, David, 226n
Abortion, 71–73, 99, 126, 158–65, 192, 209
Adams, John, 49
Affirmative action, 4, 11, 92, 129, 138–41, 184, 186
African-Americans, 7, 35, 66, 73, 81, 83–84, 129–41, 155, 168, 172, 181, 106–07, election of, 90–92
AIDS, 129, 132
Allen, Anita, 229n
Amendments to the Constitution, 7, 46, 68, 84, 114, 167, 202; First, 4, 41, 43, 47–49, 56, 59, 60, 64, 71, 81, 90, 99–127, 151, 162; Third, 148, 151; Fourth, 148, 151, 156, 176; Fifth, 148, 151; Ninth, 151; Fourteenth, 4, 102; Fifteenth, 84, 91; Seventeenth, 84; Nineteenth, 84; Twenty-Fourth, 84; Twenty-Sixth, 84; preadoption history of, 108, 109, 148, 151
American Indians. *See* Native Americans
Amish, 103, 104, 107
Amsterdam, Anthony G., 229n
Anderson, Frank, 221n
Art censorship, 73

Bad-tendency doctrine, 49
Bagdikian, Ben H., 224n
Baldus, David, 136
Baptists, 111
Barker, Ernest, 219n
Bartlett, Donald, 218n, 224n
Bauman, Richard, 232n
Bell, Derrick, 228n
Bennett, William, 70
Bernstein, Irving, 221n
Bias-related crime, 4, 11, 73–82, 189
Black, Hugo, 23–26, 30–31, 65, 161
Blackmun, Harry, 1, 67, 72, 81, 92, 135, 163, 165, 179, 189
Bork, Robert, 36, 150, 189, 210, 217n, 231n
Bowen, Catherine Drinker, 217n, 223n
Brandeis, Louis, 45–46, 149, 229n
Brennan, William, 117, 135, 142
Brown, Dee, 220n
Buchanan, Patrick, 166, 189, 210
Buddhists, 118
Burger, Warren, 69–70, 93, 103, 117, 125, 143, 177
Bush, George, 1, 8, 35, 210; administration of, 7, 62, 73

Capital punishment, 136–38, 179
Carter, Jimmy, 86, 99

Catholics, 100
Censorship, 51, 62, 66, 68, 70, 71, 73, 93; by government, 77, 79, 82, 97, 189
Chafee, Zechariah, Jr., 47, 221n
Child pornography, 51
Christians, 20, 103, 111–12, 117, 121–22, 126
Civil Rights Act of 1964, 35, 196
Civil rights movement, 99, 140
Civil War, 145, 205
Cloward, Richard A., 218n, 232n
Cole, David, 229n
Commission on Wartime Relocation and Internment of Civilians, 27; *Personal Justice Denied*, 27, 31. *See also* Japanese Americans
Congress, 7, 8, 22, 24, 29, 30, 35, 48, 88, 92, 99, 100, 115–16, 144, 156, 167, 190, 202, 209, 211
Congress of Industrial Organizations (CIO), 44–46
Connors, Richard, 221n
Constructive-intent doctrine, 49
Copelon, Rhonda, 229n
Cord, Robert L., 225n
Crenshaw, Kimberlé, 229n
Crime, 129, 132, 135, 167–68, 173–74, 179
Currie, Elliot, 231n

Davis, Edward Charles, III, 169–71
Davis, William F., 42–43, 51–52
Declaration of Independence, 19, 83, 115, 145, 205
Defamation, 51, 76, 93
Department of Health and Human Services, 71–73

Deregulation, 4, 17, 200, 208
DeWitt, J. L., 22–29, 31; Final Report, 24–29, 31
Dickinson, John, 6
Disabled, 205
Discrimination, 8, 129–45, 189; and Congress, 144; by gender, 141–45, 184, 188; governmental, 130; Pregnancy Discrimination Act of 1978, 143; purposeful-discrimination doctrine, 131–38, 143, 183–84, 186; by race, 4, 21–25, 29–31, 33, 65, 92, 130–41; by religion, 35, 100; by sexual preference, 144, 153–55
Douglas, William O., 151–52, 161, 194
Due process, 1, 3, 9, 34, 167–79, 181, 183, 185, 188, 202; and coerced involuntary confessions, 174–75, 187; and protection of reputation, 170

Economy, 6, 8, 99, 101, 148, 208; and equality, 140–41, 200; free-market, 95; laissez-faire, 17; reform of, 90
Education, 68–70, 151, 154, 196; and religion, 13–21, 30, 107, 112–14, 118–20, 122–24
Eisenhower, Dwight D., 26
Elections, 83–92, 208; and African-Americans, 90–92; and corruption, 87; influence of corporations in, 89; and mass media, 85, 93, 97; effects of money in, 4, 11, 87–90, 185, 190, 208; 1992 presidential, 85,

208; and political action committees, 89, 208; racism in, 129; reform of, 8–9, 87–90, 190, 208; third-party candidates, 86; two-party system, 84–87. *See also* Voting
Emerson, Thomas, 82
Employment discrimination law, 79
English Star Chamber, 148, 174
Environmental restrictions. *See* Deregulation
Episcopalians, 100
Equality, 1, 3, 9, 129–45, 183–85, 210; and the disabled, 205; economic, 140–41, 202; and education, 154, 196; and public housing, 202; and purposeful-discrimination doctrine, 131–38, 143, 183, 186; and women, 130, 138, 141–43, 165, 189, 205
Executive branch, 7, 203–4

Fahy, Charles, 28
Fairness doctrine, 93–94
Family planning. *See* Public Health Service Act
Federal Bureau of Investigation, 26, 28
Federalists, 48–49, 50; and *Federalist Papers*, 6
Flag, 14–15, 18, 19, 20, 205
Flag burning, 36, 40, 51, 57, 200, 209
Framers of the Constitution, 6, 47, 100, 113–16, 147–48, 151, 186

Frankfurter, Felix, 18–21, 26, 34, 36, 109, 113, 210
Ford, Gerald, 1, 87
Fraud, 51
Freedom of Information Act, 28
Free speech. *See* Speech rights
Fried, Charles, 2–3, 4, 7, 160–61, 191, 193, 217n, 218n, 230n, 232n

Gable, Clark, 71
Gates, Darryl, 171–73; and Los Angeles Police Department, 171–74
General Electric, 95, 142–43
German-Americans, 27–28
Goldberg, Arthur, 151–52
Good faith immunity, 174
Gosha, Nathaniel, 90–91
Gotanda, Neil, 229n
Greider, William, 218n, 224n
Gun control, 11

Hague, Frank, 44
Hamilton, Alexander, 6
Harlan, John, 157
Harmless error doctrine, 174–75, 187
Hill, Anita, 11
Hispanics, 35, 96, 168
Hitler, Adolf, 14
Holmes, Oliver Wendell, 42–43, 45
Holocaust, 20, 21
Homelessness, 132
House of Representatives, 6, 83; Un-American Activities Committee, 50

Incidental effects doctrine, 65, 88, 183; and election reform, 90; and religious exercise, 106
Irish-Americans, 25, 139
Irons, Peter, 28, 219n, 229n
Italian-Americans, 25, 27–28, 139

Jackson, Robert, 15–21, 27, 31, 34–35, 36, 109, 202, 209
Japanese-Americans: internment of, 21–25, 27, 65
Jay, John, 6; treaty by, 115
Jefferson, Thomas, 19, 48, 219n; and wall of separation principle, 110, 114–16, 187, 210
Jehovah's Witnesses, 14–15, 74, 102
Jews, 35, 100–101, 103, 111–12; and U.S. military, 121
Judicial restraint, 4, 5, 6, 8, 11, 18–19, 26, 34, 36, 131, 137, 162, 182, 186, 189–90, 210; and election reform, 4, 90
Judicial review, 17, 19, 152, 162; strict scrutiny standard of, 10, 32–33, 51, 54, 58, 59, 64, 74, 84, 85, 98, 102, 104–6, 107–9, 138–39, 143, 154, 201

Kennedy, Anthony, 1, 92, 159, 162, 175
Kennedy, Duncan, 232n
Kennedy, John F., 1
King, Martin Luther, Jr., 66, 197
King, Rodney, 171, 173
Klare, Karl E., 232n
Kluger, Richard, 224n
Konvitz, Milton R., 229n

Korematsu, Fred, 21–29
Ku Klux Klan, 66

Labor, 44, 50; laws, 5–6
LaFave, Wayne R., 229n
Levy, Leonard, 47–48, 221n, 224n
Liberal paradigm, 50, 53, 58, 59, 61, 64, 66, 71, 72, 73, 74, 87
Lincoln, Abraham, 165–66, 210
Lynching, 66
Lyon, Matthew, 49
Lyons, Adolf, 171–73

McCarthy, Joseph, 50
McClellan, James, 227n
McCleskey, Warren, 136–38, 179
McCloskey, Robert G., 227n
McDonnell, Michael W., 225n
McKean, Dayton, 221n
McSwain, Peter, 226n
Madison, James, 6, 109, 115–16
Marshall, John, 17
Marshall, Thurgood, 120, 135, 175
Marshall, William P., 225n
Mass media, 40, 41, 59, 94, 107, 149, 189, 207, 208, 210; centralization and monopolization of, 95–97; racial hostility as portrayed by, 96; and right of reply statute, 93; and speech rights, 55, 56, 57, 62; and voting process, 85, 93–94
Matsuda, Mari, 223n
Maxwell, Robert, 95
Meese, Edwin, III, 2, 192, 217n
Military, 24, 26, 28, 30, 33, 61, 121, 148, 169, 209

Mormons, 121
Murdoch, Rupert, 95
Murphy, Frank, 26
Murphy, Paul L., 220n

National Endowment for the Arts, 73
National Guard, 66
National Labor Relations Act of 1935, 44
National security and military necessity, 30, 33, 65
Native Americans, 32; free exercise of religion and, 104–6
Nazism, 28, 40–41
Neuborne, Burt, 231n
New Deal, 15, 44, 151
Newhouse, S. I., 95
Nixon, Richard, 1, 87; administration of, 36

Obscenity, 51, 62–63, 70, 79
O'Connor, Sandra Day, 1, 62, 138, 161, 165, 167, 186
Original intent, 10, 90, 108, 114, 162, 167, 186
Orwell, George, 64, 222n
Overbreadth, 74

Paine, Thomas, 48, 52, 148, 210
Pamphleteering, 42, 44, 51–52, 55–56, 57–58, 61, 97
Participation in the political process. *See* Elections; Voting
Pearl Harbor. *See* World War II
Pember, Don, 229n
Pinckney, Charles, 6
Piven, Francis Fox, 218n, 232n

Planned Parenthood, 150
Pledge of allegiance, 14
Police, 15, 66, 134, 136, 153–55, 156–57, 168, 169–70, 174, 177–79, 188; and deadly force, 171–74
Political action committees, 208
Powell, Lewis, 137
Presley, Elvis, 150
Presley, Lawrence, 90–91
Prior restraints, 47
Prisons, 168
Privacy, 1, 3, 9, 34, 72, 147–66, 175, 177, 181, 184, 185, 196, 201; financial, 149, 155–58, 188, 202; of gay men and lesbians, 153–55, 189; and government intrusion, 148–49, 153, 156, 190; and legal determinacy, 162, 194; in sexual and reproductive matters, 150, 152–55, 158–65, 189, 192
Probable cause, 156–57, 161, 167, 176
Protestants, 100
Public accommodations law, 35, 140, 196, 202
Public forum: designated, 59; doctrine of, 58–62, 162, 183, 188; traditional, 59, 62
Public Health Service Act of 1970, 71–72

Quakers, 23
Quayle, Dan, 7, 166
Quayle, Marilyn, 166

Rabban, David M., 221n
Race, 73; discrimination by, 4, 21–25, 29–31, 33, 65, 92, 129–41, 186, 189, 197–98; and elections, 129; integration of, 27, 35, 129, 133, 140, 181; and marriage, 152, 154; segregation by, 27, 35, 129, 132–33; and sex, 150; stereotypes of, 24–27. *See also* Bias-related crime
Racism. *See* Discrimination by race
Racist speech, 54, 57, 66, 73–82
Rape, 66, 174, 177
Rational basis standard, 33–34
Reagan, Ronald, 1, 2, 86, 89, 160; administration of, 7, 29, 70, 71, 129, 159, 181, 191, 210; and religion, 99
Reaganomics, 17
Reasonableness standard, 58, 61, 63, 156
Regulation of expression, 148–53; content-based, 63, 65, 72–82; and content discrimination, 67–68; and content selectivity, 75; and disfavored content, 73; and proscribable content doctrine, 77–78
Rehnquist, William, 1, 7, 34–36, 58, 61, 67–68, 72, 89, 113–16, 119, 126, 142, 152, 163–64, 170, 174–75, 178, 187–88, 192, 196, 210, 218n
Reinstein, Robert, 223n
Religion, 1, 9, 10, 34, 48, 99–127, 181, 190, 200–201, 202; and conformity, 13, 21, 123; and education, 13–21, 30, 107, 112–

14, 118–20, 122–24; establishment of, 64, 99–102, 110–20, 122, 124, 183; free exercise of, 64–65, 99–110, 111, 120–24, 126, 164, 184, 188; secular purpose rule, 184; and sex, 150; and taxation, 100–101, 118–19, 121, 124–26; and wall of separation principle, 110–11, 113–15, 120–27, 187
Rights of assembly, 16, 42, 45, 51, 52, 55, 56, 66
Rights of association, 72, 84, 140, 151, 158
Robertson, Pat, 166
Roosevelt, Franklin D., 15, 18, 22, 151

Savage, David, 218n, 220n
Savings and loan banks, 206
Scalia, Antonin, 73–81, 106, 107–10, 162, 163–65, 210
Schecter, Stephen L., 217n
Schubert, Glendon, 219n
Scientologists, 121
Secondary effects doctrine, 63–66, 67, 79, 88, 183; and election reform, 90
Sedition Act of 1798, 48–49
Seditious libel, 47–49
Segregation, 35
Seventh Day Adventists, 65, 102, 103
Sex, 68–71, 73, 189; harassment, 11, 79; preference, 144
Shakespeare, William, 70
Shils, Edward, 229n
Slavery, 129, 167, 199

Slotkin, James, 226n
Smith, Alfred, 104–6, 188
Smith, Bradley A., 223n
Sodomy laws, 153–54, 165
Solicitation, 57–58, 61
Souter, David, 1, 19, 162
Soviet Union, 30, 84, 141, 168
Speech rights: commercial, 51, 54; compelling government interest and restriction of, 32, 74, 93, 124; conditions of government funding and, 71–73; content barrier, 40, 54, 55, 63; of corporations, 89, 181, 190; dissent and, 42–43; draft-card burning and, 88; fighting words and, 51, 73–77; intentional infliction of emotional duress and, 76; listener's veto and, 52, 70, 74, 75, 107, 201; and offensive speech, 68–71, 75; political, 51, 54, 62, 70, 73; and proscribable speech, 79; protected, 51–56, 74, 77, 87; in public places, 44–50, 57–62; religious, 108, 126; restrictions of, 72, 74, 88; threats of imminent violence and, 76; time, place, and manner regulations, 63; unprotected, 51–56, 74–82; and wealth, 55, 181, 185, 188, 190; and zoning, 62–65. *See also* Pamphleteering
Steele, James, 218n, 224n
Stephens, James, 221n
Stern, Philip M., 224n
Stern, Robert L., 217n
Stevens, John, 1, 71, 92, 113, 131, 162

Stewart, Omar, 226n
Strict construction, 59, 162–63, 174, 178, 182–83, 186
Strict scrutiny. *See* Judicial review
Surveillance, 156–58, 176–77, 188, 202. *See also* Police

Taney, Roger, 165
Terkel, Studs, 30, 220n
Thomas, Clarence, 1, 11, 19, 92, 175
Thomas, Kendall, 229n
Thompson, E. P., 232n
Tobacco industry, 96
Tocqueville, Alexis de, 219n
Travel rights, 72
Tribe, Lawrence, 225n, 229n
Trubow, George, 229n
Turkington, Richard, 230n

United States Drug Enforcement Agency, 105
United States Navy, 28

Vietnam War, 32, 88; Veterans' Memorial, 62
Virginia Statute for Religious Freedom, 115
Vose, Clement E., 218n
Voting, 8, 40, 84–87, 185, 196, 202; early qualifications for, 6; and freedom of choice, 87; freedom of expression and association in, 84; and mass media, 85; and parliamentary system, 86, 207; and prohibition of the poll tax, 84; protest votes, 84; residency requirement for, 160, 162; restriction of, 84–87; Rights Act

Voting (*continued*)
of 1965, 8, 91–92; rights of African-Americans, 7, 83–84; rights of women, 7, 83–84; write in, 84–87, 188. *See also* Elections

Warner, Kenneth E., 224n
Warren, Earl, 22, 133
Warren, Samuel, 149, 229n
Watergate, 87
White, Byron, 1, 78, 84–87, 92, 154–55, 172, 175

White House, 126
William, Juan, 224n
Williams, Hosea, 66
Wills, Garry, 223n
Winger, Richard, 223n
Women's movement, 43
World War I, 41–42
World War II, 10, 13–14, 20, 21, 23, 28, 30, 94, 134
Wyman, David, 219n

Zoning restrictions, 62–63

WITHDRAWN